D0569489

THE MARCO POLO ODYSSEY

Above: Drawing of Marco Polo

THE MARCO POLO ODYSSEY

IN THE FOOTSTEPS OF A MERCHANT WHO CHANGED THE WORLD

By Harry Rutstein

B&H Bennett & Hastings Publishing

Published in the United States by Bennett & Hastings
Publishing in cooperation with The Marco Polo
Foundation, Inc.

Bennett & Hastings Publishing
7551 15th Avenue East
Seattle, WA 98117
www.bennetthastings.com

Marco Polo Foundation, Inc.
1501 17th Avenue, Suite 1010
Seattle, WA 98122
www.marcopolofound.org
e-mail: hrutstein2@aol.com

Library of Congress Cataloging in Publication Data:

Rutstein, Harry
The Marco Polo Odyssey: In the Footsteps of
    a Merchant Who Changed the World
Includes photographs
2008902408

ISBN 978-0-9802076-0-6

Printed and bound in the United States of America by
Worzalla Publishing, Stevens Point, Wisconsin

Designed by Geoffrey Gray

CONTENTS

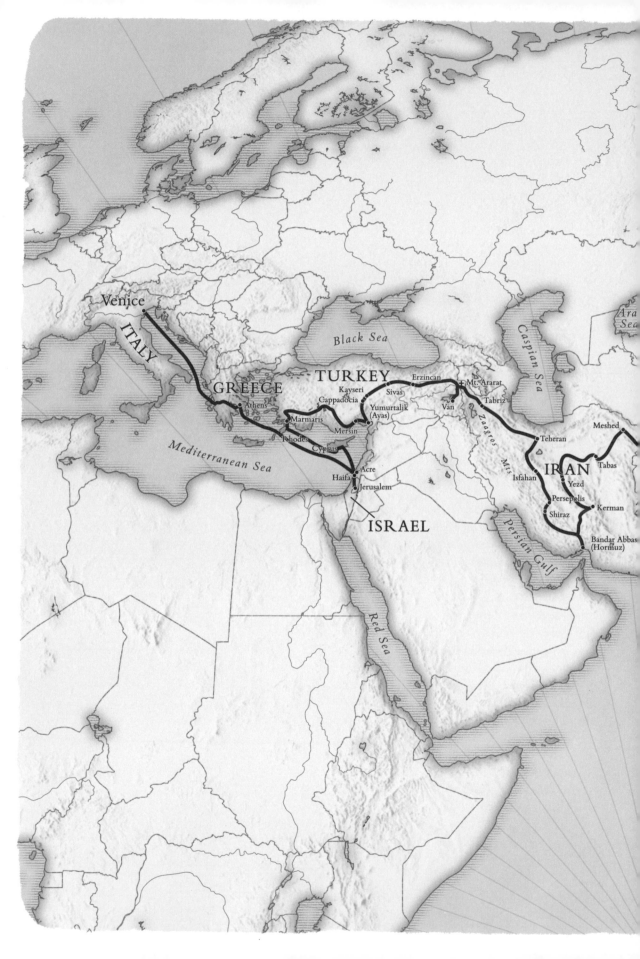

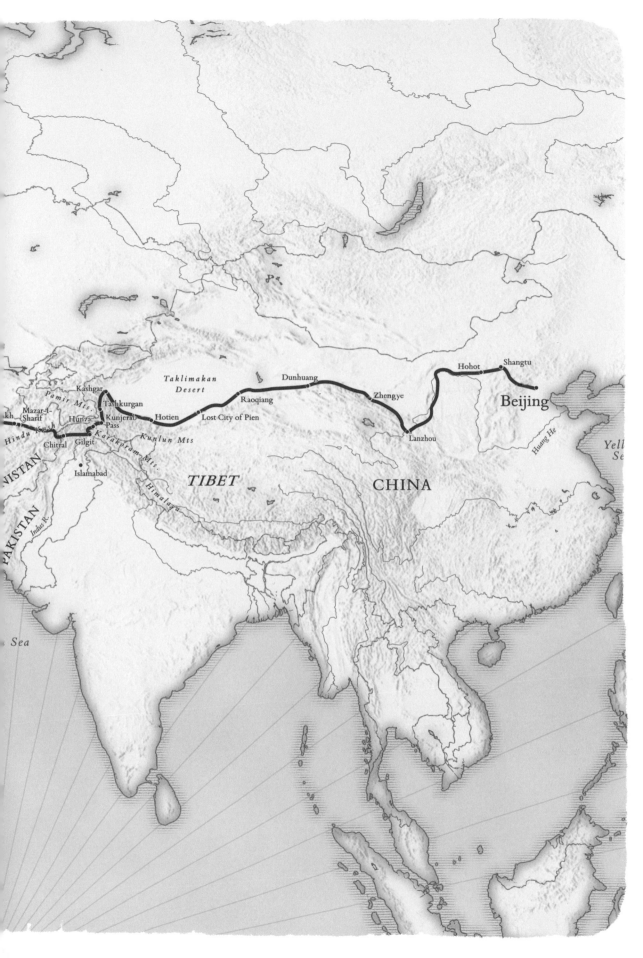

EPIGRAPH

We shall not cease from exploration
And the end of all exploring
Will be to arrive where we started
And know the place for the first time.
T.S. ELIOT

INTRODUCTION

I was eight years old. The year was 1938. On Saturday afternoons I sat in front of the large wooden cabinet that held our family's Philco radio captivated by my favorite program. The program was produced by the Smithsonian Institution and called "The World is Yours." Each program presented stories of exotic cultures in faraway lands. The world, I believed, *was* mine and I began to imagine how I would someday find my way to these places. My adventure through history had begun.

In the 1960s, I meandered most of the Americas, visiting the sites of pre-Columbian civilizations from Central Mexico through the Peruvian Andes. By 1970 I had visited over forty countries around the world...yet I knew there was more to experience and learn. I longed to trek across Central Asia and the East to study the age-old civilizations of that part of the world.

My friend Joanne Kroll and I discussed the possibility of such a trek, and we hit on the idea of following Marco Polo's path to China. This would allow us to visit the sites of the Greeks, Romans, Hittites, Persians, Turkomans and many other early societies that had lived along the old, and now abandoned, Silk Road; Marco Polo's road. What a great idea!

I reviewed the research and many translations of the story of Marco Polo. He was born in Venice in 1254, while his father and uncle were on a trading trip that eventually took them all the way to the Kublai Khan in China. By the time they returned to Venice, to pursue a project for the great Kahn, Marco was fifteen, and his mother had died. Two years later, in 1271, the Polo brothers once again voyaged to China, this time with young Marco. They traveled to Jerusalem, across Turkey, through Persia (now Iran, Afghanistan, and Pakistan) and over the Old Silk Road in China, back to the court of the Kublai Khan. This was the route I would follow; with, as it turned out, more than a few unexpected obstacles and adventures. Marco Polo worked for the Khan for seventeen years and gained great knowledge of his empire. The Polos finally returned to Venice in 1294 as rich noblemen. Still an adventurer, Marco Polo became a gentlemen captain on a Venetian warship that was part of an armada battling the Genoese. He and his ship were captured and Marco was imprisoned in Genoa.

In prison and using his notebooks for reference, Marco Polo recounted his travel tales to his cellmate, the novelist Rusticiano of Pisa. The tale, Marco Polo's *Description of the World,* written out by his fellow prisoner, has remained a best seller for 700 years. Marco Polo told of alien geography and technologies, of customs and concepts unknown at the time to Europeans. He described both overland and sea routes to China. Armed with Polo's accounts of people, places and products, Europeans could trade directly with Asia. It was the beginning of globalization. And I, benefiting as well from Polo's chronicle of his journey, could use it to map my own route to and through Asia. His book became my guide.

As journeys often do, my Marco Polo odyssey began in dreams, designed with maps and books. It began in a love of travel; an eight year old boy's craving to explore places where ancient cultures lived and still live today. In the end, my odyssey became "living history" making history come alive by traveling along the Old Silk Road and entering the world of Marco Polo.

Before setting out on my odyssey I, of course, had to know if any other adventurer had traced the same path. I put my question to the Royal Geographical Society, which chronicled such events. They reported that no traveler was known to have successfully followed the entire eastward voyage of the thirteenth century merchant. I was determined to try. And determination proved key: unpredictably, it took ten years and three expeditions to fulfill my dream.

Above: Marco Polo's home today is still
located in the courtyard of the man who was
known to tell a million lies

PART ONE

CHAPTER 1

Marco Polo's Home
Venice, July 23 to July 25, 1975

reat Princes, Emperors, and Kings, Dukes and Marquises, Counts, Knights, and Burgesses! And People of all degrees who desire to get knowledge of the various races of mankind and of the diversities of the sundry regions of the World, take this Book and cause it to be read to you. For ye shall find therein all kinds of wonderful things, and the divers histories of the Great Hermania, and of Persia, and of the Land of the Tartars, and of India, and of many other country of which our Book doth speak, particularly and in regular succession, according to the description of Messer Marco Polo, a wise and noble citizen of Venice, as he saw them with his own eyes. Some things indeed there be therein which he beheld not; but these he heard from men of credit and veracity. And we shall set down things seen as seen, and things heard as heard only so that no jot of falsehood shall mar the truth of our Book, and that all who shall read it or hear it read may put full faith in the truth of all its contents.
MARCO POLO, 1298

On January 9, 1324, Marco Polo was dying, at his home in Venice. He had just given the notary, Giovanni Gustianiani, details for his will. A priest stood by to give Marco his last rites. On his deathbed his friends asked for the truth about his journey to the East. Marco Polo replied, "I have not told half of what I saw."

Nearly 700 years later, I sat with my friend Joanne Kroll and my son Rick in the pizza parlor that had once been the first floor of Marco Polo's house. The three of us were at the site where Marco Polo's deathbed words were spoken, and were about to set out on a journey to confirm and authenticate the contents of Marco Polo's book. Our goal was to examine how much had changed and perhaps reveal the other half of what he saw. Most important, we hoped to give this great man the credit he undeniably deserved and has never received.

Our philosophy of traveling overland would be the same as the Polos'—we would take whatever means of travel was available to get from one place to the next. The excitement of our travels involved the journey as well as our destinations. It became the adventure of a lifetime, a ten year trek across half the earth.

There would be just three of us on the first leg of the voyage: Joanne, Rick, and myself, a forty-five year old merchant who traded in high-tech products from Asia, just like the Polo family. Marco Polo was nineteen when he arrived in China with his father; Rick was nineteen as he traveled with me the other side of the world. Joanne, the third member, was a cultural anthropologist, a registered nurse, and a lifelong traveler. She joined our project after just completing a 50,000-mile solo

15

bus tour, crisscrossing Central and South America. I could not imagine a person with better credentials for our expedition.

After years of planning, reading, and talking about the life and times of Marco Polo, we arrived on July 23, 1975, in Venice, home of our medieval traveler in his youth and from the age of forty-one to his death, thirty years later. Venice in the thirteenth century was a great city-state, the center of a mercantile empire that controlled most of the major ports in the Mediterranean and the Black Sea: Venice, a city of islands that grew out of a lagoon—Venice, a city still living in the thirteenth century.

Marco Polo's first and second houses were tucked behind an old church, just a hundred yards from the Rialto Bridge, the only bridge that existed across the Grand Canal in the thirteenth century. We found that one of the Polo houses was now a movie theater and the other, conveniently, the Malibran Hotel and pizza parlor. That became new temporary headquarters for our Marco Polo project. Our rooms at the hotel overlooked the courtyard and outdoor cafe. My window could have been the one from which my vicarious mentor called to his friends 700 years

Above: The back alleyway to the Polo family stables

ago. To be surrounded and totally immersed in the thirteenth-century world of Marco Polo was exhilarating!

The Marco Polo Expedition could not have had a more authentic beginning. As we sat in the pizza parlor discussing our plans, I hoped his spirit would be traveling with us, guiding us safely along his path and through his ancient world.

When Marco Polo's father, Niccolo, and uncle, Maffeo, were working as traders in Turkey, wars forced them to travel farther east to Bukhara (now in Uzbekistan). After a few years of doing business in this cultural center along the Silk Road, they received an unusual request: a visiting emissary from Peking (now Beijing) invited them to visit the Kublai Khan. The Polos saw it as a great business opportunity and trekked two thousand miles east with the emissary. The Great Khan, ruler of the Mongolian Empire, asked the Polo brothers to go to the Pope in the Vatican and petition the church to bring Christianity to his vast Empire. The Polos were then to return to the Khan, bringing holy chrism (baptismal oil) from the Church of

Left: St. Mark's Square

Right: St. Mark's Church was built in the eleventh century

the Holy Sepulchre in Jerusalem and "a hundred learned men" to introduce and teach Christianity on a grand scale in the Mongolian Empire.

As the Kublai Khan requested, Niccolo and Maffeo returned to Italy, hoping for an audience with the Pope. Unfortunately, Pope Clement IV had died the previous year. The brothers waited in Venice for two years, but a new pope still was not elected. The Polos knew the Kublai Khan was expecting their return so they decided to head east again, this time with the young Marco. They stopped in Acre (Israel) where they fortuitously met with the newly elected Pope Gregory X. Joanne, Rick, and I were now setting forth in their footsteps.

Venice's Rialto section has always been the center of the city's commercial life. In the thirteenth century, merchants sat under the porticoes, bargaining with clients, socializing with friends, and soliciting local prostitutes while their wines, spices, and precious Asian silks were displayed in nearby warehouses. Overlooking the Rialto Bridge were Europe's busiest money exchange and famous Venetian bordellos, both ready to serve the hundreds of foreign merchants who came to do business in Venice. Today the bordellos are gone and tourists have replaced the traders, but the vibrant atmosphere of the Middle Ages remains.

The Grand Canal snakes its way from the historic Rialto Bridge to the Piazza San Marco (St. Mark's Square), the hub of Venetian social life for a thousand years. The tiled Piazza stretches from St. Mark's Church—its unmistakable eleventh century architecture and cupolas bubbling across the skyline—down to the steps that lead into the blue lagoon. In this spectacular setting, medieval guilds and religious brotherhoods paraded before the Doge, bearing banners and jeweled incense burners that perfumed the salty air. The Doge, Venice's titular leader, celebrated his election in Piazza San Marco, scattering coins to the cheering crowds as the craftsmen who built Venetian galleys carried him, in vivid velvet splendor, to the nearby arsenal (dockyard). This was the Venice that Marco Polo knew.

During our stay at the Malibran Hotel we became friends with the suave, strikingly handsome Angelo Saivezzo and his partner, Paolo Dorigo, who helped with our exploration of the area. One evening, as the sun settled behind the surrounding buildings, we sipped Chianti and nibbled on cheeses while we talked with Mr. Saivezzo about our travel plans. He was obviously envious…traveling for him had been limited to the Italian peninsula. He said, "Tomorrow, I will show you something very special."

In the morning, Angelo took us to a secluded courtyard and a stable hidden from the public: it was where the horses of the Polo family had been kept 700 years before. Over the arch of a darkened entrance to the courtyard, weatherworn and partially hidden beneath centuries of grime, was the Polos' original coat of arms—three crows on a shield with a knight's helmet—carved in the stone. A scarf appearing to flow in the wind was chiseled into its background. This was a good omen to Joanne because crows were her favorite-feathered friends.

The plaque in the courtyard entryway proclaimed it to be the *Corte Prima Del Milione,* a reference to Marco Polo's nickname, "the millions." This was not a term of endearment, but one of ridicule, because Marco so often used the number in his tales of the East. Marco told stories his fellow Venetians thought were fantasies and lies; describing things in the millions, telling tales of a world they could not believe existed, a world about which all of Europe knew nothing. I can easily see Marco entertaining his listeners, gesticulating wildly as he tells of fireproof fabric that he called salamander (asbestos). He would say, "When it is dirty and gray, you throw it into a fire and it becomes clean and white." Now, who could believe that in thirteenth-century Italy?

I found it a great tragedy that Venice had not declared the home of its most illustrious resident a shrine, a sacred place, a museum, or at least a historic monument restored and preserved for posterity. Instead, the city fathers had put up a plaque identifying the courtyard as one owned by a man who was believed to have told a million lies. Marco Polo should be properly recognized for his importance to world history: his book impacted expansion of the European economy starting in the fourteenth century. *Description of the World* provided the Western World its first detailed knowledge of the East and offered a wealth of know-how: it allowed Polo to widely disseminate information he had brought with him from the Orient. Polo's influence was staggering. For the next two hundred years Polo's book would be the prime source of knowledge about Asia. Even Columbus used it as his guidebook to the East.

The waters, strewn with garbage, lapped at the edges of the canal. One evening on our way back to Marco's old house, a man dressed in green swim trunks (or underwear) walked out from his house, placed a towel on the knee-high wall of the canal, and with soap and a razor in his hand jumped in for his evening bath and shave. To us, as visitors, this was a bit startling, but to a Venetian it was part of a daily regimen.

The singing of the gondoliers, clad in blue and white, interwove with the sounds of church bells, wailing babies and the animated conversations of late-night diners in the courtyard below. We could have easily imagined ourselves to be in Marco Polo's medieval Venice, that is, if we could have ignored the television antennas and the roar of polluting motorboats.

After three days in Venice, it was time to go. In the bright morning sun, we walked across town toward the shipping docks and past the old iron works known as the "Ghetto," where Venetian Jews were once walled in. Things have changed since that time, including the meaning of the Italian word "ghetto": it is universally used today, but not for foundries and blacksmiths.

What should one carry on a thirteen-thousand-mile odyssey across Asia? As little as possible! Especially, since we would have to transport it all on our backs through a myriad of climates and conditions, from the scorching heat of the great deserts of Iran and China to the bitter cold heights of the Hindu Kush and the many mountains and high plateaus in Afghanistan, Pakistan, and China. Each item had to be weighed carefully in importance and ounces.

During the early planning for the first expedition our travel expert, Joanne, had suggested we find backpacks large enough to accommodate all our gear and protected by the toughest waterproof material available; everything was to be secured on the inside of the pack, including the tent and down-filled sleeping bags. Because she had found that most bus, donkey, or camel loaders invariably grabbed the weakest part of the pack while doing their job, she specified that the pack was not to have any outside appendages that could be used as a handhold, including a metal frame or tent poles: nothing except for the mandatory back straps. All pocket and flap closings were to be fastened with heavy-duty zippers. Drawstrings, often used on backpacks, were unacceptable, as they tended to work loose in the constant jostling. We finally found a pack that met these criteria, and others, such as lightweight, padded straps, accessibility, and balance. The pack came in only one perfect color: bright yellow!

Medieval travelers wrapped their belongings in a carpet or in heavy cloth, threw them across the backs of mules, camels, or yaks, and proceeded across Asia. Our packs were always stored with the bundles of our fellow passengers, which were wrapped as they were in Marco Polo's time. They would often leak fluids, some familiar and some strange, with indefinable aromas. On occasion a harried helper would toss the luggage into the sewage troughs that ran along the roads or streets of most Asian towns. Rain was only one reason for waterproof packs.

Besides having the luxury of all their baggage being carried by donkeys, the Polos had carried a gold tablet (*paizah*) that the Kublai Khan gave to Niccolo and Maffeo and which provided free and protected passage throughout the Mongolian Empire:

hen the Prince had charged them with all his commission, he caused to be given them a Tablet of Gold, on which was inscribed that the Ambassadors should be supplied with everything needful in all countries through which they should pass—with horses, with escorts, and, in short, with whatever they should require. And when they had made all needful preparations, the Ambassadors took their leave of the Emperor and set out.

MARCO POLO, 1298

It was the same as having an American Express card today with no credit limit and no payments. The Polos also carried documents from the new Pope to deliver to the Kublai Khan and gems for currency. We, instead, carried a few traveler's checks and official letters of introduction written by the ambassadors and cultural attaches of the countries we would visit. Hopefully, they would help us open doors to ancient places as we pursued Marco Polo to the other end of the earth.

On July 25, we filled a mesh bag with bread, cheese, and fruit for a four-day sea voyage to Israel.

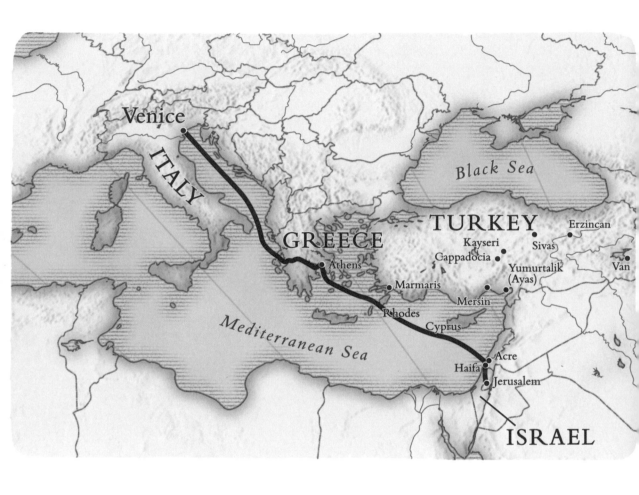

CHAPTER 2

First Steps into the Past
Jerusalem, July 26 to August 6, 1975

he two brothers departed from Ayas and came to Acre, arriving there in the month of April, in the year of Christ 1269, and then they learned that the pope was dead. And when they found that the pope was dead (Pope Clement IV), they went to a wise Churchman who was legate for the whole Kingdom of Egypt, and a man of great authority, by the name of Theobald of Piacenza, and told him of the mission on which they were come. When the legate heard their story, he was greatly surprised, and deemed the thing to be of great honour and advantage for the whole of Christendom. So his answer to the two Ambassador Brothers was this: Gentlemen, ye see that the Pope is dead; wherefore ye must needs have patience until a new Pope is made and then shall you be able to execute your charge." Seeing well enough that what the Legate said was just, they observed: "But while the Pope is a-making, we may as well go to Venice and visit our households." So they departed from Acre and went to Negroponte, and from Negroponte they continued their way to Venice. On their arrival there, Messer Nicolas found that his wife was dead, and that she left behind her a son of fifteen years of age, whose name was Marco; and 'tis of him that this Book tells. The two brothers abode in Venice a couple of years, tarrying until a Pope should be made.

When the two brothers had tarried for two years and saw that never a Pope was elected, they said that their return to the Great Khan must be put off no longer. So they set out from Venice, taking Marco along with them, and went straight back to Acre where they spoke to the Legate. They had a good deal of discourse with him concerning the matter, and asked permission to go to Jerusalem to get some oil from the lamp on the Holy Sepulchre to carry with them to the Great Khan as he had enjoined.

MARCO POLO, 1298

From the deck of a Greek liner we bade farewell to the Piazza San Marco and the rest of a brilliant, pastel Venice, as our ship passed the narrow islands and the beaches of the Lido. Soon we were plying the waters of the Adriatic, with Greece and then Acre, Israel, our next destinations.

The sea was the deepest of blues and quiet, and the days passed in an easy rhythm. The three of us ate and read. We watched an occasional school of dolphins, kibitzed with the cribbage players in the lounge, and talked for hours with our fellow passengers. I was once admonished with, "Don't forget to talk to strangers," and that became an important rule of the road for me. It is a rule easier to follow on trains and ships than on planes, since you have easy access to your fellow travelers. The people we met on the ship to Israel represented a diverse spectrum of humanity. We met elderly Greeks and their families: Costa, the cheerful bartender from Cyprus was going back to work in his son's tavern; and an unhappy college professor from the United States, talked of Mediterranean archaeology and remained just a little bit drunk throughout the journey. When his wife had died he had decided to give up twenty-seven years of teaching for a new life in Israel. We met Israelis and relatives of Israelis, and a vivacious young couple from Los Angeles, who had decided that there must be more to life than what was available in "La La Land." They'd quit their jobs, sold their home, and were immigrating to Israel.

There were a hundred shipboard faces at which to smile, and a hundred stories to be told. For the brief moment of that smile or encounter, we were part of our fellow travelers' lives. This was the romance of traveling. It made the inconveniences, indignities, frustrations, and untold obstacles with which we were confronted, tolerable. During those fleeting hours on ship, many friendships were established, and while it's likely that most did not remain active beyond arrival in port, the connections and experiences remain indelibly etched into each passenger's tablet of life.

Perhaps the Polos slept on their Venetian galley's deck, under the stars, with the sea mist in their faces. Perhaps they ate bread and cheese and dried apricots with a little wine for dinner, as we did. They surely did not lounge late into the evening listening to the sounds of harmonicas and guitars and to voices singing Greek and Israeli songs, songs that we soon heard only faintly as we drifted into sleep. Our ship provided its own twenty-knot breeze, and sleeping was easy with the boat gently rocking as its bow split the smooth Mediterranean, creating the soft sound of the spray as it drizzled back on us and the sea.

At about five-thirty in the morning of the second day we awoke to see sheer, red-orange sandstone walls rising up on either side of the ship, so close that we could almost touch them. They bracketed an enormous red-orange sun rising from the rose-colored haze directly in front of us. This was probably one of the two days of the year in which the sun was in perfect alignment with the Corinth Canal for the sunrise. We pulled ourselves out of our sleeping bags to watch this dreamlike event.

A tugboat was leading us through the clear waters between the Peloponnesus and mainland Greece. It was about a sixty-minute tow through the Canal and two more hours under the ship's own power to the port of Piraeus, outside Athens. Athens is not too many miles from Euboea, the modern name for Negroponte, the Polos stopping point on the voyage from Venice to Acre. We decided to take a too-brief tour of Athens; a few minutes to experience a millennia of history. And then back to the ship and the sea.

On the third morning at sea we were told that the ship had stopped before sunrise off the island of Rhodes. We hadn't even heard the anchor chain roll out, although we had slept just a few feet away. After four days at sea the ship slid into the humid, smog-filled, modern port of Haifa, not far from Marco Polo's Acre (now called Akko in Hebrew) but on the deeper side of the bay. Late the evening before, the ship's personnel had taken everyone's hastily repacked bags away from

25 *First Steps into the Past*

Top: The shaded streets of Acre
Below: A Palestinian child runs past the well in
the courtyard of an Islamic Medressah (school
of theology) in Acre

them. Upon arrival, passport stamps, a formality unknown in the thirteenth century, were issued on the upper deck where we shuffled and sweated our way along with the throng of debarking passengers.

We traveled by local bus to the area where the Polos had touched shore 704 years before. It was less than a mile from the port to the now silted and shallow harbor of Acre, on the north side of the Bay of Haifa.

Inside the palm-fringed, crenellated sea walls of Acre, ancient solid stone arches straddle the dim and constricted streets. The fortress-like walls of the houses include Christian ones with a rare window high in the air and Arab structures totally sealed off from the outside world, all testifying to the millennia of invasions and occupations Acre has endured.

Acre's long and colorful history goes back to the nineteenth century B.C.E., when the Egyptians mentioned it in their sacred texts. This once critical center of commerce, where the western world met the East, has been the focal point of many bitter wars fought under many flags. The Egyptians captured the city in the fifteenth century B.C.E. Phoenician traders brought their vessels into the harbor three thousand years ago. It was here that Hercules of Greek mythology found an herb called *aka* to heal his wounds. This could be the origin of Acre's name since *aka* in Greek means cure. Alexander the Great established a mint there in 333 B.C.E., and it operated for six hundred years. England's King Richard the Lionhearted and others sacked Acre in the name of Christianity during the Crusades.

The Polos most likely shared dinner with the knights who were there to fight the Muslims (whom Polo called "Saracens"). If so, they would have visited the Grand Meneir, the operational center for the Crusader government. Marco Polo describes what subsequently happened:

or you must know that, when the Sultan of Egypt marched against the town of Acre and captured it, to the great loss of the Christians, this sultan of Aden contributed to his forces fully 30,000 horsemen and 40,000 camels, much to the advantage of the Saracens and the detriment of the Christians.

MARCO POLO, 1298

In Acre we were rarely allowed so much as a glimpse of the activities behind the blank walls of the dwellings, except perhaps a child's face in a doorway or laundry fluttering high above the street. We wandered along shaded cobblestone paths and unpaved alleys, or passed time in the bazaars for the pleasure of smelling a myriad of fragrances, strolling about just to see and feel something of the local life.

In the bazaar or *souq*, lovely, unfamiliar music greeted us. Conversations were shouted with laughter. Street talk was always at a level leaving me to believe that most of the people of Israel were partially deaf. Cries of "shalom" (peace) came out of doorways on all sides as we meandered through the maze of lanes and shops

where splinters of light barely penetrated roofs and canopies. A man sweeping away dust from his doorway asked in English, "Are you lost?"

Almost anything could be bought. Well, almost anything, if we could identify the object in the dingy light: beige deck shoes or a finely hand-woven, hand-embroidered dress, a tooled-leather camel saddle or glow-in-the-dark paintings of the Last Supper. We could choose between silk prayer rugs or more economically priced ones in lively colored plastics. We watched elderly Bedouin women with blue-tattooed mouths and cheeks picking through the vegetables, covered from head to shoes with yards of dark heavy fabric. The aroma of freshly baked bread and spices and goat hides mixed with the pungent smell of ammonia from puddles of evaporating urine. Some travelers find that roaming the bazaars of the East offers a beautiful, exotic experience while others think it just nauseating. For me, visiting markets in Asia was like being lost in a surrealistic fairy tale: surrounded by peculiar produce and products, encountering strange people wearing curiously different clothing and speaking unrecognizable languages in primitive facilities (even in modern Israel) run by lethargic merchants.

As we left the bazaar to enjoy the full sunlight again, bands of clowning, unruly children danced in and out of the shadows ahead of us and behind us. Some had blue eyes and pale yellow hair; some were very dark. All repeatedly arranged and rearranged themselves in briefly serious and unsmiling poses for our cameras. And then they continued clowning.

A large herd of goats, tossing up thick puffs of dust, accompanied us through the gate leading from old Acre to the modern town. The goats were herded into a nearby ravine where they waded into the murky waters.

We boarded the bus that returned us to Haifa; a modern city of industry and commerce, so to linger had no purpose. We left the next day for Jerusalem, about a hundred miles and a three and a half hour bus ride from Haifa. For the Polos, the trip took three and a half days. We arrived on August 1, 1975.

King David captured Jerusalem and made it his capital three thousand years ago. From antiquity through the Middle Ages geographers called Jerusalem the center of the world, although it was located near neither a waterway nor a major

Above: Mosque of Quabbat-al-Sakhra
(Dome of the Rock)

caravan route. The ramparts of Old Jerusalem are surrounded by a large and thoroughly twentieth-century city. Within the walls of the Old City were structures, the remains of structures, and the widespread debris of structures that were old when the Polos made their visit. The foundations of the immense, substantial city wall were ancient, some parts dating perhaps from the reign of King David's son, King Solomon. A section of the original supporting western wall of the Second Temple of the Jews remains, known as the "wailing wall"; the Roman Army destroyed the rest in 70 C.E.

The great mosque within the old city is called Dome of the Rock. It was from this site that the prophet Muhammad was said to have made his visit to heaven on his horse, Lightning. Twelfth-century Crusaders converted the great mosque into a Christian church, but its form and much of its decoration remained as they appeared when it was built in the seventh century over the ruins of a Roman Temple of Jupiter. Walls were once encrusted with sparkling mosaics and the golden tiles of the dome had been replaced with gold-plated aluminum that could be seen for miles, the most outstanding structure on the skyline. The mosque's name refers to the rock in its interior, which, ancient custom has it, is the rock on which Abraham prepared to sacrifice his son, Isaac. This makes it a sacred site for three of the world's great religions: Judaism, Islam and Christianity.

Also within the ramparts of the Old City, in the Christian quarter, close to the bazaar entrance and down an unmarked alley, was the Church of the Holy Sepulcher, nearly hidden by the surrounding buildings. This, the most sacred site in all of Christianity, was lost in the labyrinth of the narrow streets of Old Jerusalem. Immediately as we stepped inside the three-foot-thick-walled church, street noises were no longer audible. Down a few stairs, the oil-filled lamps burned at the head of a low, oblong sepulcher resting over the traditional site of the tomb of Christ. Investigating the deep and shadowed spaces around and behind the lamplight, we saw that the church interior was divided into chapels, some large, some small, with wooden construction scaffoldings alternating with golden altars in dim and quiet recesses. In the chapels, prayers were offered and priests of the Greek Orthodox, Roman Catholic, and Armenian churches, as well as the Syrian, Coptic, and Abyssinian, held services.

Near one chapel we met a soft-spoken gentleman with kindly eyes and a dark black beard. He was wearing a deep blue cassock. With warmth and patience this gentleman, the Archimandrite Cyrill of the Armenian Church, answered our questions and talked of the history of this church and of the much-needed repairs and restorations that were taking place around us.

"The church is now much the same as it was in the twelfth and thirteenth centuries," he said, adding that minor alterations had been incorporated into the original structure over the years and a wooden dome was destroyed by fire and never replaced. He also knew of the holy chrism oil that the Polos took to the Kublai Khan, "after it was blessed by the bishop." It was a mixture of balsam and olive oil used from antiquity to anoint priests, prophets, and the kings of Christian states; most likely, the intended use by Kublai Khan. There were workmen everywhere. But the peaceful stillness as we talked was hardly disturbed by the taps of the artisans' chisels as they carved ornamental stones to replace those lost or crumbling.

Outside the church everyone was concerned about Arab hostility. Radios blared at all times in public places and on the local buses, ready to announce a war and call their military reserves into immediate mobilization. A new anti-terrorist urban designer had come to town. The buses had bars at the windows to prevent bombs from being thrown inside. Trashcans had special covers that accepted only small pieces of garbage. Stores had solid fronts instead of windows. The mailboxes were fixed with metal strips across the openings, so that only thin letters and postcards would fit. Anything thicker or larger was handed directly to a post-office attendant. Guards at the entrances to every public building and every public area examined you and whatever you were carrying. Soldiers and police continually patrolled the streets. One could easily distinguish between the two because the soldiers carried automatic rifles and the police carried handguns. Security was evident everywhere.

During a visit to my friend at the Israel Broadcasting Authority facilities, we asked the receptionist for directions to the engineering building. A scenario right out of a James Bond movie ensued. The guard-receptionist called for an aide to man his post at the desk. He had taken a 45-caliber pistol from his desk, cocked it and held it pointing up. He walked the twenty feet to the door, carefully looked around outside, then pointed to the building with his left hand while he kept his gun in a ready position. This type of experience was part of everyday life in Israel.

My fifteen-year-old daughter, Sonia, was visiting Israel during our stay, and we all got together at Zion Square in downtown Jerusalem. Sonia was a bit embarrassed by her father and brother showing up at a nice restaurant with grubby clothes and scrubby beards, carrying monstrous yellow backpacks—but she was happy to see us. I had arranged a four-week holiday for Sonia in Israel to study and experience Judaism and live and work on a kibbutz. Before heading to the kibbutz she was staying at a nearby hotel. She told us that the balcony to her room had been blown off two weeks before by a Palestinian car bomb. As I said, this was everyday life in Israel.

Before leaving Acre for Turkey, the Polos visited again with the Legate of the Catholic Church, hoping to get support for Kublai Khan's request to introduce Christianity into the Mongolian Empire. Without the blessing of the Pope, the Khan's Christian state would not be possible. The new pope was still not elected. Disillusioned, the three Polos set sail again across the Mediterranean for the Lesser Armenian (Turkish) coast and the port of Ayas. Soon after the Polos left, the Vatican

announced that the Legate with whom they had spoken in Acre had been elected Pope Gregory X. Here we find the Polos enjoyed the same type of good fortune as experienced by our modern-day Polo expedition. The Cardinals in the Vatican had taken two years to elect a new Pope. Within a week of their meeting with the Legate Bishop in Acre, he was chosen to be Pope. The chances of this happening and its timing were astonishing.

Realizing the importance of the Polos' mission, the new Pope sent a messenger to Ayas to get them to return to Acre for another visit. This time Pope Gregory X laded them with the holy chrism oil, gifts of glass, credentials, and two learned friars—Friar Nicholas of Vicenza and Friar William of Tripoli—for their return trip to Ayas and China. This was far less than the Khan's request of "a hundred learned men," but it was apparently the best offer available from the new head of

the Catholic Church. Apprehensive about the long journey, which they perceived as dangerous, the fainthearted friars chickened-out halfway across Turkey and returned to Acre. The Polos carried on with their mission.

The Persian Gulf was the Polos' new destination. They followed a circuitous route north of Iraq to avoid the Mongols' wars in the Levant. The Persian Gulf was also our destination. We were soon to find that serendipity was to take us on an even more indirect route, to avoid a modern war.

Left and right page: Church of the Holy
Sepulcher, Jerusalem

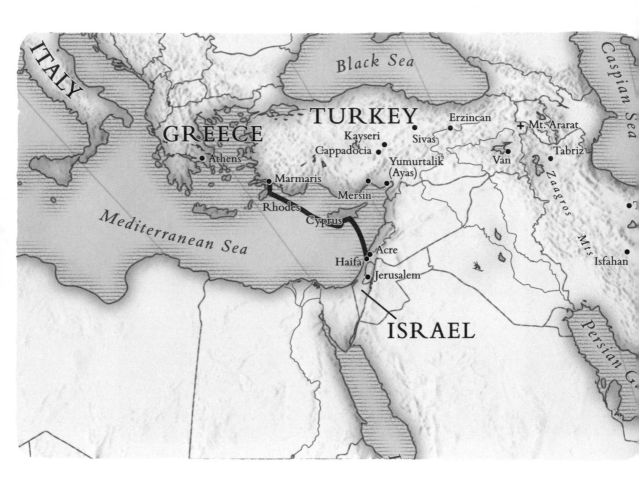

ITALY

GREECE

Athens

TURKEY

Black Sea

Kayseri
Cappadocia

Erzincan

+ Mt. Ararat

Sivas

Van

Tabriz

Yumurtalik
(Ayas)

Marmaris

Mersin

Rhodes

Cyprus

Mediterranean Sea

Acre

Haifa

Jerusalem

ISRAEL

Caspian Sea

Zaagros Mts

Isfahan

Persian G

CHAPTER 3

No Problem
Cyprus and Rhodes, August 7 to 9, 1975

or let me tell you that since our Lord God did mould with his hands our first Father Adam even until this day, Never hath there been Christian or Pagan, or Tartar, or Indian, or any man of any nation, who in his own person hath had so much knowledge and experience of the divers parts of the World and its Wonders as hath had this Messer Marco Polo! And for that reason he bethought himself that it would be a very great pity did he not cause to be put in writing all the great marvels that he had seen, or on sure information heard of, so that other people who had not these advantages might, by his Book, get such knowledge.

MARCO POLO, 1298

"No problem." These two, small words—heard frequently in the months ahead—were usually the precursors of our confrontation with obstacles and "problems" of every magnitude.

A commercial sea route no longer existed between Israel and Turkey. For thousands of years, vessels made regular sailings between the two coasts, but these sailings ended during Israel's October War of 1967 with its Arab neighbors. The modern-day follower of Marco Polo was told he could go to Turkey only by way of the island of Cyprus.

Cyprus had been divided by its own war the previous year, with almost half the island controlled by the Turks. Suspecting that we might have difficulties crossing from one zone to the other to find passage across the sea, we visited a variety of consulates before leaving Jerusalem—Greek, Turkish, and American. We wanted to know if our planned journey by boat to Turkey would be possible.

Everyone was very helpful. At each stop we presented our itinerary and discussed it, and telephone calls were made to the appropriate embassies in Tel Aviv. At each stop we listened to declarations that it was indeed possible for us to continue with our plans, that there would be "no problem."

At this point we still retained our innocence…so we bought plane tickets from Ben-Gurion Airport outside Tel Aviv to Larnaca in the Greek-controlled half of the island of Cyprus.

We boarded the plane, after a lengthy and extremely thorough two and a half hour security check during which random socks and assorted small items became mixed forever with the possessions of others and examiners tossed toothpaste and shampoo into our yellow backpacks with caps and bottle tops loosely replaced, if replaced at all. Capsules in our medical kit were opened and sniffed, cameras were clicked, tape recorders dismantled, and every part of our body and clothes thoroughly examined. Joanne was taken into a small room and strip-searched. A gentleman in a fashionable business suit had the heel of his shoe removed in search of some sort of contraband. The guards found nothing, and the young man calmly hobbled down to the plane with his baggage, apparently accepting the inconvenience as a necessary precaution for survival.

The flight from Ben-Gurion Airport took one hour in a prop-driven, 1950-something Viscount without air conditioning. We perspired. The plane landed in an even hotter Larnaca at 9:30 p.m.

Arrival stairs were rolled up to the plane, and we descended into the hot sultry night, collected our packs, and went into a corrugated aluminum, brightly-lit customs shed. Our passports were spread across the metal counter, and we offered simple answers to questions about how we intended to spend our time in Cyprus. The men in black uniforms promptly informed us that our plans would be not merely a problem, but impossible to carry out. After explaining to us what we could not do, the customs officer could not tell us what we could do, nor did he know what to do with us. Our plan to cross over to the Turkish side of the island and take a ship to Turkey was illegal. He placed a call to the Larnaca police station and spoke with the immigration officer, Sergeant Andreas. I hoped that this was going to be a simple bureaucratic delay; that once they realized we had no political motives and our Marco Polo expedition was simply a cultural venture, we would get the necessary permission to travel to the Turkish/Cyprus port of Famagusta, less than twenty miles away... I hoped this would be "a *small* problem."

Within a few minutes the sergeant was in the shed and listening to our story. He was visibly upset with us for even thinking about going to the Turkish-held side of the island, much less discussing it with him. Again and again he reminded us that a quarter of a million refugees from the north of Cyprus had been forced to live in tents around Larnaca: some of these refugees were members of his own family, all of whom had lost their homes, their livelihoods, and most of their belongings.

But we continued to explain, and the sergeant continued to listen. After a while he said that he understood and accepted our arguments and believed that our plans were peaceful and nonpolitical ones, however...

He was still not happy about our need to get to Turkey, but the sergeant tried to find some way to help us. It was now after midnight, but he decided to call the head of the immigration department in the capital, Nicosia. He translated for us what he was being told on the telephone and what we had been hearing for two hours: we could not go to Turkey from Cyprus. It was not legal and would not be permitted. This was now a serious problem.

What were we to do?

We knew that the new Greek-Turkish frontier was just a five-mile hike from Larnaca. Privately, we considered the idea of simply walking across this line and locating the ferry that would take us to Turkey. Anticipating this possibility,

Sergeant Andreas quietly informed us that if we had been thinking about leaving Greek territory by foot, we should know that we would be promptly arrested.

With this final caution—given with a firm invitation to visit him at the central police station in the morning—the sergeant at last directed the customs official to stamp our passports. We were issued a twenty-four-hour transit visa to give us "time to find an acceptable way off the island" through a Greek port. The Polos had managed to bypass politically turbulent areas. We had boarded a plane and flown directly into the middle of one.

Perplexed and more than a little tired, we tramped slowly down the gravel road into Larnaca and attempted to find a place to spend the one night we had been permitted to stay on Cyprus. It was amazing how much heavier a sixty-five-pound pack could get when accompanied by dejection, frustration and a problem with no obvious solution. The town seemed asleep. We could hear nothing but the quiet roar of the invisible ocean to our right, and we could see only the motion of bats flapping and diving through the light of the street lamps, eating the insects congregating there.

Refugees occupied not only tents outside the town but all the hotel space in Larnaca that was not filled by the few tourists. There were no rooms for us anywhere. The only accommodation we could find was in the cocktail lounge of the Four Lanterns Hotel. The man at the reception desk turned on a few lights in the stale-beer smelling lounge and said that what we saw was the best he could offer. He brought three small towels and a bar of soap and told us to make ourselves comfortable.

This was not the type of accommodations that my wife back in Baltimore would accept, which was why she was not accompanying us. To Rick, with his camping experiences, and Joanne, with her years of traveling under far worse conditions, a night on the floor of the Four Lanterns' bar was far better than what might be expected—and what we would experience—further along Marco Polo's route. We distributed our sleeping bags and our weary bodies on the dance floor and the stage—Joanne wanted to sleep on the stage—and quickly fell asleep.

Our unorthodox lodging was a surprise to the early-rising hotel guests, who wandered through the lounge on their way to breakfast. We rose early as well and headed for the police station.

It was still quite early when we arrived at the police station, but everyone seemed to have been expecting us. We apparently had been under police surveillance throughout the night, no doubt to keep us from scurrying across the border; a sort of "house arrest" or more appropriately "hotel arrest." Immediately, before we even asked, we were directed upstairs. The officers all knew who we were and where and how we had spent the night. Sergeant Andreas was waiting for us in his office on the second floor.

The scene was a familiar one. We have all seen it in old black and white movies. We were on a hot Mediterranean island. The three of us, Rick, Joanne and myself, sat facing the glare of the sun through a window in a police official's office. Above us a large, slowly revolving fan barely stirred the dusty, still air. Palm branches hung motionless outside. The sergeant—possibly playable by Omar Sharif—was young and dark and handsome and had, fortunately for us, a friendly smile exaggerated by a bushy mustache. He offered us cigarettes. He ordered coffee. He leaned back in his chair, lit a cigarette, and began to discuss our dismissal from his country. I expected Humphrey Bogart to casually walk through the door and rescue us...

Contrary to our speculations of the night before, there was no indication or hint of the possibility of bribery by the good sergeant. After a number of telephone calls and much conversation in Greek, the sergeant announced something we understood, "You are sailing tonight on a ship to Rhodes." The Greek island of Rhodes! This was definitely in the wrong direction: four hundred miles to the west. But, he continued, we would have "no problem" finding a ship on Rhodes to take us to Turkey.

We expressed our thanks and farewells and joined three Cypriots for a hot, fast taxi ride along the coastal plain to the port of Limassol, about sixty miles away.

At the shipping office we discovered that there was already "a problem." No one could sell us tickets because it was by no means certain that there would be room for us on the fully-booked ship. But we could, the agent said, "Go to the pier at the 10:00 p.m. sailing time, and wait to see if there would be any extra space on the deck." There was, and at the very last minute we paid for our passage, rushed through customs, and ran up the gangplank to look for our space on deck where we could camp for the night. We were sailing on the *TSS Apollonia* of the Olympic Lines, the very same ship we had taken to Israel.

Unlike the sea on our eastbound trip, the Mediterranean this night was livid and stormy. It started to rain. The sea began to roll. It seemed prudent to go below deck to find more "luxurious" accommodations. Essentially, we were traveling steerage with about fifty students and other low-budget passengers. We found berths below the appropriately named "poop deck" at the stern of the ship. The cavernous, green-painted cargo hold had no portholes or ventilation: perhaps it had been used to haul coal or grain in the ship's previous life. Our berths were airline-type recliner seats: there were over four dozen spread out across this lower deck.

The storm outside intensified, and the rolling, rocking, shaking ship started to take its toll on our fellow cabin mates. One after another they became sick. The stench and the retching sounds of nausea forced us outside, where we had ringside seats to watch and an exciting battle between the ship and the sea.

Throughout the night, tall waves washed over the forward decks. The wind blew hard, screeching fiercely around the ship's stacks and pipes and through the railings and cables. Sleeping under the stars as we had done previously was not only impossibly damp but dangerous as well. Yet, none of us would even consider returning to that lower deck. In an attempt to look optimistically at this travel crisis, we spent the night by a stern rail talking about rerouting ourselves across Turkey and all the exciting places we would have the opportunity of visiting.

The following afternoon, after another rough ride from the ship to the island by launch, we arrived on the Greek island of Rhodes. As we gathered up passports and backpacks at the ubiquitous aluminum customs shed, an official remarked that there would be no ships to Turkey for awhile. Nor would there be, for another eight days, a ship to Athens, from whence to fly to Turkey. Maddeningly, only a short stretch of sea separated us from the Turkish mainland, but apparently we would not be progressing very rapidly over it.

With this information we realized our new sorrowful predicament and began to feel just how tired we were after an uncomfortable and sleepless night. The backpacks were getting even heavier, and we became suddenly and unpleasantly aware of the muggy air and the blinding light from the sun and sea.

Disappointed and discouraged, we trudged away from the shed, along the concrete pier, toward the town. We were scheduled to be in Mersin, Turkey by then, to meet the guide arranged by the Turkish government. There was no way to contact him. Based on the information I received at the customs shed, we would be at least two weeks late—this would have a domino effect, screwing up all our plans. With each step our predicament became more worrisome. And then—before we could even think about beginning to plan our next move—the three of us sighted something that immediately lifted our spirits and adrenalin level: a forty-some-foot sailboat at the dock, flying the red-and-white Turkish flag!

We made cheering noises. I dropped my backpack, jumped over a low wall, and raced down to the pier where the boat was moored. I asked the tiny blond woman sunbathing on the deck, "Do you know of any boats going to Turkey?" The answer came in accented English: "Yes, ve vill soon leave for Turkey." The boat had been rented for a Mediterranean cruise by a young man from Vienna who was celebrating getting his Ph.D. in philosophy. He looked more like a football player than a philosopher. His shipmates were three beautiful young ladies. The crew was busily preparing to set sail within minutes. After hearing the account of our problems, they came to our rescue and asked if we would care to sail with them. We were, to say the least, ecstatic. "*Jawohl!*" (Yes, indeed, to be sure!)

Here we were, almost a thousand miles from our planned route, but, just possibly, we were finally on our way to Turkey. Hitchhiking on a sailboat was not on our original itinerary, but why not? What could be more authentic than sailing to Turkey, and weren't the Polos diverted from their original course of travel by wars between and among the Seljuk Turks, the Mongols, and the Mamelukes of Egypt? So 700 years later it was a war between the Turks and the Greeks that mirrored history and diverted our modern Marco Polo odyssey. We once again set out to sea.

The waters had been dark and rough the previous night. They were no less menacing this evening in a boat that was less than one hundredth the size of the

Apollonia. It was an ominous start. As we left the pier the main engine stopped. "No problem," we were told—there was an auxiliary engine. We sat on the afterdeck, sipped tea and watched waves half the height of the mast, roll menacingly towards us. Then we watched them slip gently beneath the heaving hull. The auxiliary engine was now straining to push the boat through the heavy seas. A sailboat of this size can barely make ten knots headway under power and, with the wind against us, we were moving even more slowly than that towards Turkey. It was going to be a long night.

Attila, the Turkish helmsman, fought the wheel to keep us from being swamped. With both hands, the slender, deeply suntanned Attila gripped the wheel for hours without relaxing. Knowing, perhaps, that we watched and admired his skill, he frequently gave the wheel a fast turn with two or three fingers. This apparent offhandedness was belied, though, by the tautness of his biceps and triceps.

Rhodes faded away behind us. The misty purple mountains of the Turkish coast came into view. Isolated shore lights winked on as darkness fell. Then…the auxiliary engine coughed to a stop!

The crew began shouting at each other in obvious panic. They ran from foredeck to afterdeck and in and out of the cabin and jumped into and out of the space below the deck—all in an attempt to restart the engine. The fragile-looking, aged, and toothless boat captain began to calmly pull the sails from their lockers, moving about with unfaltering steps on the wildly rising and falling boat. He had been hiding somewhere below until now because, as the blonde quietly told us, "He's afraid of the crew."

On the edge of all this activity we continued to sit where we had been sitting, wet, petrified by the violent movements of the ship as it was tossed by the sea, yet mesmerized by the lights on the shore. Our ship was a dervish beginning to spin, dancing and whirling as the still fierce winds turned the boat in foreboding circles and nudged us precariously back into the open sea. I tried not to show the terror I felt and quietly prayed, bit my lips and pondered the fact that no one knew where we were. What would happen if the boat sank in all this black water? I berated myself. What kind of father would take his oldest child, his son, on a monomaniacal journey around the world only to be lost in the middle of the Mediterranean Sea? Nicolo Polo, for one: the reality was that he also took his son on a life-threatening journey. I wondered if waiting for the ship to Athens would have been, after all, a more prudent thing to do. I wondered and worried and prayed, holding tightly to the arms of the chair that was bolted to the deck.

The youngest member of the Turkish crew came up with the brilliant idea of pouring boiling water from our teapot into the battery. Tempers had cooled, as had cylinders—enough to allow the extra energy that the battery now possessed to get the engine purring once more. The crew stopped shouting and running. The shoreline ceased to dance and swirl. Attila returned to the helm.

Near midnight we rounded a breakwater and slipped into a bay, headed toward the cluster of flickering lights that marked the little resort town of Mamaris.

At the dock the police, dozens of curious townspeople, and the tall, imposing owner of the boat, Mr. Karabenlis, dressed in a ship captain's white uniform, welcomed us. They'd heard of our emergency by radio.

A quick stop at the police station provided us with amiable instructions to remain on the boat for the night and take care of passport formalities in the morning.

Everyone—Rick, Joanne and I, the crew, the Viennese, Mr. Karabenlis; eleven in all—then proceeded into town and celebrated our safe arrival with massive amounts of food at a waterfront restaurant. Platter followed platter to the table—fish and shish kebabs, vegetables and tons of rice. Beer bottles were opened, and we toasted each other with raki (a strong clear liquor that turns milky white when mixed with water) in English and German and Turkish.

We had, finally, arrived in Turkey.

CHAPTER 4

Gateway to Asia
Western Turkey, August 10 to August 23, 1975

*I*n Turcomania there were three classes of people. First there are the Turcomans; these are worshippers of Mahomet, a rude people with an uncouth language of their own. They dwell among the mountains and downs where they find good pasture, for their occupation is cattle-keeping. Excellent horses known as Turquans, are reared in this country, and also very valuable mules. The other two classes are the Armenians and the Greeks, who live mixt with the former in the towns and villages, occupying themselves with trade and handicrafts. They weave the handsomest carpets in the world, and also a great quantity of fine and rich silks of cramoisy and other colors, and plenty of other stuffs. The chief cities are Konia, Sivas and Kayseri, besides many other towns and Bishops' sees, of which we shall not speak at present, for it would be too long a matter. These people are subject to the Tartar Khan of the Levant.

MARCO POLO, 1298

After several nights without sleep and after our many beers and raki, the boat bunks and sleeping bags looked very inviting. We could still hear music and voices from the town, punctuated by water slapping the pier. The helmsman, now quite drunk, laughingly, vigorously, noisily swabbed the deck until a voice pleaded, "Enough, Attila, enough!"

Early the next morning, in the company of the police, Mr. Karabenlis, and our hosts, we walked into town. We climbed a tall, narrow flight of wooden stairs to the second story of a white clapboard building and knocked on the door. After a long pause, a short, dark-haired woman with disheveled hair opened the door: she was the customs agent, whom we had obviously gotten out of bed. She looked at the police and told us to enter. She drowsily welcomed us to her house and her country while she opened and closed several desk drawers, looking for her paraphernalia. Ceremoniously, she stamped our passports and showed no interest at all in the three matching yellow backpacks, which the police had insisted we bring with us.

After thanking our hosts and saying good-bye to our new friends, we seated ourselves near the harbor to await the eastbound bus. Our maps and guide books directed us to a bus trip from Marmaris (here on the southwest coast of Turkey) to Mugla (just thirty miles away), where we were to buy tickets to Aydin. We would change buses again in Aydin and head east on a five hundred mile, zigzag passage to Mersin on the southeast coast of Turkey. This would have been our ingress to Turkey had the ferry sailed from Haifa as originally planned. Beyond Aydin the bus wound through gray limestone mountains, weathered and rounded, with strange and foreboding formations. For the next three hundred miles, the narrow road was

41

lined with eucalyptus trees and flame-red hibiscus blossoms. On the bus to Aydin we traveled with a young Turk named Mehmet Ali Sayarer, who owned a tobacco and pipe shop in Marmaris, which, of course, specialized in meerschaum. Pieces of meerschaum are usually only a few inches in diameter and are the remains of fossilized sea creatures that were buried by nature millions of years ago. Mehmet was short and thin and wore large thick glasses, a white pressed shirt, and a narrow black tie. He was a graduate economist from Ankara University and looked the part. His family was from the area of Eskisehir in West Central Turkey, where the white meerschaum used in making pipes was mined.

The bus continued through scrub forest and over dry mountains, past tobacco and cotton fields and olive groves, past tiny villages with red tile roofs on mud houses.

The Turkish men, almost without exception, had thick, neatly-shaped black or, later, grey mustaches, a tradition dating back to the days of the harem. Eunuchs, the castrated men who guarded the women of the harem, could not grow facial hair; therefore, the growth above a man's lips proved his masculinity. (I had always wondered why the moustache was almost universal in the Islamic Middle East.)

Most men in the major cities of Turkey wore Western-style clothing, but the streets of a small village provided a very different experience. It was like walking onto the back lot of an early twentieth-century Hollywood movie. The clothing worn by men in the villages consisted of dark suit jackets with narrow lapels, white shirts, very narrow black ties, and the incongruous baggy pants. We often saw men cutting and tossing hay in the fields, dressed in this same manner, including the tie securely pulled up to the neck in the hot noonday sun.

In 1923, the Turkish leader Mustafa Kemal Attaturk decreed that women would not cover their heads with a veil nor men wear the turban or the colorful baggy pants with a crotch that crossed at the knees. This design for pants also goes back a millennium or more when certain Muslims believed that the next Islamic messiah would be born of man and they all wanted to make sure there was enough room in their pants if they were the chosen one. It was curious to see men wearing standard Western leather shoes but bending down the back of the shoe to use them as pre-1923 backless shoes i.e., slippers.

As we traveled east, we also traveled back in time. More and more women wore a sort of pants called the salvar: a large quantity of fabric draped from the waist, down and between the legs, and tucked in at the waist on the opposite side. As the fashion transitioned to more modern styles, we saw standard skirts sewed together at the hemline except for the two places for legs, giving somewhat the same effect as the draped fabric. It was fascinating to see a culture try to hold on to its ancient traditions after so many generations during which these were forbidden.

The heat was unbearable, but the windows on buses were never allowed to be open, not so much as a millimeter. We could therefore be assured that the "dangerous" moving air with demons wouldn't enter and that no sickness-bearing spirits could join the passengers inside. Apparently we were the only ones who found the heat oppressive. A chorus of male-voiced protests began if there was an attempt or even a suspicion of an attempt to open a window. The women seemed content, clothed in their voluminous, heavy skirts worn with warm stockings, pants and two, three, or more sweaters with the ever-present headscarf, which had replaced the veil of the old Muslim Turkey.

At noon on the second scorching day along the Mediterranean coast we watched a group of nomad women bathing in the sea. Each was modestly covered with their waterlogged flowing skirt-pants, a scarf, and excessive layers of wool sweaters. Only their slippers had been removed and left at the water's edge.

After two days of bus riding east in Turkey, we found no one goes anywhere, no matter how long or brief the bus ride, without the required bag or basket of food. To refuse an offer of food or to eat only a small portion of that which was offered was to risk hurt feelings; or worse, the refusal can be considered a grave insult, even if one finished a large meal only fifteen minutes before. Although we never stopped trying to order small portions at the rest stops that served food, most meals turned out to be enormously large. So we ate rice and chicken and eggplant and lamb. And then, with as much enthusiasm as we could, we ate the food proffered by those traveling with us: grapes, cucumbers, raisins, nuts, and more. Much more! I was certain that starvation was not to be our problem in Turkey but traveling the deserts of Iran, Afghanistan, and China could be a different story.

We held out our hands at least once between stops for a cooling splash of the lemon cologne distributed by the "conductor" assigned to our bus—a refreshing and matchless custom that we found in Turkish bus travel. The conductor was a young boy of about twelve years who also served tea at each stop out of a glass kettle in an ornate metal carrier and small glass cups in nickel-plated metal holders. Greyhound Bus Lines, please take notice.

Music was an essential part of bus travel in Turkey. The bus drivers seemed to like it, even to need it, while traveling. The passengers tolerated it. We usually arrived at our destinations with throbbing headaches. Called, we were told, *dolmush* [taxi] music because no one other than bus or taxi drivers would listen to it, the taped music was always played at brain-piercing volume. In the music world, my daughter Sonia, who is a musician, told me this is called setting the sound to 11. It was always set at 11, and always, always played.

Our travel plans, altered by our passage through Cyprus and Rhodes, serendipitously gave us the opportunity to visit places not exactly on Marco Polo's route: We found the Roman ruins of Hierapolis now in possession of a few Italian archaeologists and thousands of bats. And there was Pamukkale with its hot calcium springs where the ancients worshiped and which have formed a series of giant, white, petrified waterfalls cascading down three hundred feet of a mountainside. The pools of mineral water looked cool and inviting under the hot sun so we joined the crowds and took a dip. We dried our mineral-encrusted skin and got an afternoon bus to Konya. Our discomfort from the heat was compensated by a magical sunset, a delicate pink and gold sky over a lake speckled with tiny white caps and surrounded by misty, purple mountains. It was almost midnight when we arrived in Konya and the best we could find for dinner was some pastry and a Coke. The only hotel we could find did not have water. As travelers in the Third World you just have to make do.

Konya was the five-thousand-year-old city that Polo mentions in passing but through which he probably never passed. For eight hundred years the Mevlevi Monastery, with its green conic cupola has been the home of the world famous Whirling Dervishes. These exotic, Islamic male dancers practice their faith and pray through a dance that reminds one the earth is always spinning on its axis. We watched, fascinated, as the white-robed dervishes with tall cylindrical hats continually spin round and round on their left foot to agitate the soul, see God in all directions and get what is comparable to a "high." The dance was called the "sema." With flaring skirts, the Whirling Dervishes resembled giant, inverted white tops spinning in the main hall of the elaborately decorated monastery in Konya. Melvana Celal E. Rumi founded this religious sect just prior to Marco Polo's journey through Greater Armenia.

The bus ride eastward took us past bleak fields of boulders, fields that were salt-crusted and gray, and then through green fields of corn, wheat, tobacco, and cotton and more cotton; crops irrigated, as they have been for thousands of years, by troughs and water wheels and buckets. Men cut hay while their wives and daughters scrubbed clothes in the distance. At times I felt we were traveling in the thirteenth century, on the coattails of Marco Polo.

The bus overtook and passed donkeys carrying straw piled three times their height, often with a child perched on the very top of the straw, waving and grinning as we went by. Undulating masses of gray and white sheep crossed the cracked, burned mountain slope, and their tiny shepherds—some of whom seemed to be little more than toddlers—scampered alongside the flocks with their dogs. Here and there were the brown felt tents marking the residences from which the diminutive nomadic shepherds had come.

One humid evening, after a week of travel, we arrived in the rather unlovely, modern seaport town of Mersin at the west end of the Cilician Plain, near ruins of an old Roman port and near ancient Ayas. At last, we were where the Polos had landed after their sea journey from Acre. How near, we had no idea.

Arrangements had been made with the Turkish government to have a guide meet us in Mersin, and he was there, waiting for us. Mersin was chosen since that would be the terminus of the ferryboat from the Turkish side of Cyprus. Ertan

Akbayar was an engineer by training, a photographer by preference, and a well-informed, enthusiastic guide. Ertan also folded down the back of his shoes to wear them as slippers. He was a very warm person and an excellent cook, as we discovered when we stayed at his apartment in Ankara. Ertan's welcome gift to us was a much-needed Turkish-English dictionary and an invitation to visit Ankara for a few days before continuing along Marco Polo's trail.

owbeit, they have a city by the sea, which is called Ayas, at which there is a great trade. For you must know that all the spicery, and cloths of silk and gold, and other valuable wares that come from the interior, are brought to this city. And merchants of Venice and Genoa, and other countries, come thither to sell their goods, and to buy what they lack. And whatsoever persons would travel to the interior (of the East), merchants or others, they take their way by this city of Ayas.

MARCO POLO, 1298

Marco Polo thus told of his arrival in Ayas from Acre. We did not find Ayas on any modern map of Turkey. Through research we found Ayas to be an ancient port and trading post, which dated from the eighth century B.C.E. This was the time of Hittite settlements in southern Turkey and the Greeks, who built up a major port there called Aegae. Later it became Ayas, as did two other ancient towns on the Turkish coast. Of the three, we decided to visit the fishing village now known as Yumurtalik. The coastline of this town most resembled that shown on an ancient and detailed British Admiralty map we had discovered a few years before in an old Turkish history book. The map also showed a castle on an island a few hundred meters from shore. There was an island of this description at Yumurtalik.

Discovering Yumurtalik to be Ayas was a combination of good luck, good guessing and a little research. Without these three factors providing our support, our expedition would have been a disaster at almost every turn.

Led by Ertan, we set off to see and photograph Yumurtalik and to look for new clues to its past. We were not disappointed. Almost immediately we found a section of a fluted column buried in the wall of the ruined castle near the shore. This was a Greek artifact. (Roman columns are smooth.) Later in the afternoon more of the 2,500-year-old column drums and fragments could be seen protruding from the rubble of the town's breakwater or lying loose and eroding beneath the waves.

While Rick, Ertan and I continued to search for an older Yumurtalik and for confirmation that it had once been the Ayas of which Marco Polo wrote, Joanne went off to explore the rest of the tiny, somnolent town and to drink tea with a half dozen teenage girls. Few of the inhabitants were visible. Windows had been shuttered and doors remained closed. Most of the houses and sea walls seemed to be turning to powder, bit by ochre-colored bit, falling into the dusty lanes.

A paved road and the railway now follow Marco Polo's trail to Iran. Over the next few weeks, with the guidance of Ertan, we would photograph and explore most of the towns along the old trade route at the western end of the Silk Road.

We left Yumurtalik by the ubiquitous Turkish bus, traveling north to the area of Cappadocia, a weird wonderland where nature's fingers had clutched the fragile tuff stone and molded it into bizarre shapes: humps, irregular pyramids, and surrealistic cones rising to the height of three or four stories. Everything was a sandy rose color. Where soil had accumulated at the top of nature's strange structures, we found grass growing, resembling green hair on Martian creatures. There was little other vegetation.

The Byzantine monks carved apartments out of these cones in the sixth century. Their work had survived these many centuries. Where erosion had worn away a side, we could see the holes for storage shelves, and benches for sitting and sleeping. These were chiseled out of the walls to create living space in these simple, primitive residences. They still provide low-cost housing for the local community. Our two days here amongst the rocks of Cappadocia was like living in a fairyland

Nearby was the city of Kayseri, where the trail turns to the east to Sivas, as mentioned by Marco Polo.

The landscape of Eastern Turkey was barren and treeless. Indeed, except in town parks, trees were rarely seen throughout our entire journey. Green pastures or a patch of cultivated field infrequently interrupted the rock-strewn terrain.

There was, however, no lack of color wherever we looked. Snow-capped mountains in the distance constantly changed from gold to brown to purple with the climb and descent of the sun in the luminous, clear blue sky. Donkey trains followed one after another, stepping synchronously by the side of our bus; donkeys with grasses and brightly dyed sacks, donkeys with clanking pots and pans

Above: Monastery of the Whirling Devishes in Konya

and other multicolored household goods tied to their backs. Small, grimy children and their mothers used switches across the donkey's forward shoulders to keep the animals moving along to a rhythm, the way a bass drum sets the pace in a parade. The train drivers were all gaily-dressed in velvets of reds and pinks and greens or in other shiny, colorful fabrics. White herons stood in the irrigation ditches, and rust-colored hawks soared overhead. Bright, tiny yellow birds flew up, and then resettled on the shoulders of grazing cows. It was a world painted from a palette of enchanting colors both natural and exciting.

Once in a while we skirted small settlements of houses built of sun-dried bricks. These little dwellings—huddled together with windowless backs turned to the road—seemed dwarfed by enormous stacks of hay and by large pyramids of drying animal dung on their roofs. In this treeless part of Turkey, dung was the fuel of choice for the cooking and heating fires. The haystacks and dung piles reminded us that the harsh winter was soon expected to replace the heat that enveloped us as we traveled east.

Again and again during the journey we had the sensation that time had long ago stopped its progress. Villagers stooped in the fields, swinging scythes; huge hand-hewn wooden pitchforks tossed and winnowed the dried wheat; yoked oxen plodded around and around, dragging a stone, grinding the grains, while other oxen carried off the yield; bent elderly men seated in blue-painted wagons with wobbling, solid-wooden, spokeless wheels rumbled along the roads.

Marco Polo traveled as we traveled through Kayseri (ancient Caesarea) at the foot of Mount Erciyas. Kayseri has the sorrowful honor of being invaded and destroyed by almost every major conqueror in the Middle East since the beginning of the first millennium when the city was named after Caesar. They were overrun by Romans, then King Chosroes II of the Sassanids, followed by the Arabs, the Mongolians and Tamerlane in 1402 with many other invaders in between. An imposing citadel built in the seventh century did little to protect its people, except occasionally by providing temporary shelter. Nineteen rectangular towers and thick black lava stonewalls stood as bastions against conquest, but the huge double gates did not keep us out. Inside we found a truly picturesque market. Ertan and I realized the best place from which to take photos of this colorful scene was from the forty-foot walls or the towers above them. Ertan led me up some dark stairs in one of the towers that had an entrance to a wall, and we walked straight out along the top of the wall towards the next tower. I followed without thinking where I was or what I was doing except I was following Ertan to get a great shot of the market. Suddenly my acrophobia kicked in as I came to my senses and realized I had just gone some forty paces on the top of a high stone wall that was less than eighteen inches wide. I panicked. Slowly I lowered myself to all fours and carefully crawled back to the tower. My heart must have been pounding at its aerobic maximum rate. I'll never be a James Bond.

Further along the Silk Road, our bus stopped at the once Roman city of Sivas with its many ancient structures. As usual, Ertan found a place for us to spend the night. The next morning we crossed the River Euphrates to Erzincan (pronounced Er-zin-john in Turkish) and Erzurum. The arid land along this route was crossed by dry riverbeds and speckled with the small, white summer tents of nomadic shepherds. This rainless area gave way to flowing creeks and much more agriculture as we moved to the East, where fields and hills glowed golden with ripe wheat as far as we could see. Then the terrain, barren again, became red rock, then rugged, naked, green, copper-bearing hills.

The cities were fairly modern, or trying to be, in a dusty, somewhat shabby fashion. Modern city or not, we found at every turn, often a few steps from an air-conditioned hotel, the very structures that the Polos also passed. Much of the handsome, bright Seljuk blue tiles and the chiseled stonework had survived as part of the twelfth- and thirteenth-century buildings, mosques and minarets. Domed, polygonal twelfth-century red brick mausoleums sat between twentieth-century houses or were stranded alone on a grassy divider of a four-lane street.

Some of the mosques had been in use over the centuries; others were being renovated. The call to prayer by the muezzins through long voice trumpets was distorted and quavering, and echoed from ancient minaret to minaret five times daily.

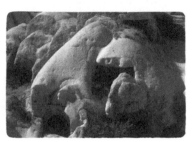

Active seven hundred years ago as theological schools (madrassahs), mosques, or hospitals, many buildings were now empty, elegant silhouettes against the sky, lovely shells, gray and silent. If the gates to the buildings had disappeared or had been left ajar, sheep and chickens wandered in to graze or scratch at the ground in weed-filled courtyards where once students of medicine or Islamic studies worked and slept. Intricate, delicate patterns in the tiles of the walls and vaulted ceilings with honeycombed, high relief carvings framing doors and windows, offered a somber and symmetrical beauty.

We saw carpets in a great variety of patterns and colors, carpets of wools and silks in all the hues one could dream of, carpets spread everywhere, from the primitive tent to the richest mosque, from bazaar floor to teahouse. Exquisite Turkish carpets adorned all level surfaces and a few walls as well. Marco Polo called them the most beautiful in the world. Turkish knotted carpets can last for centuries. On many occasions we saw new carpets laid out in front of mud huts to be trampled by people and animals to soften the wool.

Erzurum was the last good-size town before reaching the Iranian border. Its 70,000 inhabitants lived at an altitude of 6,500-feet surrounded by 10,000-foot mountains. In Erzurum we had an opportunity to watch the process of carpet making at Ataturk University, School for Carpet Making, where girls began at twelve years of age to learn this ancient art.

Left and right page: Cappadocia

A few of the students made kilims at the looms, a specialty of the individual villages. Kilims were woven carpets in which the bold, color-filled geometric patterns appear on either side of the finished piece. Most carpets or kilims made by Moslems and decorations on mosques and other buildings have only geometric designs. We were told that living things were never reproduced in Islamic art since only "Allah" can create life.

The majority of the students practiced the more exacting, traditional method of making Turkish (or Persian or Afghan) carpets: knotting separately and by hand each wool or silk weft yarn on a wool or cotton warp. The weft yarn was twisted into a figure eight around two- or four-warp threads, tied, and cut, all in a blur of flashing fingers.

Only by looking carefully could we see any difference between the work of the novice students and those with more experience. The twelve-year-olds had before them smaller or simpler designs, and their fingers didn't move with the agility of those of the older girls, but their carpets were all skillfully produced.

Above: Cifte Minare (The Twin Minarets) in the city of Sivas was completed the year Marco Polo came to this trade center

The school director, who showed us the workrooms and explained the girls' tasks to us, said that an experienced student could, in one minute, make and trim perfectly with her knife about thirty-five knots, and working at this speed they would complete a ten-meter carpet in about two years. Usually two or three girls sat before the work frames, rhythmically knotting and cutting, selecting a different yarn color when their drawings showed a change, creating the designs of these handsome, softly dark carpets. The school paid the girls three and a half Turkish lire per one thousand knots, or about twenty-five cents an hour. The ten-square-meter (eight by twelve foot) carpet was made for about $1000 in labor. If my math is right, that is over eight million knots for one carpet.

In the town center, men would sit in coffee houses smoking and sipping. The coffee was black, extra strong and extra sweet. They filled half their cups with sugar and played backgammon, a game that came from nearby Babylonia (Iraq) five thousand years ago.

Above: A church in Cappadocia carved out of the stone by the Byzantine monks

CHAPTER 5

Noah's Place
Mt. Ararat, August 26 to 31, 1975

his is a great country. It begins at a city called Arzinga (Erzincan), at which they weave the best buckrams in the world. It possesses also the best baths from natural springs that are anywhere to be found. The people of the country are Armenians, and are subject to the Tartar. There are many towns and villages in the country, but the noblest of their cities is Arzinga, which is the See of the Archbishop, and then Arziron (Erzurum) and Arzizi (Van)...

And you must know that it is in this country of Armenia that the Ark of Noah exists on the top of a certain great mountain [on the summit of which snow is so constant that no one can ascend; for the snow never melts, and is constantly added to by new falls. Below, however, the snow does melt, and runs down, producing such rich and abundant herbage that in summer cattle are sent to pasture from a long way round about, and it never fails them. The melting snow also causes a great amount of mud on the mountain]...

On the north it is bounded by the Land of the Georgians, of whom also I shall speak. On the confines towards Georgiania there is a fountain from which oil springs in great abundance, insomuch as a hundred shiploads might be taken from it at one time. This oil is not good to eat with food, but 'tis good to burn, and is also used to anoint camels that have the mange. People come from vast distances to fetch it, for in all the countries round about they have no other oil.

MARCO POLO, 1298

The bus left Erzurum on the caravan route that climbed and wound its way over the Tahir Pass at 8,000 feet. Guardrails on these narrow roads were unheard of, and along the way lay memorials to those who had, once too often, driven the tight curves at life threatening speeds: carcasses of trucks and cars lay at the bottom of roadside ravines. "Allah will provide" was the fatalistic justification for not helping Allah just a little by driving with more care. Allah provided for us as the bus took the treacherous tight curves at high speed without mishap. Ertan took it calmly as if he were on a horse drawn cart driving down a country road; on the other hand, Rick, Joanne and I had white knuckles.

When we were safe again on the plain below, an army officer routed our vehicle off the highway and onto a path through harvested fields for awhile. Some horrible disaster that required military involvement had no doubt blocked the road ahead.

Nothing much taller or greener than a thistle grew along the way to Lake Van, but the cattle were abundant and plump so there must have been something edible somewhere. In the fields little boys, dragging white cloth bags twice their size, gathered cow dung. We passed a bright red bus returning to Pakistan from

Mecca with dozens of Muslim pilgrims (Ertan translated the banner on the side). The thistles and shrubs along a creek were festooned with the shirts and pants of the pilgrims, all male, who vigorously washed their half-naked bodies and their clothes under the afternoon sun. They waved to us as we passed. Nearby a baby howled at the world while his mother scrubbed his small body in a public fountain. As we crossed a hilltop we saw a shining dot of water dozens of miles away...Lake Van.

The lake was a brilliant turquoise in contrast to the tawny hills. On its southern coast was the little hamlet of Gevas where a burly, craggy-faced fisherman, Yusaf, took us in his boat on the three-mile excursion to the island in the center of this high and saline body of water, lifeless except for a few ugly carp. Yusaf showed us one of the whiskered monsters he had just taken from the lake.

In the tenth and eleventh centuries Van, the city on the other side of the lake, was a major town in the kingdom of Armenia, and here, early in the tenth century, on the bare rock of the island we were visiting, the Aktamar Basilica, a Church of the Holy Cross, was founded. The building stood solid with its golden-brown stone, framed by the blue sky and the distant hills, alone on the island except for gulls and mosquitoes and pigeons, and now us.

After a thousand years the interior fresco had faded, but we could easily follow some of the painted scenes from the life of Christ, around the dome. Clear and vivid Bible stories were cut in stone around the church exterior; among them Adam and Eve in the Garden of Eden, and an unhappy Jonah being pitched over the side of a boat into the waiting mouths of ugly beasts with ferocious doglike faces and the bodies of fish. It was truly amazing that this ancient building had survived so well, just frozen in time. There was no graffiti, no vandalism: a dry climate and isolation from the world—except for a few visitors like us—all helped its survival. From the outside it looked as if it was built just twenty or thirty years before.

We climbed down the stony side of the island to Yosuf's waiting boat. As the late afternoon light started to fade, we watched the last bit of color being squeezed from the bald mountains: brown, rust, gray, and then nothing but dark shadows.

The nearby town of Van was an ancient oasis. It fell, over the ages, to the Medes and the Persians and, like every other place of importance from Poland to the Yellow Sea, the Mongols came and went, but it survived. It survived, until Tamerlane (also known as "Timur") the fourteenth century Turkic conqueror, totally destroyed it. A year after our visit, on November 24, 1976, a devastating quake rocked this town, leaving 3,800 people dead and over 10,000 homeless. Even Tamerlane could not have wreaked such havoc and ruin in so short a time.

The following morning we left Van and continued again toward Iran by bus.

The snow-covered peak of Mount Ararat came into view, visible through the cloud of white road dust in which we traveled and with which, floured and phantom-like, we had been smothered. We were told this was a rare sight since the top of Mt. Ararat was almost always shrouded in clouds. Below us, in the northeast corner of Turkey, was the town of Dogubayazit, our last stop on the main caravan route before we entered Iran.

Above the town on a mountainside we found what remained of a fairy castle; the vacant Palace of Abdi constructed of red sandstone for a seventeenth-century pasha. The different levels of the building unevenly climbed the hillside in a mélange of architectural styles, from Armenian to Seljuk Turk to pure fairy tale. Rick, the future architect, was especially taken with its beauty. Joanne and I were in awe of this jewel perched on the hilltop.

Balconies overlooked spacious gardens and courtyards. Carvings in stone and stucco twined thickly around and up every pillar and arch, and outlined the numberless windows, doorways, and spaces that appeared to be doorways but turned out to be windows. Joanne discovered this when she threw open what she thought was a door, and was about to step forward onto nothing but the mountain slope from two stories up.

Ceiling paintings had dimmed only a little, and the chains that suspended many dozens of lanterns still hung in place. We found interior balconies reached by hidden staircases, and cozy niches or tiny rooms set high in the walls from which women could watch unseen through filigreed screens, the activities of the men in the rooms below.

This was such a surrealistic place it felt extraterrestrial: as if we were in the Land of Oz, Dorothy, the Tin Man, and the Warm Hearted Lion traveling arm in arm down the yellow brick road—this time to Xanadu.

The untidy, dust-blown town of Dogubayazit had nothing to compare with the romantic castle that looked down on it. Emaciated cows and horses stood here and there in the streets. Little was for sale in the market except a small and sad assortment of aging fruits, vegetables, and rotting meats infested with flies. This might have been the cause of what was to become a near disaster for Rick and me. One evening we had our dinner at an outdoor restaurant in which the meals were prepared in a nearby shed. To say it was not clean would be a gross understatement. Joanne had ordered rice and vegetables and Rick, Ertan and I had shashlik, their one meat dish. Ertan left for Ankara the next day. Rick and I soon became ill with major stomach problems. Over the following weeks the "problems" became progressively worse for both of us. This was a bigger issue for Rick because he was a vegetarian before signing up for this expedition. The foods available in Turkey were both against his dietary principals and physically disagreeable to him. At first I thought he was just being a good sport about his acceptance of the overwhelming amount of meat and few vegetables that were proffered in the places we ate, but I was now concerned about the implications of his new forced diet.

The thirty-year-old manager of our hotel, Fahrettin Kolan, a tall lanky guy, had been a guide for expeditions that searched Mount Ararat for the legendary remains of Noah's Ark. At the time of our visit, non-Turkish climbers were not allowed on the mountain, and since most of the would-be explorers were not Turkish, Fahrettin hadn't led an expedition since 1972. He climbed solely for his own pleasure.

He described for us the ascent on the east, the easy side of the mountain, as one would describe a pleasant three-day stroll. The climb on the north, on the "difficult" side, he said, took a good climber about a week over ice and snow. Son of nomads, a Kurd, Fahrettin spent the early summers of his life in the rich pastures halfway up the 17,000-foot mountain with his family and their herds.

His climbing methods might not appeal to the nervous or frail. He began his climb, he said, in the dark of night "when the air is cool." "Tea at night only" was all the fluid he allowed himself, and he slept little, "a few hours, but not the first night." For supplies he needed only the tea and "a little chocolate, butter, and biscuits" and the single ski, an early version of a snowboard, on which he made his descent, "like the village children use in winter for sport."

The Iranians called the mountain, an extinct volcano, Koh-i-nuh, "Noah's mountain." It has long been sacred to the Armenians, who have lived in this area for thousands of years and who believe that the ark does rest at the summit but that man has been forbidden by God to find it or see it.

As to whether any of the expeditions had learned something about the existence of the ark, or where it might be if it did exist on this mountain, Fahrettin admitted that no one had yet seen or found anything, but he related the traditional story that Marco Polo had heard and recorded seven hundred years before, as he passed below Mount Ararat.

Fahrettin said, "The ark is there, buried eighty meters down in the glacier on the Russian side of the mountain." He even drew us a map of the area of the mountain and marked the location of the ark. Was it only an age-old local fable or a real possibility? Fahrettin wanted very much to be able to climb again with those who want to continue the search.

About one hundred years before Marco Polo came to Mount Ararat, another traveler of the East passed this way, the Rabbi Benjamin of Tudela, Spain, whose writings were translated from Hebrew into Latin in 1575. His story may hold the answer as to why the ark was never discovered. The Rabbi writes about an Islamic leader, Omar Ben Al-Khataab, who removed the wooden ark from the mountain, dismantled it and built a mosque with its timbers on an island in the Aras River four miles away. I found no modern record or memory of the mosque. The mystery continues.

We wished Fahrettin good luck in finding the truth about this biblical story and the whereabouts of this famous Ark of Noah.

Top: Mount Ararat, legendary home of Noah's ark
Bottom row and right page: The Palace of Abdi, a fairy-tale castle and caravanserai

On August 31, 1975, we had a party of yumurta, ekmek and coke (eggs, bread and coke) to celebrate our departure from Turkey and to say goodbye to Ertan who had become our cherished friend.

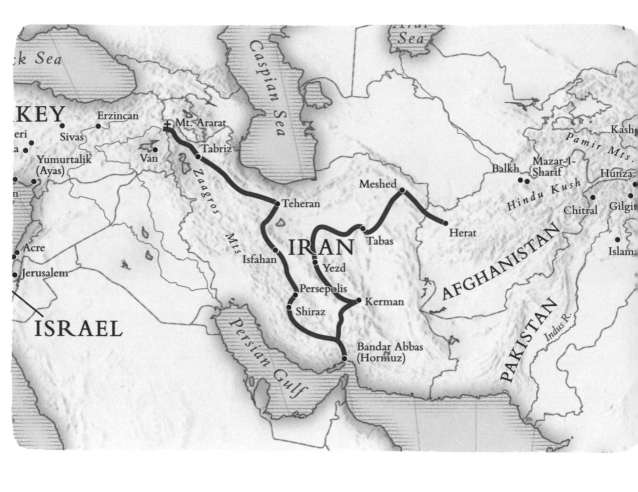

CHAPTER 6

A Persian Paradise
Iran, August 31 to September 9, 1975

Persia is a great country, which was in old times very illustrious and powerful; but now the Tartars have wasted and destroyed it.

In Persia there is the city of Sava, from which the Three Magi set out when they went to worship Jesus Christ; and in this city they are buried, in three very large and beautiful monuments, side by side. And above them there is a square building, carefully kept. The bodies are still entire, with the beard and hair remaining. One of these was called Jaspar, the second Melchior, and the third Balthasar. Messer Marco Polo asked a great many questions of the people of that city as to those Three Magi, but never one could he find that knew aught of the matter, except that these three kings were buried there in days of old. However, at a place three days' journey distant he heard of what I am going to tell you. He found a village there which goes by the name of Cala Ataperstan which is to say "The Castle of Fire-worshipers." And the name is rightly applied, for the people there do worship fire, and I will tell you why.

They relate that in old times three kings of that country went away to worship a Prophet that was born, and they carried with them three manner of offerings, Gold, Frankincense, and Myrrh; in order to ascertain whether that Prophet were God, or an earthly King, or a Physician.

So it came to pass when they came to the place where the child was born, the youngest of the Three Kings went in first, found the Child apparently his own age; so he went forth marveling greatly. The middle one entered next, and like the first he found the Child seemingly of his own age; so he went forth again and marveled greatly. Lastly, the eldest went in, and as it had befallen the first two, so it befell him. And he went forth very pensive. And when all three had rejoined one another, each told what he had seen; and they all marveled the more. So they agreed to go in all three together, and on doing so they beheld the Child with the appearance of its actual age, to wit, some thirteen days. Then they adored, and presented their Gold, Incense and Myrrh. And the Child took all three offerings, and then gave them a small closed box; whereupon the Kings departed to return to their own lands.

And when they had ridden many days they said they would see what the Child had given them. So they opened the little box, and inside it they found a stone. On seeing this they began to wonder what this might be that the Child had given them, and what was the import thereof. Now the signification was this: when they presented their offerings, the Child accepted all three, and when they saw that they had said within themselves that He was the True God, and the True King, and the True Physician. And what the stone implied was that this Faith which had begun in them should abide firm as a rock. For He well knew what was in their thoughts. Howbeit, they had no understanding at all of this signification of the gift of the stone; so they cast it into a well. Then straightaway a fire from heaven descended into that well wherein the stone had been cast.

And when the Three Kings beheld this marvel they were sore amazed, and it greatly repented them that they had cast away the stone; for well they then perceived that it had a great and holy meaning. So they took of that fire and carried it to their own country, and placed it in a rich and beautiful church. And there the people kept it continually burning, and worship it as a god, and all the sacrifices they offer are kindled with that fire. And if ever the fire becomes extinct they go to other cities where that same faith is held, and obtain that fire from them, and carry it to the church. And this is the reason that the people of this country worship fire. They will often go ten days journey to get of that fire.

Such then was the story told by the people of that Castle to Messer Marco Polo.

MARCO POLO, 1298

With Mount Ararat still in view behind us, we said good-bye to our guide, Ertan, and crossed the frontier into Iran. The landscape didn't change. The hills were still treeless. Where the land was irrigated, it was green; the rest was covered with patches of scrubby grass. The countryside was stark; as the hills became mountains, the vista we saw ahead of us was overpowering. The frontier town of Maku sat at the bottom of a long gorge only two hundred yards wide with almost vertical walls. The mountains stood like giant jaws ready to take a bite from the blue skies. Mud-brick buildings seemed to be glued to the sides of this canyon, and near the top was the ruin of a fortress. Beyond Maku the mountains' giant mouth spread apart as the road rolled along a level plain to Tabriz. Ahead of us was modern Iran and much of ancient Persia.

We left Turkey but Rick and I took a little of Turkey with us—severe food poisoning.

Rick's ailment was so bad that it was necessary for him to return home a few days later when we reached Teheran. He was much more afflicted with the curse of bad food than I. After all the strange, exotic and unclean foods that I have eaten all over the world, my digestive system may not have been as sensitive to food with bad bugs as was my son. But there was little I could do. Joanne felt fine.

Never in my life have I ever been as lost and confused in the middle of a major city as we were after our arrival in Tabriz. We had city maps both in English and Farsi (Persian). However, none of us could correlate the words on our maps with the few Farsi street signs we found. Asking directions from people on the street without knowledge of Farsi was impossible. Our bewildering situation and despair digressed into throwing angry words as we tried to delegate blame on each other for our irresolvable predicament. In addition to the frustration of being lost, Rick wasn't feeling well and this made it all the worse. We stood on a street corner, totally exasperated and bewildered. A fifteen- or sixteen-year-old boy apparently recognized our dilemma and with a kind face and a smile, offered to help. Not one word of English was used but by exchanging a few gestures and showing him the letter we received from the Ministry of Culture, he understood our needs. We followed him through the winding streets of this rather nondescript city to the Ministry's office. Modern Tabriz was a disappointing spectacle for a city with such an ancient and colorful heritage. This important Silk Road way station had been essentially paved over and historically white washed.

We presented our letter and described our project to the officials at the Ministry. They were to have met us at the border and neglected to do so. We had waited at the border post for three days pestering the guards every hour or so. Since there were no public accommodations, we set up our tent by the side of the road. This would not have been so bad if it were not for the literally hundreds of trucks that were going back and forth in front of us with their noxious fumes. We felt to camp further away would not be prudent or safe. If this were in Polo times I would not have been as concerned about camels going by instead of trucks since the only really smelly thing about camels was their breath and occasional farts, but they are much quieter.

We even learned how to say in Farsi "Have you heard from the Iranian government?" Finally, the three of us realized that they had truly forgotten us, and we decided to go on to Tabriz and take our chances on finding this obscure government agency. The arrangements for our travel across Iran were to be made by the Ministry of Culture in Teheran by direction from the Iranian Ambassador to the U.S., and someone really screwed up.

Frank Shore, Associate Editor of National Geographic, had introduced me to the Iranian Ambassador, Ardeshir Zahedi, a few months earlier. The Ambassador's support of our project included his promise that the Iranian Ministry of Culture would help in every way possible. The officials at the office in Tabriz were very concerned about the political implications of not meeting us at the border town of Maku. Ambassador Zahedi was also the brother-in-law of the Shah and politically very, very powerful. To atone for their oversight at the border, they arranged to handle the details for our visits to each of the major points of interest along the Marco Polo trail on our journey across their country.

Accommodations were arranged; local transportation and guides knowledgeable in the history and culture during Polo's time were assigned to us. It was very much like the "Tablet of Gold" the Kublai Khan gave the Polos for their travels across the Mongolian Empire. Marco Polo's benefactor was the Kublai Khan and ours turned out to be the Shah of Persia, Mohammad Reza Pahlavi.

Our first few disastrous days in Iran serendipitously turned into more than a month of real royal treatment.

The Ministry made arrangements for our accommodations in Tabriz and told us a guide would meet us in the morning. With our world turned around, we went out to celebrate with a lunch of orange juice and ice cream. As we sat in the sidewalk café enjoying our new fortunate situation, we watched a man in a dark black suit literally pushing his three reluctant sheep across the street. At the next table, a cat was finishing the meal of the previous patron. So goes life on the other side of the world.

In Teheran, a rental car instead of a camel became our ship of the desert that would carry us across the sands of "Persia." We rented an English Hillman, made here in Iran, and hoped it would help make up for the days we had lost getting from Cyprus to Turkey. We hoped it would provide us more freedom to investigate less accessible areas of the country. The car did give us the opportunity to spend time with many warm, friendly people we would not otherwise have met, but it also caused us to suffer a number of minor disasters and major challenges to our survival. I learned during this voyage that disasters and good fortune are the balance of life on the road. Too much of one would be chaos and too much good fortune could be boring. After all, an adventure would be a journey when something went wrong.

Driving in the city of Teheran was an adventure in itself. The trip across town from our hotel into the open countryside was as perilous as anything I had experienced in driving on six continents…even worse than Rome or Boston. Part of the reason for the traffic turmoil was that the Iranian laws were written for four-wheeled vehicles. Half the vehicles on the streets of Teheran were three-wheeled motorized bicycles that were obviously not subject to the law. They avoided traffic by riding on the sidewalks. They ignored traffic lights and signs. It was like a citywide game of "chicken." By the time I left the city of Teheran I was certain that the name of the city should have been spelled "Terror-ran."

For my son, Rick, to leave our project at the halfway point was sad and upsetting for him, as it was for me, for many different reasons. He was sick and there was little we could do for him in Iran. I was concerned his illness could get worse. I was worried about his long journey home alone, but he would get far better care in Baltimore than in Teheran. A year earlier I was truly elated when he asked to go on this journey with me across most of Europe and Asia. Now, he was to miss seeing and experiencing places that may never be the same. This was also the part of the expedition where there were fewer hotels and sleeping under the stars was what he preferred. He contributed a great deal to the project and I would very much miss Rick.

It was September 5, 1975. We walked along the many streets searching Teheran for a bank to cash my American Express Travelers Check. All the banks were closed for some unknown (to us) holiday, but we knew the Hilton Hotel would exchange it for dollars or local currency. According to the map the hotel was just a short distance, but maps can be deceiving and sometimes wrong. There were no taxis. Today, the streets were almost empty of traffic. We stopped for lunch at what Joanne called a "semi-posh restaurant." The omelets were good but more important they gave us change from my travelers check. This plus the money I had in my pocket, seemed enough for his trip home since there would be plenty of food on each of his flights.

Rick was to fly to Beirut with a short stopover and then on to Rome to change planes for the trip back to the U.S. They said there would be no problems. Part of the tent and a few other items that he was carrying were transferred into my backpack and we exchanged long hugs. It was not easy.

Rick got into a cab and headed for the airport. His flight arrangements did not go as planned. The "no problem" phenomena pursued Rick.

When he arrived at the departure area he was told that the one Pan Am flight out of Teheran was full, in contradiction to what we had been told earlier. Since his was a complimentary ticket from Pan Am, it had a very low priority, and he would have to wait until the next day's departure. There was no way for him to contact me. He knew no one in Teheran or even in all of Iran. The cash he had was almost all spent on an orange juice and a book to read on the plane ride home...Jaws. Now there was no more money for food much less for a place to spend the night.

The solid-plastic, gray chairs in the departure area would have to be his home for the next twenty-four hours. Rick started to read Jaws. As night came, hungry and tired with no medication for an angry stomach, he tried to sleep in the chair. Teheran had rules against sleeping in the terminal and the security people to enforce them. Rick said there was a man with a cane who walked through the terminal and probed him with the cane whenever he found Rick asleep. That was Monday night.

Tuesday morning the attendant at the Pan Am desk told him the flight to Beirut was again full, and he would have to wait another day. Somehow he managed another day without food and read Jaws again. After scouring the area around the airport he found a clump of bushes where he could hide and sleep in his sleeping bag unprobed by the security guard.

The Wednesday flight was also full; in desperation he asked to speak to a supervisor. After explaining his predicament, the manager of the Pan Am office tried to see what could be done. It was possible to get Rick on that day's flight to Beirut, but the continuing flight to Rome was full. After changing planes in Rome there were many seats available on the flights to London and Washington, DC. The supervisor told him of the risk if he stopped and waited in Beirut for a later flight to Rome. Lebanon was at war with Israel. His passport showed that he had stopped in Israel and not only was he not allowed in Lebanon, but he could be considered a spy and possibly shot. This was pretty horrifying news for a nineteen year-old who was hungry, sick and just trying to go home. His empty stomach prevailed, and he decided to take his chances in Beirut since he knew there was something to eat on the flight. The last thing the Supervisor said to Rick as he left was "Don't leave the Beirut international area and don't show your passport to anyone."

In 1975 international flights did have some security restrictions; there were, for instance, limits to the size of the blade on knives. Rick's folding knife had to be handed over to the flight captain. This gave Rick a chance to briefly tell his story, and the pilot sarcastically responded with a strong British accent "Cheer up, it could be worse." Later that day this same pilot saved him from a very dangerous situation.

When the stewardess heard that Rick had not eaten in two days she loaded him up with multiple portions of everything she had to serve plus some crackers and biscuits as a backup for the future.

The Lebanese civil war had started a few months before Rick arrived in Beirut. It was amongst every local faction including the Christians, Shi'i Moslems, Druze, PLO, but Israel and Syria were now the main contenders.

Rick could not have arrived at the Beirut airport at a worse time. Tripoli was overflowing with blood and flames. Exceptionally brutal fights between Tripolitans and Zghortiotes caused fires, street riots and kidnappings. Beirut was a cauldron of trouble—plastic bomb attacks, brawling in the streets and fires that Rick could see from the airport. Unable to communicate, Rick had no idea of what was going on, but he could tell by the anxious faces on everyone that this country was in real trouble. The gun-toting soldiers did not make him feel any more comfortable. Carrying an Israeli-stamped passport did not diminish his terrible predicament. He knew he had to get out of there quick. Since it worked in Teheran he asked to speak to the Pan Am manager. Luckily, someone had not shown up for the flight to Rome and that gave Rick the one seat that was available on the same continuing flight. Nothing can be that easy. All the baggage had been removed from the plane on its arrival and, since he was not scheduled to leave, Rick's was somehow lost. Departure time had come and past. A short Lebanese baggage helper ran all over the airport looking for that big yellow backpack, with Rick in pursuit. Finally they found it, and Rick headed across the tarmac towards the plane that was parked a hundred yards from the terminal. This time the little man was chasing Rick and caught him by the shirt and wouldn't let go as Rick tried to climb the roll-up stairs to the plane. He wanted a tip. Rick of course had no money but he did have a big hand full of almost worthless coins—Turkish Lira that was being saved as souvenirs. There were no Arabic words stamped on the money, and the baggage handler broke out in a big smile…"Amerrikin!"

Even though the British pilot was indifferent to Rick as they left Teheran, he held up the flight to Rome and waited for him to board. It may have saved his life.

The layover in Rome was overnight. With twenty-some hours and a handful of crackers to eat Rick decided to walk to Rome and see some sights. The sign on the road outside the airport said "Rome 26 Km." "It's better than sleeping at the airport."

He wasn't hitchhiking but as he walked down the road a car pulled up and the motorist asked in accented English, "Where are you going?" "Rome…" "It is 26 Km…" "Yup." The driver offered Rick a lift. Rick told him about his adventure and the dark, curly-haired man who worked at the airport shared his dinner that

evening with Rick and gave him a couple of transit tokens to take a short sight-seeing tour around Rome. After sleeping the night on his couch, the kind Italian took Rick back to the airport for an uneventful trip home to America.

Since the sixth century B.C.E., Persia has been a wealthy nation. The wealth of Persia still lingers today in the center of Teheran at the Melli Bank, the state bank of Iran, and it was confirmed by what we saw in its underground vaults. It was mind-boggling. The Ministry of Culture arranged for us to visit these subterranean vaults—guarded behind a succession of highly armored doors and dozens of armed guards—the Persian (Iranian) Crown Jewels were kept here. The collection started thousands of years ago as booty of military expeditions and conquests, bequests and excavations from the Persian Imperial mines. We entered the darkened, green-marbled room and were immediately confronted by a twenty-foot long display case made of heavy, obviously bulletproof glass. Three conical piles of precious stones in heavy crystal bowls exploded with their natural brilliance like totally molten volcanoes. Each pile was over two feet high. The first was of brilliant cut diamonds—thousands of them, the second of ravishing rubies, and the third of emeralds radiating an electrifying green, all perfectly polished and of substantial size, ranging from a few carats, about the size of a pea, up to gems the size of cherries. This same display also held a bowl of identical giant pearls of such perfection that they were of equal value to these other precious stones. We were awed by all of the thirty-seven displays, including the many jewel-encrusted crowns, swords, scabbards, coronation chairs, and gowns. Each object of the Imperial collection contained a wealth of diamonds plus many other jewels and pearls. The "Peacock Throne" of seventeenth century Nader Shah, was the centerpiece of the exhibition. It was last used in the coronation of the Reza Shah in 1925. We did not attempt to count the 26,733 gems embedded in this royal chair. It had been valued at one billion dollars.

Above: Grinding grain in Tabriz

To me the most extraordinary object on display was the Daryu-I-Nu (Sea of Light), the largest pink diamond in the world, weighing 182 carats. It has been part of Persian crown jewels since Emperor Cyrus wore it in 558 to 529 B.C.E. And what we saw represented just part of the royal wealth with the balance in even greater protected storage. These treasures are still used to back the currency of the country. It was a peculiar feeling to be surrounded by billions of dollars in untouchable wealth.

The Ministry of Culture had made arrangements for guides at most of the places we were to visit. It was our responsibility to find our way from one town or city to the next, so Joanne and I set off on the next leg of our journey to the Persian Gulf. We looked forward to exploring this remote, deserted, and mostly uninhabited part of the world.

Our car began to die before we left Teheran. Malfunction followed malfunction as we followed Marco Polo's route. Retreating would have been as difficult as advancing, and more dispiriting. We could not remain where we were—on narrow roads of the Zagros Mountains with oil tanker trucks screeching and speeding past in both directions. So we advanced, often very cautiously, for 250 miles, from Teheran to Isfahan. To add to our car problems we were faced with the nemesis of the desert traveler...a sandstorm. It was late in the afternoon when its dark almost black cloud moved towards us from the horizon. The sun disappeared. Soon we were enveloped in this darkness as we pulled to the side of the road and just waited it out. Now this sounds like a simple solution; however, one must realize this was in the middle of a desert in August. The temperature in the shade—if shade could be found—was over 100 degrees. The car in which we had to take refuge was not air-conditioned. The windows must be tightly closed for protection from the fine grains of sand trying to grind their way inside. Outside, it was impossible to see or breathe anything but sand. People traveling by camel would crouch down on the leeward side of the sitting beast. The women would cover their faces with shawls and men would undo their turbans and cover their heads to help keep the sand out of their lungs. We sweated for hours that seemed like days, unable to move, trapped in our motorized oven, as we waited for the storm to pass. It did, and we continued to Isfahan.

Occupied in the seventh century by the Arabs, Isfahan served as the capital city of Persia from 1051 to 1063, from 1072 to 1092, and again from 1590 to 1722. Today Isfahan is sprinkled with architectural reminders of its long history. The city resembles two handfuls of monumental gems that some ancient colossus set carefully in the desert.

It was long after midnight when we drove into town. Street lamps produced a muted amber glow that transformed the eroding mud and plaster of shop walls into works of art, as golden and splendid as the domes of the mosques we passed.

The town was a treasury of soft-colored buildings faced with earthen color and pastel tiles. Even such mundane structures as twentieth-century gas stations had been covered with tiles of the same delicate colors. There were innumerable flower-filled gardens and fountains at almost every intersection made rainbows as fine sprays of water fell into basins and reflecting pools.

The Zaindeh River, invisible in the darkness, was spanned by the simple, harmonious curves of yellow brick bridges softly illuminated at night. On the Khaju Bridge, a double stack of Roman-type arches supported the roadway and added to its splendor.

In the bazaar the following morning, smells and sounds enveloped us: the fragrance of herbs and fruits, saffron and vine leaves and pomegranate peel used to make dyes for the carpet yarns, the hushed sounds of bargaining, the greetings of people who ran a hundred yards to stop us and say in sixth-grade English, "Hello, how do you like Isfahan?"

Passing through dimly lit shops, past enormous vats of dyes and out the rear doors, we came upon courtyards crisscrossed with racks of newly, brilliantly dyed wools hanging to dry, or large yellow sheets of freshly block-printed cottons showing teahouse scenes and polo matches in greens, browns, and oranges.

The main plaza was almost a mile in length: a place where polo matches and public executions were held. Women sat on benches in front of the shops, making carpets of silk with the pattern sketches tacked to the top of their work frames. In another shop we passed, very young apprentices squatted on ledges and rugs, with piles of thin wood strips and ivory and bundles of copper wire, gluing and piecing together inlaid boxes. Others hammered designs into sheets of brass and copper, embossing unattractive souvenirs for the few tourists that passed this way and more agreeably decorated kettles and samovars for Iranian homes.

A few steps from the covered bazaar stood the gifts of the Shah Abbas to Isfahan. All the numerous buildings commissioned by the Shah in the seventeenth century: mosques, theological schools (madrassahs), palaces were all works of rich beauty, each differing subtly from the other in colors and decorative themes, each with its own park or garden. We discovered the older buildings in Isfahan had been constructed of baked topaz-colored brick and of stucco with little ornamentation. The eleventh-century Friday Mosque and the adjacent Winter Mosque were examples of this. Both were constructed over the foundations of Zoroastrian fire temples, and both contained large, dark spaces with low tent-like ceilings. It was very moving to us to see the diffused light as it passed through sheets of alabaster, and the spaces in between were adorned with only the changing shapes and surfaces of brick and plaster. Joanne and I both remarked on its warmth and feeling of utter serenity.

The Shah Abbas initiated in Isfahan the use of painted tiles. He apparently wanted as many structures as possible built without delay so that he could enjoy them in his own lifetime. Because of the haste with which they were erected, many of the structures were in need of some or considerable renovation. There was no time to embellish the works with designs, which in a more leisurely period would have been composed of tiny mosaic tiles. Instead the designs were painted onto two-inch-square ceramic tiles, glazed and unglazed.

We walked from one edifice to the next around the gigantic main plaza. Entire walls, archways, and domes were covered with cut terra-cotta stalactites, painted rosettes and vegetal forms, or arabesques and scrolls of every curved and swirling decorative motif imaginable. The effect somehow remained controlled and tranquil. Colored sand textures and designs caught and scattered the light, which changed with the movement of the shadows and brightened the unlit spaces with iridescence, like that from countless precious stones.

I can't explain how much the breathtaking beauty of this city took me.

From the quiet interiors of mosques and madrassahs we heard only the most peaceful of sounds: birds calling outside the high, tiny windows; someone sweeping leaves from the walkways with a handful of twigs; at prayer time the whisper of carpets being pulled into place for the faithful to kneel on.

The cannons boomed at dawn on our first day in Isfahan, announcing the beginning of Ramadan, the month-long period of pilgrimage, fasting, and prayer set by the Muslim lunar-religious calendar. We had been warned that it wouldn't be easy for us, non-Muslims, to find food and drink during this month, and it was true that most restaurants and market stalls remained closed until sundown, when the fast could be broken until sunrise. But, as usual, lack of food was not one of our problems. As we walked around the town we continued to eat well and frequently, from secreted pistachios and raisins in the pockets of our clothes.

Marco Polo claimed Isfahan to be the most beautiful city in the world. The 19th century French writer-diplomat Gobineau calls Isfahan "A town as enchanting as a dream, the triumph of elegance and the model of loveliness…" and I agree with both. There is no city in the world that can compete with the beauty and elegance of this ancient place. In the beginning of the twenty-first century, this is beginning to change as developers start to tear down some of these priceless relics and build condos.

The oasis of Isfahan opens into mile after mile of desolate, glistening white salt flats. We left trees and gardens behind us, except those we glimpsed through gates in the high walls of an occasional village. We passed endless gray-white flats and cone-shaped mounds of salt scraped from a prehistoric seabed, and then drove over a new range of mountains in the direction of the Persian Gulf. After another beautiful, blinding sunset, on our way to Shiraz in southern Iran, yet another sandstorm stopped us in our tracks. As darkness descended, so did the temperature, and the wind-blown sand relinquished its fury, allowing us to proceed in a southwesterly direction. We were entering a different Iran.

CHAPTER 7

Looking for Hormuz
Persian Gulf, September 9 to 15, 1975

he Plain of which we have spoken extends in a southerly direction for five days journey, and then you come to another descent some twenty miles in length, where the road is very bad and full of peril, for there are many robbers and bad characters about. When you have got to the foot of this descent you find another beautiful plain called the Plain of Formosa. This extends for two days' journey; and you find in it fine streams of water with plenty of date palms and other fruit-trees. There are also many beautiful birds; francolins, popinjays and other kinds such as we have none of in our country. When you have ridden two days you come to the Ocean Sea, and on the shore you find a city with a harbor called Hormuz.

MARCO POLO, 1298

It was like crossing over into a new country. Increasing numbers of black wool tents and camel herds appeared along the roadside. In this area the nomads spoke Turkish. The women were unveiled and exuberantly dressed in vivid full skirts and gauzelike multicolored blouses trimmed with metallic threads. Ribbons and laces and velvet strips hung from every item of clothing. All the women had wavy black hair swinging from beneath thin, lacy bright head coverings. The kilims they wove were as bright and colorful as the clothes they wore. This area, once known as Fars, spawned the Iranian national language of Farsi. These nomadic people were called Qashqai, and up to the twentieth century had been a continuous threat to cities and towns of southern Persia, as Polo described. During the past hundred years, they had been subdued by the Iranian government but to Joanne and me they were in no way a threat, just a colorful contrast to other Persians.

The road to Shiraz took us near Persepolis. Marco Polo made no mention of this ancient site, but we couldn't pass without stopping. Now practically bare of vegetation of any kind, these hillsides were once heavily forested and were chosen twenty-five hundred years ago to be the site of the capital of the Persian Empire. Construction of the extensive group of palaces, halls, and temples was begun during the rule of Darius I, in the fifth century B.C.E.

All the structures rose from a vast elevated terrace. The east side was at the base of a mountain into which were hewn the tombs of later kings; the other three sides were contained by walls. To approach this imperial complex, we climbed one hundred and ten stone steps on either side of a double staircase and passed through the few columns that remained of Xerxes' gate.

Darius lived to see the ceremonial stairways completed and an audience hall that once had a sixty-five-foot-high ceiling supported by thirty-six stone columns. Thirteen of the columns still stand. Successive rulers continued to add monumental

architectural works: soaring pillars and gateways, a grand throne room, a profusion of megalithic slabs still in situ, worn very little by time: a dry climate helps. The slabs were covered with bas-reliefs of animals and of processions of gift-bearing representatives from distant corners of the empire, led by Medes and by Persians or watched over by the Zoroastrian god Ahura Mazda. One such participant in the parade carved in this wall was that of a man leading a Bactrian camel, the two humped camel. This confirmed that the Persians also traded with Western China, the land from which these animals emerged.

Persepolis continued to be an important reminder of Persia's imperial past and unimagined wealth after it was plundered and burned by Alexander the Great in 330 B.C.E. It was buried under two to three feet of ashes. The empire continued to be ruled from Susa or Babylon because of the mountainous and rather inaccessible location of Persepolis.

Even after the devastation by Alexander and twenty four hundred years of time, the delicate beauty of many of the stone carvings remained intact. We noticed the feathers of a winged lion cut into the stone portal of an ancient building that still displayed the detail of the almost microscopic hair—like barbs along each feather's shaft as if they were molded from a live bird yesterday.

Persepolis existed mainly for show and for the celebration of the ceremonies of the New Year and the springtime reception of the gift-bearing visitors. The show was an awesome one, if the immense and beautiful gray stones that remained were an indication; polished two thousand years ago, they still mirror the gold of sunsets and the honey-colored mountains. I would have given anything to have been a visitor to see these spectacular events 2,500 years ago but, instead, the two of us sat on a balustrade in the middle of the complex and just imagined the experience.

Above: Isfahan

Joanne and I have had hundreds of thousands of miles of travel experience, and we liked to think of ourselves as experienced and sensible travelers who would never, if we could avoid it, set off uninformed into the unknown, especially if the unknown was a large section of Persian desert. In Shiraz we carefully inquired about travel conditions on our route to the Persian Gulf in the South. The assurances came from the Ministry of Culture and others: the roads were "adequate" (we had in our hands a newly printed map with a red line that testified to that), and there would be "no problems." The two of us climbed in our Persian-English dune buggy and off we went.

Actually there was a problem. For miles and miles and hours and hours we looked longingly at a thoroughly barricaded and as yet unpaved raised roadbed slicing across the empty landscape. Our path paralleled the would-be road, plowing through the blowing, billowing blizzard of desert grit. Construction trucks for the soon-to-be road had at some time passed this way. We occasionally spotted interrupted traces of their tracks in the shelter of a dune. The red line on our map was more of a prediction than a reality. Our delicate and dying four-passenger Hillman in no way resembled an off-road vehicle. As we struggled onward for hundreds of miles, the car slowly filled with sand and began to resemble a barely mobile sandbox. Being alone in this vast empty desert was scary. To paraphrase the words in an old Noel Coward musical "Only mad dogs and Americans cross a desert in the mid-day sun."

Finally we came to within a few hours of the Persian Gulf. The car had no power. It slowed down, as would a mule with too big a load. The strong, warm wind continued to blow from the Persian Gulf in the south, and with our descent

Above: Joanne at the bazaar in Isfahan

Above: Along the great square of Isfahan

from the elevated plain, the damp heat became swiftly and increasingly oppressive. A temperature of 130 degrees Fahrenheit was not unusual in this area. It probably was not quite that warm, but it felt like it. The heat was so intense that the people of the area take to the rivers for relief, just as they did in Marco Polo's time:

In summer (the people) do not stay in the cities, or they would all die of the heat; but they go out to their gardens, where there are rivers and sheets of water. Here they build arbors of hurdles, resting at one end on the bank and at the other on piles driven in below the water, and covered with foliage to fend off the sun. Even so, they would not escape were it not for one thing, of which I will tell you. It is a fact that several times in the summer there comes a wind from the direction of the sandy wastes that lie around this plain, a wind so overpoweringly hot that it would be deadly if it did not happen that, as soon as men are aware of its approach, they plunge neck-deep into the water and so escape from the heat. To show just how hot this wind can be, Messer Marco gives the following account of something that happened when he was in these parts. The king of Kerman, not having received the tribute due to him from the lord of Hormuz, resolved to seize his opportunity when the men of Hormuz were living outside the city in the open. He accordingly mustered 1,600 horses and 5,000 foot soldiers and sent them across the plain of Rudbar to make a surprise attack. One day, having failed through faulty guidance to reach the place appointed for the night's halt, they bivouacked in a wood not far from Hormuz. Next morning, when they were on the point of setting out, the hot wind came down on them and stifled them all, so that not one survived to carry back the news to their lord. The men of Hormuz, hearing of this, went out to bury the corpses, so that they should not infect the air. When they gripped them by the arms to drag them to the graves, they were so parched by the tremendous heat that the arms came loose from the trunk, so that there was nothing for it but to dig the graves beside the corpses and heave them in.

In this district they sow their wheat and barley and other grains in November, and they have got in all their harvest before the end of March. And so with all their fruits: by March they are ripened and done with. After that you will find no vegetation anywhere except date palms, which last till May. This is due to the great heat, which withers up everything.

MARCO POLO, 1298

The final part of the journey to the coast was uneventful. We enjoyed the scenery as much as we could. Through the glowing haze of the heat everything seemed to be slightly out of focus and pink-tinted: the hill and rock formations, the sand and sky. An antelope sprang across the road. A herd of camels crossed in front of us, leaving one female unmoving and staring disdainfully down at us from the center of our path. Had the car horn still worked we could have honked. She looked at us as long as she cared to, and then leisurely stepped off to the side, giving the car fender a deliberate thump with her right hind hoof as we went by.

The Polos had come to the Gulf at the old port of Hormuz to find a ship to China. They inspected the available vessels and decided that all were of poor con-

struction and not seaworthy enough for such a long voyage. The boats of Hormuz were never taken further than the nearby coast of India:

Their ships are very bad and many of them founder, because they are not fastened with iron nails but stitched together with thread made of coconut husks. They soak the husk till it assumes the texture of horsehair; then they make it into threads and stitch their ships. It is not spoiled by the salt water, but lasts remarkably well. The ships have one mast, one sail, and one rudder and are not decked; when they have loaded them, they cover the cargo with skins, and on top of these they put the horses, which they ship to India for sale. They have no iron for nails; so they employ wooden pegs and stitch with thread. This makes it a risky undertaking to sail in these ships. And you can take my word that many of them sink, because the Indian Ocean is often very stormy.

MARCO POLO, 1298

The Port of Hormuz as described by Marco has disappeared, replaced by Bandar Abbas. Our new challenge was to find the old original port.

It was obvious that Bandar Abbas was growing rapidly in size with an exploding population. The hotels were overflowing with visiting salesmen, engineers, naval officers, businessmen, and transient laborers but little room for the traveler. Only a few years earlier ten thousand people lived in Bandar Abbas. Now, the city had fifty thousand permanent city residents, plus another fifty thousand living on

Above: The honey-comb ceiling in the Palace of Forty Columns on the great square in Isfahan

ravine required a four-wheel-drive vehicle or a donkey, and we were still driving the Hillman. Should we turn back? How important was Hormuz, and was it worth the risk?

We decided to go on. After all, one of the purposes and focus of this project was "to follow authentically and verify the route of Marco Polo across Asia," and ancient Hormuz was an important way station in his thirteenth-century odyssey. The Hillman found firm footing in the rocky riverbed and with a little coaxing with appropriate curse words, we made it to the other side.

After many more miles of crawling across the desert, our car came to the end of the trail at a village on the Persian Gulf on the banks of what must have been a wide river centuries ago. There were a few thatched-roof mud houses set on the muddy beach, with two weathered gray and disintegrating fishing boats littering the shore. We finally found ancient Hormuz. The town looked deserted and defeated, not the thriving metropolis of the thirteenth century. One camel sat in the shade of a palm tree. If there were people, they were hiding. To look further into where these people were hiding may have resulted in looking down the barrel of a gun. This was truly a "one camel town," and we were intruders. We decided not to disturb the tranquility of sleepy Tiab and our Hillman somehow got us back to Minab.

The town of Minab appeared to be as impoverished as the settlement at the old port site. Abdullah, a bartender in Bandar Abbas, told us that drinkable water and food were scarce in this area: "Not much more than dates and some goat milk or cheese to eat." While some of the adults seemed to be well nourished, most of the children we saw had large, rounded bellies and sticklike arms and legs. Skeletal beggars also lined the town's streets.

Because of the heat, not all Muslim women on the Gulf wore chadors, a one-piece black cloth that covered the body down to the ankles, over the head and one cheek. Here in the South they cover their bodies thoroughly with long-sleeved shirts and long, close-fitting, lace trimmed pants under skirts. Instead of concealing their faces with khumurs (veils), they wore fabric or leather masks of shiny reds, blacks, browns, edged with lace, hiding all but glimpses of chins and dark eyes. The masks allowed some air to circulate around the face and were in themselves pretty but gave the women a strange wolf-like appearance. The Koran, Islam's holy book, orders the Muslim people to dress in a modest fashion:

...and say to the believing women that they should lower their gaze and guard their modesty; that they should not display their beauty and ornaments except what must ordinarily appear thereof; that they should draw their 'khumur' over their bosoms and not display their beauty except to their husbands, their fathers, their husband's fathers, their sons, their husband's sons, their brothers or their brother's sons, or their sister's sons, or their women, or the female

slaves whom their right hands possess, or old male servants who lack vigor, or small children
who have no sense of the shame of sex;....

24:30-31 OF THE KORAN

Hormuz—now Tiab—and the Persian Gulf coast is not a place where one would
want to linger in the summer, and we soon, as did the Polos, turned north again.

Top left: The fluted columns of the Apadana
Palace in Persepolis
Bottom: The main staircase show merchants
bringing tributes to the Kings of Persia from
the East

Top right: A bas-relief of the colossal winged
bull on the Xerxes porch in Persepolis

CHAPTER 8

The Tranquil Soils of Kerman
Kerman, September 15 to 24, 1975

The return journey from Hormuz to Kerman passes through a fine plain amply stocked with foodstuffs. It is blessed with natural hot baths. Partridges are plentiful and very cheap. Fruit trees and date palms abound.

Kerman's kingdom formerly had a hereditary prince. Since the Tartars conquered the country the rule is no longer hereditary, but the Tartar sends to administer whatever lord he pleases. In this kingdom are produced the stones called turquoises in great abundance; they are found in the mountains, where they are extracted from the rocks.

MARCO POLO, 1298

The road to Kerman was paved with asphalt as part of the main north-south route through Iran. I did not see a single partridge but the plain was amply stocked with foodstuffs, and there were fruit trees. Some things do change over the centuries.

The Hillman barely crawled up to the drier, cooler 6,000-foot plateau through multihued, heavily eroded mountains. The green mirage ahead became the town of Sirjan. As we entered the town, by the side of the road, we saw a shack housing an auto repair shop. Our Hillman was really sick and needed help. The manager came out, and I pointed to the car and then pointed my two thumbs down. He looked at and listened to the car and said, "OK," which represented a large part of his English vocabulary. He walked over to a man working deep inside the hood of another car and touched his shoulder. Out popped a runt of a man who could not have weighed more than 98 pounds…wet. He wore overalls that were riddled with acid holes and held together with the thick patches of the grease that covered it. His eyeglasses must have been ground from the bottom of a couple of coke bottles and held together with the wire of an old coat hanger. The manager gestured to us that our mechanic could not hear or speak. His name was Mohammed and as his name suggested, he turned out to be both a prophet and a saint. Mohammed took our keys and restarted the car. He lifted up the hood and placed his hand on the engine just as a doctor would take a "pulse." Our car coughed and spat and shuddered as if it had a bad cold. After this one-hand diagnosis, the little guy came over to us and put both of his greasy hands to his neck in a choking manner. After taking it apart, we found he was right, the choke in the carburetor had a hole in its rubber diaphragm. Mohammed got the new part from the shed, and with the tools from his deep pockets he soon had our car purring like a cat and ready to run like a puma. The part was $1.19 and labor about $2.00. We called this our "miracle of Sirjan."

Marco Polo recounts a story about the character of the people of this part of Persia:

79

*N*ow let me tell you about an experiment that was made in the kingdom of Kerman. It so happens that the people of this kingdom are good, even-tempered, meek, and peaceable, and miss no chance of doing one another a service. For this reason the king once observed to the sages assembled in his presence: "Gentlemen, here is something that puzzles me, because I cannot account for it. How is it that in the kingdoms of Persia, which are such near neighbors of ours, there are folk so unruly and contentious that they are forever killing one another, whereas among us, who are all but one with them, there is hardly an instance of provocation or brawling?" The sages answered that this was due to a difference of soil. So the king thereupon sent to Persia, and in particular to Isfahan aforementioned, whose inhabitants outdid the rest in every sort of villainy. There, on the advice of his sages, he had seventy camels loaded with earth brought to his kingdom. This earth he ordered to be spread out like pitch over the floors of certain rooms and then covered with carpets, so that those who entered should not be dirtied by the soft surface. Then a banquet was served in these rooms, at which the guests had no sooner partaken of food than one began to round on another with opprobrious words, and actions that soon led to blows. So the king agreed that the cause did indeed lie in the soil.

MARCO POLO, 1298

During Iran's 1979 revolution against the Shah, Isfahan was the site of many killings, the sacking of public buildings, continuous turmoil with violence- the worst in all Iran-whereas in Kerman, not one incident occurred. There was no question that after 700 years the soil has not changed its influence on the people of these cities.

High altitude and dry air made Kerman famous for the brilliance of its starry nights, as well as for its carpets and pistachios. Clouds and city lights at night prevented us from appreciating the celestial glitter, but the deep-colored carpets were indeed handsome and fresh Kerman pistachios were plumper and infinitely more flavorful than the nuts available at a neighborhood supermarket in the United States.

Many of the mosques and madrassahs and portals to the Kerman bazaar were built after the fourteenth century. Even though some of the buildings were quite lovely, they generally lacked the rich colors and forms of earlier constructions. Glowing neon tubes over the dome of a fifteenth-century dome spelled out in Arabic a prayer; to me they were quite garish and just did not seem appropriate.

As that king of bygone days would have predicted, we found the people of Kerman warm, friendly, and beautiful; offering a smile, maybe a sample from their shop-always with *Salaam Aleikum* (peace be with you). This expression has about the same pronunciation in every language of the Middle East and Central Asia. We hoped its sentiments would be not only on the lips of the people but also in the hearts of their leaders.

Of interest to the thirteenth-century traveler and to us was a tall (sixty-foot) conical shaped structure at the edge of Kerman: an icehouse called *yakhchal*. An icehouse in the desert may sound strange but they have been used in desert towns in Persia since the fifth century B.C.E. These large hollow cones were built with a wide gutter spiraling around the outside, from the top to the ground and below. Water spills down the spiral into a shallow trench where, on cold desert nights, it freezes. (Kerman is at an altitude of over 6,000-feet.) The trench was well protected from the sun's warmth by the two-meter thick walls of the cone. Ice was broken up and moved to caverns deep in the ground, where it was stored until needed. More water could then run into the trench, and the process repeated. This design allowed kings and leaders over the centuries to enjoy Persian ice cream all through the summer.

Badqirs, or wind traps, are towers often seen around the icehouse cones: they cool the underground caverns. Built of mud or mud-brick, these badqirs, mentioned by Marco Polo, were further examples of the creativity that has permitted survival in a harsh desert. Whether box-shaped or rounded, the operating principle of the various badqirs is the same: they catch the slightest breeze in the vent openings at the top (on two or four sides of the structure) and funnel the cool night air downward—through internal, vertically-placed wooden slats—to the rooms below, then out the badqir on the other side. In this way, life in the desert can be made bearable.

Towns and villages unexpectedly appeared as we crossed the Iranian plateau. The land was flat and the dust and haze obscured what little might be otherwise visible in the vacant landscape. Much of the great interior plateau is still unexplored. The plateau, called *kevir,* consisted of salt wastes: large areas with unstable salt crusts overlying mud. Nothing could grow. Few people wanted to venture here, much less settle, and so a town or village was always a welcome surprise.

The presence of *qanats* suggested that a town was somewhere ahead of us. Like giant molehills in a line, these openings in the sand about every hundred yards were the entrances to shafts leading below ground, to water flowing from distant springs through man-made channels to cities and towns. These channels continued for great distances: the mountain streams or springs feeding water to a qanats could be 50 km (30 miles) or more away. These were amazing feats of engineering accomplished by people equipped with small hand tools thousands of years ago and still in use today. Marco Polo spoke of seeing qanats in his travels, although he apparently thought they were natural formations.

he traveler arrives at a stream of fresh water that runs underground. In certain places there are caverns carved and scooped out by the action of the stream; through these it can be seen to flow, and then suddenly it plunges underground. Nevertheless, there is abundance of water, by whose banks wayfarers, wearied by the hardships of the desert behind them, may rest and refresh themselves, with their beasts.
MARCO POLO, 1298

The qanats along the road we traveled were leading us to Yezd.

Top: Turquoise-colored dome of mosque in Kerman. Marco Polo tells the legend that turquoise is the color of the bones of people who died of a broken heart

Bottom: Tiab, once the great port of Hormuz on the Persian Gulf

CHAPTER 9

Zoroastrians and Assassins
Yezd and Tabas, September 24 to 27, 1975

ezd also is properly in Persia; it is a good and noble city, and has a great amount of trade. They weave there quantities of a certain silk tissue known as 'Yezdi' which merchants carry into many quarters to dispose of. The people are worshippers of Mahommet.
When you leave this city to travel further, you ride for seven days over great plains, finding harbor to receive you at three places only...
MARCO POLO, 1298

We continued north until we saw the low, sand-colored, barrel-vaulted roofs that mark the town of Yezd. At the crossroads of many major caravan routes, Yezd has been—since ancient times— both a commercial and a religious center. Fifteen centuries after its founding, it continues to be commercially important, mainly in the manufacture of silk fabrics, just as Marco Polo observed. The Ministry of Culture (tourist office) used almost the same words as Polo in describing modern Yezd.

The further I traveled along this Marco Polo trail, the more I realized how relevant his book was for a modern day traveler; moreover, I realized how important a document it was to the merchants of Europe: its contents opened the door to direct trade. As these merchants expanded their business activity into Asia by water, the Silk Road began to die and the English, Dutch, Portuguese and the other nationalities of Europe started to build their mercantile empires. That expansion could be traced to Marco Polo's travel and book.

Yezd continues to be important to the Zoroastrians, those who still practice the religion of Persia since the third millennium B.C.E.

On our first day, we paid a visit to a Zoroastrian Fire Temple. How many times in a lifetime do you get to say that? After we covered our heads and removed our shoes, the young priest took us inside the small white building. The head covering ritual is a tradition still followed by Muslims and common to Abrahaminic religions: Jews have always covered their heads before entering a synagogue.

The sacred fire burns in a giant brass urn, set in the middle of a marble walled cell at the center of the temple. The urn was about four feet high and five feet across at the top. The fire itself was isolated from all except the priests and was carefully shielded from the direct rays of all external light, artificial or natural. This fire, the priest told us, has been charged five times a day for the past thousand years; that is, prayers were said while new wood and incense were added to the urn and the ashes removed. Although Zoroastrians are known as fire worshipers, the priest wanted to be certain we understood that this was a misnomer. "The fire," he said, "is an intermediary between man and God. For the followers of the prophet Zoroaster, the one god is known as Ahura Mazda. The fire is a symbol of truth and good, not the thing worshiped." It should be noted that in the Old Testament, Moses sees God in the burning bush that was not consumed by the fire (Exodus 3:2).

Outside of Yezd, in the desert, on a quiet, windy mountaintop, stand two stone towers, one of which was about six hundred years old. Unused since 1970 (at "government request," said the temple priest) these towers, Towers of Silence, open at the top to the sky. The inner walls are arranged in three concentric circles on which the Zoroastrians for centuries placed their dead. Rather than, as their religion forbids, "contaminate earth, air, or water," the dead were dealt with by birds of prey—birds called "living tombs"—and the natural decaying process fostered by the dry, hot, sun. The religious beliefs haven't changed, but the authorities have insisted that the Zoroastrians bury their dead in the new cemetery below the towers. A few graves could be seen in this small, grassy space at the foot of the mountain.

Because of Ramadan, the shops in the Yezd bazaar remained closed throughout the day, and we encountered few people in the covered passages. But men continued to sit, hunched over in gloomy, half-hidden rooms, weaving with silk yarns. The patterns of plaids and other simple, geometric designs weren't very pretty, but the colors were, and the tedious work process with the fine threads was impressive to watch.

As always, there were old mosques and madrassahs to explore and photograph, with the aid of old and toothless doorkeepers, who first helped Joanne to cover her body with a chador and then helped us both to find our way through the buildings. We found a prison, built during the time of Alexander the Great, which was being restored, the subterranean cells now covered and sealed, the structure above converted into a madrassah. Near the prison stood an empty but well-preserved ninth-century mausoleum protected by two young bulls munching hay, and a proud, grinning, very bent old man.

Leaving Yezd was quite an event. We gave up the car and bought bus tickets. A half-dozen loudly vocal males were commandeered to push the bus through the gates of the bus yard and past a mountain of cucumbers piled for sale in the street and on the sidewalk. The motor started and we were on our way, our feet resting on a cushion of grape seeds, which the driver continued to build up, driving and spitting seeds in all directions. When not eating, he joined in the prayers being chanted at intervals by his passengers.

To reach what is now Afghanistan from Yezd, the Polos had to cross the Dasht-e-Kavir, the "Great Salt Desert." Marco Polo describes the region as an area of *"utter drought and neither fruit nor trees and where the water is…bitter."* We found it about as inhospitable in the twentieth century.

A corrugated unpaved trail crosses the near-empty expanse of sand and salt. The only fruit to be seen was carried in the bags of our bus companions or spread out over the dashboard of the vehicle within easy reach of the driver. The ancient bus that was our transportation across this vast, bleak desert must be called an "off-road vehicle" since the sand/salt over which we traveled could not be called a road. But where there was any settlement of people, there often grew a lone, spindly, lovingly nurtured tree. Once or twice in a day's travel we came upon a *chai khanna*. At these teahouses the traveler can take off his shoes and sit on carpets spread over the hard, dusty earth. The spindly tree might have produced enough leaves to cast a little shade over the carpet. Or a ragged cloth awning would be draped between poles to shield the traveler's head from the sun.

It was Ramadan, but in the chai khanna we still could have a pot of tea and some bread—the enormous flat sheets of nan carried over the arm of the server like muslin dishtowels. With luck, an egg or two might be available. This describes where we ate when in villages large enough to have a small amount of food to sell. This also describes where, daily, we made new acquaintances.

Even if we had wanted to, we could never sit alone at the teahouses. Almost as soon as we had loosened our bootlaces, someone would come over and ask us to join them and their friends or family groups. Everyone quickly moved babies and baskets and bundles aside so we could squeeze into the circle. We would sit down with legs folded under us, and the introductions would begin.

When there is little shared language, one can at least exchange and understand names, and then the answers to "Where are you from?" and "Where are you going?" Numbers are easy to convey, so "How old are you?" was a popular question. Somehow, after drinking our tea and passing the fruit basket around—and after a lot of laughter and gesturing and consulting the dictionary—we would all part with some faint idea of who everyone was, what each was doing that day on the road, and, very likely, the ages of everyone in the group.

The fact that I was a Jew in an Islamic world was not a factor regarding the acceptance we received wherever we traveled in the Middle East and Asia. As Americans we were honored guests. This universal, gracious greeting led me to believe that the first commandment of the culture in this part of the world was "Thou shalt be hospitable," as it says in the Koran.

There were toilet stops from time to time to relieve the passengers if there were no teahouses. The driver had designated places where small dunes on either side of the road provided privacy for segregated groups: the women squatted behind the dunes on one side of the road, and the men squatted on the other. As a participant in these rituals, I became aware of an interesting phenomenon. At the European end of Asia men would stand upright when urinating, but as we traveled east they changed their position for this purpose to kneeling on one knee. Further east, Iran and beyond including all of China, everyone squats.

The bus had to pause only once for repairs during the two-day journey, and at some point during the cold, star-decorated, desert nights, the driver stopped to sleep for a while in the aisle between the seats. Shortly after sunrise on the third day we arrived in the town of Tabas.

Tabas was in the middle of an arid nowhere, but within the boundaries of this oasis grew pine trees and an abundance of date palms. We walked through several large, rose-filled parks, around splashing fountains and past swarms of orange butterflies. Enormous mounds of melons were on sale in every storefront and on every street corner. Almost everyone we passed had a dripping melon slice in his mouth or a round green melon tucked under an arm or tied to the back rack of a bicycle. Dates were also plentiful. A young doctor told us that the second major crop of Tabas was, surprising for the center of the desert…rice.

Underground water was more than enough to satisfy the thirsty plants and people of Tabas, but the middle of the two great Persian deserts can be more than hot. Almost every house and building in this community of some 14,000 people had the wind catching towers, badqirs, to help adjust to life in a nasty desert. There was a below-ground-level living room that was cooled by the badqirs. During the hottest part of the day this was where the people lingered.

Left: A sixty-foot high ice house in Kerman   Right: Windcatchers in Tabas

Tabas, "queen of the desert," contains the ruins of a large ancient fortress that belonged to the sect of the "Assassins." Marco Polo tells the following fascinating story about these people and their leader known as the "Old Man [or Sheikh] of the Mountain."

In the twelfth century, the Old Man of the Mountain built a luxurious garden in a beautiful valley to the east of Tabriz, enclosed by two mountains and protected by a citadel. Palaces, of various sizes and forms, decorated with paintings, works of gold, and furnishings of rich silks, were scattered about the grounds. Flowers, fruits, and vessels of wine, milk, honey, and pure water were everywhere. Within the palaces dwelt beautiful women, skilled in singing—playing all types of musical instruments—and dancing, especially the dances of amorous allurement (probably a medieval version of the modern belly dance). The women were all richly and exotically clothed. The object of establishing this fascinating garden was this: Muhammad had promised that all those who followed his will and the Koran would reach a paradise where all forms of sensual gratification would be found. The Old Man of the Mountain claimed that he was a prophet and peer of Muhammad, and that he too had the power of admitting into his paradise all those he favored.

He looked for youths between the ages of twelve and twenty who were skilled in the martial arts and appeared to possess physical strength and a special courage. The youth would be given hashish until he would be half dead with sleep. Then he would be carried into the garden of The Old Man of the Mountain's paradise. When the youth awoke, he found himself surrounded by lovely ladies singing, dancing, attracting his attention with fascinating caresses, and serving him delicate, exotic foods and exquisite wines, until he was drunk with the excess of enjoyment and truly believed he was in paradise. After a week he was again drugged and taken out of the garden. He was then given an audience with the Old Man of the Mountain and told, "He who defends his lord shall inherit his paradise, and if you show yourself devoted to the obedience of my orders, that happy lot awaits you." Each young man was then glad to receive the commands of his new master and was not at all concerned about dying in his service, since dead or alive he would get to go to paradise. With this kind of dedication, the young men were sent on missions all over the world to kill whoever was marked for elimination. The service of these disciplined assassins was in high demand. Even mothers of young boys were eager to have their children join the ranks of the Old Man of the Mountain. The word "assassin" comes from the Arabic word for the drug hashish; *hashshashin.*

Older citizens saluted us with "salaam" as we walked, and the children said "goodbye." Not, we hoped, because they wanted us to leave but because it was the one English expression they had learned. In some towns the one word was "hello" or a shrieking "Eeengleesh?" shouted by little children in the general direction of our armpits. We once heard a shouted but dubious "Japanese?"

Tabas hadn't been a stop on the way to anywhere since the days of the cara-vans, so we were somewhat surprised to find three other guests at the only hotel. They sat in the cool, shady garden behind the hotel, eating melon and playing backgammon. They said they were businessmen from Teheran who had come to Tabas "for a rest." Although fashionably and expensively dressed, they all wore the one-size, one-style, pink-colored plastic slippers placed for the guest under every bed in every hotel from western Turkey to eastern Afghanistan.

Two of the men offered to take us with them the next day to Meshed in their air-conditioned Range Rover. We couldn't refuse.

The next afternoon, after a lunch of thick yogurt and salad, we sped off into the desert. During the ride we discovered that the older gentleman was the owner of a chain of department stores in Teheran. His younger companion was the chauffer. The real reason they were in Tabas was that the Shah was looking to arrest this businessman. In order to cut back on inflation that was hurting the economy of Iran, the Shah had come up with a very simple solution. He decreed that on the first day of Ramadan all prices of all goods must be reduced by ten percent, period! Our traveling companion had decided he would not go along with this crazy idea and had refused to lower the prices in his stores. He felt if he hid out for a week or two the laws of commerce would kick in, prices would again stabilize, and he could go back to Teheran.

Three years later, on September 16, 1978, I was horrified to hear that Tabas, this quiet Iranian town that grew peacefully in the middle of a vast desert, was totally destroyed by one great tremor of an earthquake. Only two thousand of the fourteen thousand inhabitants were found alive. It struck at the time of the evening meal. Most of the people of Tabas were in their lower living room that was cooled by the badqirs, eating, when the earthquake struck at about 7:00 p.m. The vibration of the seven-point-seven quake melted these mud-built homes like ice cream on a hot day. Everyone inside was buried alive.

Aid was sent from all over the world to help the survivors of Tabas. The U.S. Air Force built a runway on the outskirts of the town to facilitate bringing in supplies. Less than two years later, the U.S. used this same Tabas landing strip outside the abandoned city for a historic military project: it was the infamous aborted attempt to free the U.S. Embassy hostages being kept in Teheran by the Islamic regime that had overthrown the Shah. Somehow the U.S. military forgot that there was sand in the desert, and this incapacitated the helicopters that were to be used in rescue.

Top: The sacred fire in a Zoroastrian Temple
Bottom: The ruins in Tabas of a twelfth-
century outpost of the murdering sect of
the "Assassins"

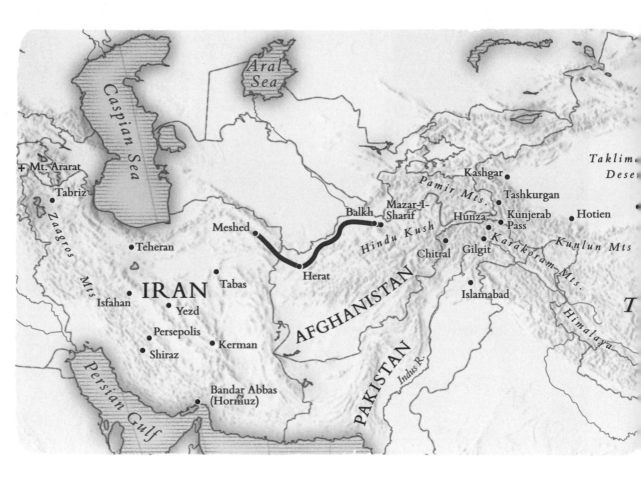

Caspian Sea

Aral Sea

+ Mt. Ararat

Tabriz

Zaagros

Mts

Teheran

IRAN

Tabas

Isfahan

Yezd

Persepolis

Kerman

Shiraz

Persian Gulf

Bandar Abbas
(Hormuz)

Meshed

Herat

Balkh

Mazar-I-
Sharif

Hindu Kush

AFGHANISTAN

PAKISTAN

Indus R.

Islamabad

Pamir Mts.

Kashgar

Tashkurgan

Hunza

Kunjerab
Pass

Hotien

Chitral

Gilgit

Karakoram Mts.

Kunlun Mts

Himalaya

Taklim
Dese

T

CHAPTER 10

The Emperor's Palace
Meshed, September 27 to October 3, 1975

The terrain was mainly flat sand, rimmed by wind-carved rocks and bare pink and amethyst-colored mountains. On either side of the Range Rover as we drove north, we passed occasional qanats lining the sands and leading toward occasional, desert-colored villages, or we saw camel herds parading toward unseen tents. The drive took nine hours at thunderous speeds, across the desert plains and around hairpin curves on treacherous mountain roads. These were unpaved corridors over which heavy trucks traveled as a short cut from Persian Gulf ports to Afghanistan. This type of traffic caused the roadbed to become corrugated like a continuum of one-foot diameter logs lain side-by-side. When we had tried to drive our English Hillman down a road such as this, we could barely exceed 15 mph. The Range Rover raced at 60 mph across the desert with a ride almost as smooth as driving on a well-maintained Interstate highway back home.

It was dark when we arrived in the spacious, thick-carpeted, chandeliered lobby of the Hyatt Omar Khayyam Hotel at the entrance to Meshed. Our Iranian companions managed to look appropriately clean and well pressed. We managed to look as though we had just hiked here from Timbuktu, even though we had actually ridden luxuriously in cool splendor.

Everyone, everywhere seemed to be related to, or at the very least a close friend of, everyone else we met. We stopped at this elegant place because our new friend, Mr. Rezai, the entrepreneur from Teheran, was a relative of the manager. This was fortunate, because our arrival in Meshed was not well timed. It was still the month of Ramadan. The weekend of our arrival was the beginning of special religious celebrations within Ramadan. Meshed, long a sacred city for Shi'ite Muslims was bulging with pilgrims. Finding rooms anywhere, we quickly discovered, was impossible. That included the hotel in which we were standing.

It hadn't occurred to us that we might not find shelter for the night. We always had. So, surrounded by beautifully dressed people, we stood in the luxurious lobby, chatting and cheerful and brushing the dust from our clothes.

We could see that some telephoning and a lot of spirited discussions were taking place at the reception desk between clerks and the hotel manager and his relative, our friend from Tabas.

Soon Mr. Rezai announced to us that behind the hotel, beyond the swimming pool, and down the white gravel path to and through a storybook rose garden, was a villa. This special place was kept for the Shah on his visits to Meshed...and for our stay in Meshed it was ours. The Emperor of Persia's palace!

Laughing maids prepared king-sized beds and left dozens of thick, soft towels in the tiled bathrooms. Joanne and I each had our own suite. They didn't ask if we were married. As we traveled in these very conservative Muslim countries, no one asked about our marital relationship. They took a "don't ask, don't tell" attitude towards us. It is part of their philosophy of hospitality.

We were able to shower to an unending flow of hot water. Ice water was placed at each bedside, and fresh flowers on the tables, and dainty silver-wrapped chocolates on the pillows. "The Six-Million Dollar Man" was effortlessly speaking Farsi on the television screen as we languished in a lush, modern day castle of the "Billion Dollar Man," the Shah. This was not only the lap of luxury; it was a cradle of paradise.

After the hovels, rooms, and campsites to which we had become accustomed, and before long would once again become accustomed, this was a shock to our lifestyle. No rusting iron beds with one threadbare sheet, if that, here; no single 15-watt light bulb dangling from the ceiling at the end of a frayed cord; no bathrooms that could be safely entered only while wearing waterproof boots. There weren't even the one-size-fits-all pink plastic slippers under the beds. The Good Fairy had sprinkled her magic dust on us once again.

It would not be long until we discovered that the worst accommodations in Iran were better than the best accommodations available to us in Afghanistan.

Marco Polo doesn't speak of Meshed, although he tells of traveling through its province of Khurasan. Meshed was old long before the Polos passed this way, and it was located only a short distance from the ancient juncture of caravan routes coming from the south, east and west, as well as northern routes from Russia.

Meshed began as a neighboring village to the once-important town of Tus. Tus, then six centuries old, was said to have had a half million inhabitants when the first Mongols rode over the hills and began the process of conquest and systematic destruction. The collapse of Tus was completed—as Tamerlane completed the collapse of so many other cities—two centuries later. The remains of the extensive walls, fortified citadel, and watchtowers of Tus were eroding and blowing as dust, back into the surrounding desert.

The Mongol warriors did not ignore Meshed, but the shrines there had been rebuilt or repaired. The city continued to grow and more recently had become a center for the wool trade. Since the ninth century Meshed has been a pilgrimage site; only Mecca and Medina are more sacred.

The shrines and burial places to which the Muslim faithful travel are those of Caliph Harun ai-Rashid and of Ali Reza, the eighth Shi'ite Muslim imam. The twelve imams (descended from Ali, son-in-law of the prophet Muhammad) are considered by the Shi'ites to be their absolute spiritual authorities and leaders. When we visited, it was said the spiritual community was still led by the twelfth imam who, although he had disappeared long ago "will return at the end of time with truth and peace."

Non-Muslims cannot enter the shrine or pass through the mosaic-and-mirrored walls of the antechamber of the venerated imam's tomb. But its gilded copper dome can be seen from most points in Meshed.

On our way to Afghanistan we stopped outside Meshed at a seventeenth-century caravanserai. We found it at the crossroad where an earlier one had stood as a protective way station in the desert. Caravanserais were essentially a combination hotel, restaurant, stable, and mosque that in Polo's time were located some twenty-five miles apart. That distance was what Polo called a day's journey—the distance a camel traveled in ten hours. This ancient hostel had a single, heavy door opening into a rectangular, mud-brick structure that continues to shelter passing shepherds within its massive walls. Animal smells lingered, and straw and the evidence of recent cooking fires could be barely distinguished in its shadowy interior. From the watchtowers above the high walls we could see distant villages and dry barren hills rolling to the horizon.

Several meters from the caravanserai were the adobe walls of the village Sang Bast; the third of three successive villages of that name, according to the aged mullah who came out to greet us. The mullah, whose age we estimated by his looks to be more than a hundred years, was the village authority in charge, as well as teacher, and religious leader. This gentleman was slightly deaf and possessed a very dry, and brown, and wrinkled face. He was dressed in a tattered shirt and pants, with a tattered white turban wound around his head. He stood there talking to us…most dignified.

Stretches of this eroding citadel wall and a mausoleum with traces of blue paint lingering on the inner walls, a minaret, and many scattered bricks were all that remained of the abandoned eleventh-century second village. The village, said the mullah, may have been occupied as recently as a hundred years ago until an earthquake tumbled homes and fortifications. His father had told him stories of repelling invaders from the parapets of the second village. These were nomadic invaders (who came to pillage the towns and carry off the women) with whom the villagers in the present Sang Bast were still doing battle only thirty years before. All this he told us in English, a language he had learned many decades before.

Men drifted out of the village to listen to the mullah, and little boys stopped. The women glanced at us quickly and continued walking, except for one small, sobbing female who saw us and paused and stopped crying to stare at the strangers standing outside her town. Then she pulled her tiny black chador into place, continued sobbing, and scurried on.

From the ruined citadel we could see and walk to the modern town of Tus. Here we discovered the marble edifice with the tomb of the poet laureate Ferdowsi, the Shakespeare of Persian literature, who was born in Tus and died early in the eleventh century.

Around the inner walls of this twentieth-century structure we found large, high-relief carvings of scenes from Ferdowsi's epic poem, "Shah-nameh" or "The Book of Kings." Called the first history of Persia, the three-part poem describes historical events and recounts creation myths and heroic tales of mythological Persian kings. Written nearly four centuries after the Arab military invasions and linguistic incursions, the poem was best known for having revived the use of classical, literary Persian. For this Ferdowsi was honored.

The caravan route east followed a paved highway from Meshed, past Sang Bast, to the frontier. On the other side of the Afghan border waited another and older time, and yet fewer highways.

CHAPTER 11

The Russian Truck
Herat, September 30 to October 3, 1975

Crossing from Iran to Afghanistan gave us the feeling that we had stepped even further into antiquity and closer to the world the Polos had experienced when they had come this way.

The Polos had followed the fifteen-hundred-year-old "Silk Route" along Afghanistan's northern border, along the Amu Darya (the ancient Oxus River), and had eventually entered the area known as the Wakhan Corridor. This narrow finger of land, three hundred miles long and only twenty to forty miles wide, pushes itself between the Pamir Mountains of Russia on the north and the Hindu Kush range and Pakistan to the south, ending at the back door to China. This border with China is only twenty-five miles long. The Wakhan Corridor was established at the end of the nineteenth century by the British to isolate Russia from what was then India.

Officials at the Afghanistan Embassy in Washington, D. C. had urged us to avoid the northern route across their country because it would be "too difficult" and, more importantly, "too dangerous" due to bandits, disease, religious fanatics, and the general uncertainties of desert travel. But as Marco Polo had established our itinerary in 1274, we had no alternative but to follow in his footsteps, and consider the consequences later.

More than once during our journey we felt as if we had stumbled onstage during the performance of some little-known surrealistic play. The Afghan customs ritual was one of those times.

Scene One: The elderly, baggage inspector with baggy-pants never sorted out who was entering the country and who wanted to leave. He rushed hysterically from one heap of luggage to another, rapidly opening and closing bags, examining some bags two or three times and others not at all. When he finally despaired of trying to establish who and what was going where, he threw up his hands, cried, "Finished, finished," and disappeared.

Scene Two: One official in the small customs hall had an extended and noisy tantrum when he discovered that the brick doorstop had been removed from in front of his office door. Another wrote camera and money information in his notebook and asked all who came before him if the word "custums" on his desk sign was correctly spelled. Of course it wasn't, and all who entered his office dutifully told him so and probably had been telling him so for years.

Scene Three: The official who stamped passports had worked up a routine in which, with each visitor, he reached across the length of his desk for the stamp on the ink pad, stamped the passport, and then—with hardly a glance—flipped the stamp through the air and back to the ink pad three feet away, right side up. He never missed his target while we were there. Didn't I say it was weird?

The first, "bus" (for lack of a better term) we boarded in Afghanistan did not fortify our confidence in desert transportation. In some bygone day this decrepit vehicle may have been painted red, but the sun and the sand had worn the color away. There were about a dozen travelers—several Australians, some Europeans, the rest Afghans—and all wanted to go to Herat. We packed ourselves onto the wooden slabs and old tires that would be our seats in what *had* been, in some bygone era, a ten-passenger van. If the outside scenery was not interesting you could look down at the ground through the holes in the floorboards. To keep them from flying open, the side doors were secured with a chain and padlock looped through the window frames. The brakes obviously were not the best because the bus began slowly to roll down the hill on which it was parked. This presented more of an opportunity than a problem, really, because rolling the bus down the hill was the only way the motor could be started. Noticing that his bus was leaving without him, the driver jumped in, and we started toward Herat.

We sputtered along the desert road, past abandoned caravansaries and dome-shaped brown yurts, until the last of the twilight was fading. At that point the driver stopped his decaying vehicle and began to collect fares, holding money in one hand and his flashlight in the other. After some arguing he accepted the previously agreed-upon fares from those of us who had obtained local currency. He then tried to extract much more from those who hadn't anything other than dollars or Persian money. After a lengthy and heated conversation about reasonable currency exchange rates and agreed-upon fares and whether we would pass the rest of the night in the desert or move onward, everyone paid something.

The male passengers, thoroughly irate about the financial discussion, now had to climb out and push the bus in order to restart it. We clattered and sputtered once again into the darkness.

In Herat the lodgings, unsurprisingly, were not of quite the same quality as those at the Meshed Hyatt. Not one laughing maid (women weren't allowed to work in hotels in Afghanistan), nor chandelier, nor rose in sight. We found, in-

Above: The crumbling walls of a fifteenth-century citadel in Herat

stead—under lights so dim they hardly deserved the title—creaking metal beds with no blankets, and no chocolates on the pillows. But the sheet on each bed appeared to be clean, even if the bathrooms unquestionably were not, and the broken windows let in cool, fresh night air and the soothing sounds of horse-drawn carts, *gurdis*, passing in the street below. We did of course, find, in this case, mismatched plastic slippers under the beds.

Those who worked in the hotel were delightful, friendly people. We spent many hours over tea with the educated and youthful manager, Reshed. He told us his life story, a story that sounded like the plot of an adventure film. It included a wicked stepmother and a politically powerful and unloving father who wanted to have Reshed arrested for holding "unacceptable political views." It included obtaining a university education that led only to restlessness, difficulty in finding a job with adequate pay and, therefore, little hope of ever accumulating enough money to purchase the bride he wanted or to attend medical school, which he wanted more. We heard similar tales of disappointment and discouragement from many educated young Afghans. The sunny, beautiful, curly-black-haired ten-year-old "assistant manager" of the hotel met us on the stairs the night we arrived in Herat and assured us that his was a "very fine hotel." He boiled eggs for us, and made us laugh, and treated us as though we were valued friends from the moment we introduced ourselves. Friendly enough, too, was the dazed-looking young man who brought the tea and the scanty meals from the kitchen, burping and using his messy apron to wipe grease from the plates, even as he set the table.

Several ancient cities stood where Herat is now, including one built by Alexander the Great after he first sacked the existing town. The site was settled by the Persians 2,500 years ago and for a thousand years or more it was a major stop on the caravan route. No longer the center of science and culture it once was, Herat is not quite modern either. The water flowing alongside paths and sidewalks in the *djubs* (small curbside sewer channels) was nauseatingly dirtied with everything from pigeon feathers to human excreta mingling with mud and goat feces. Children

97   *The Russian Truck*

played in the water and drank it, and the adult males washed their faces and hands in it before spreading their rugs and mats on the ground to pray. Camels made complaining noises as they paced through the broad, unpaved streets to the bazaar or back into the desert. Nomad's tents had been placed next to houses at the edge of town under the watchtowers of a disintegrating fifteenth-century citadel.

Nan accompanied everything we ate, whenever we ate, and although once in a while it tasted and looked like warmed cardboard and was made of who knew what, usually it was crusty and flaky and very good. Near the Herat bazaar we stopped to watch the bread being baked. Five men squatted around a deep, circular, clay-lined pit at the bottom of which a fire burned. The first man dug a handful of dough out of a pot and rolled it and passed it to the man on his right. This man flattened the roll into an oval shape and handed it on to the next person. The third man pulled the oval into a thin, broad sheet—like a small hand-towel and patted it onto a wooden paddle. The fourth man in the production line leaned forward, slid the paddle down into the pit, and slapped the dough onto the clay wall, where it began to bake. Meanwhile the final member of the group had been picking browned bread out of the oven with long tongs. He also would pull out the kettle of water, for tea, that had been heating in the depths of the pit.

In our travels, we hadn't met many people who spoke more than a few words of English. In Afghanistan we were surprised at the number who did speak it, some nearly fluently; for instance, Reshed and the young "assistant manager." One youth called out to us from a shop doorway and offered to purchase all the clothes we had on our bodies. Well, if we didn't want to sell anything, perhaps we would "like to buy some French perfume, the real thing!" After we talked for a while longer and then started to leave, the young merchant called out again to ask if he had used the word "obtrusive" correctly. He had.

This widespread knowledge of English, we discovered, resulted from a large infusion of visitors from the Anglicized world. Most of these were from the drug culture and had heard that the world's best and cheapest hashish and opium was to be found in Afghanistan.

We had two things to do in Herat: obtain a permit to make the journey across the northern Afghan deserts and find transportation for our trek. We located the police commandant, who knew only a few words of English. He telephoned someone who knew more English, and the telephone voice instructed us to cross the courtyard and go to the passport office. The gentleman in this office sent us back to the street to buy a sheet of "official" stationery from an old man who sat on a chair outside the fence of the police station. He was a professional scribe who, for a few Afghani (the local currency not the people), would sell you the paper and then write the document in Dari; a form of Persian spoken mostly in Northern Afghanistan.

The elderly scribe wrote our names as instructed and very carefully wrote out our request for permission to follow the itinerary we had outlined for the passport official. We all knew that it must be written carefully; without error. I am certain Marco Polo experienced waiting for a scribe to carefully complete some work, since this process of hiring a scribe to write documents goes back to biblical times. This is another way in which Herat is not quite "modern," but they are not alone; another example of this practice in modern times is the ritual that an Orthodox Jew must follow to obtain a "get"—the Hebrew word for a divorce document is "get." The man to be divorced buys the parchment paper, a quill, and the ink. He then hires a scribe who writes the "get"—perfectly and without error—in exchange for a silver coin. Credit cards or paper money are not acceptable. In several ways an instant gratification culture was not present in Herat: waiting was part of our journey.

When the scribe had completed his work, we were again sent back across the courtyard to the commandant, who went away with the papers, saying something about "checking visas." He never did ask to see our passports, which contained the visas he apparently wanted to check. Twenty minutes later the commandant sent us once more to the passport office, where all the numbers, names, requests, signatures, and approvals were copied into a ledger. Our official paper with the official stamp was signed. We had our permit to travel across part of Northern Afghanistan to another town, Maimana. Just imagine the chaos at a New York police station if our government had imposed the same requirements for a tourist to go from New York to Chicago! Now we had to find transportation.

With Reshed's help we arranged to go by truck to Maimana. There was no way of knowing what several days in a truck in an unknown desert would mean, but we were prepared. Our folding water jugs had been filled and, as usual, we had added a few drops of iodine as a purifier. We bought fruits and raisins and pistachios and a fresh fruit-filled cake. After sampling the cake, we ran back to the shop and bought another one. We also bought butter because Reshed had insisted we have butter to go with the cakes. It seemed about as practical as setting forth with a bag of ice cubes, yet the butter stayed quite solid and continued to taste like butter even after several days in the desert heat. It must have been made from camel's milk.

Early on the third morning in Herat we went to the truck yard, as requested. Someone tossed our now almost-yellow backpacks into the rear of the brightly painted, open flatbed truck and told us to get into the front cab and sit down. We got in and sat down. One by one, other passengers crawled into the back. About an hour later the driver appeared. He started the motor, listened to it for a minute or two, turned it off, and left again. We continued to sit.

At long last the truck was loaded with twenty-two male passengers and Joanne, plus bundles of food and clothing and whatever. The driver returned, and the truck left Herat.

The driver was a very suntanned man of about twenty-two. He was immaculately dressed in the traditional knee-length shirt and full cotton pants, both pale green and spotless, and a dark blue wool vest with little decoration. Over his short, black hair he wore an embroidered and beaded skull cap.

The road was briefly a road, then a road that was actually a dry riverbed, then a road that was a riverbed in which flowed about eighteen inches of water…and then no road, only desert.

Toward sunset on the first night we saw vineyards and pistachio groves on the mountainsides, then rare encampments of nomads near the equally rare rivers and camels kneeling at the sides of tents beneath red rock cliffs, waiting for their burdens to be untied and removed. Little girls and their mothers—all unveiled and each wearing two or three or more vividly colored, silver-spangled dresses—stirred the evening meal over small fires. (We were told that a married nomadic woman never, during her married life, removes her wedding dress but wears it next to her body.) These camera-shy women were proudly visible. Fierce-looking, earless dogs guarded the encampments, women, and the herds.

The driver maneuvered his Russian-built, orange truck with the flair of an artist wielding a broad brush over the countryside: flying through seemingly unfordable streams and somehow over trackless, impossible-to-climb dunes. He found his way through the night when one section of this rock-strewn landscape without roads looked exactly like every other section visible in the headlights. His hands moved with a graceful coordination that was absorbing to watch, and he was obviously enjoying his difficult job.

Inside the truck, penetrating cold alternated with intense heat. We were surrounded by the aroma of gas fumes mixed with the scent of the ever-present collection of melons, with dust and sand permeating everything. Outside was a different and silent reality: masses of sun-baked, barren ridges, a desiccated land of white sand and sandstone, cracked and waterless gullies and ravines. Nothing moved.

Our Russian truck continued across Afghanistan's northern desert.

In the larger towns we often passed an entire day without seeing one Muslim female, adult or child. When we did see one, she would be totally hidden beneath her screened veil; not even her eyes were visible behind the thick brown or gray fabric of the finely pleated *burqa*. Sometimes we glimpsed only the tips of shoes. We watched these shapeless, ghostlike figures sorting through bolts of fabrics in the bazaars. We hoped that the gaily-printed yardage they bought would be used to make gaily-printed dresses to wear beneath their burqa. In this way they might bring some color into their somber life. On extended trips in buses with seats, when the male passengers got off for tea or meals, the Muslim women remained on the bus. Crouched behind the seats, they raised their veils just enough so that they, too, could eat.

CHAPTER 12

Decapitating Tourists
Shebergan, October 3 to 6, 1975

n leaving the castle, you ride over fine plains and beautiful valleys, and pretty hillsides producing excellent grass pasture, and abundance of fruits, and all other products. Armies are glad to take up their quarters here on account of the plenty that exists. This kind of country extends for six days journey, with a goodly number of towns and villages, in which the people are worshippers of Mohammed. Sometimes you meet with a tract of desert extending for fifty or sixty miles, or somewhat less, in these deserts you find no water, but have to carry it with you. The beasts do without drink until you have got cross the desert tract and come to watering places.

So after traveling for six days as I have told you, you come to a city called Shebergan. It has great and plenty of everything, but especially of the very best melons in the world. They preserve them by paring them round and round into strips, and drying them in the sun. When dry they are sweeter than honey, and are carried off for sale all over the country. There is also abundance of game here, both of birds and beasts.
MARCO POLO, 1298

Long after sunset on that first night after leaving Herat the truck followed the fast-moving River Murghab into the oil-lamp town of Bala Murghab, a few kilometers from the Russian border. In Bala Murghab we stopped at a large teahouse for a meal of rice and yogurt soup and shared several pots of tea with the driver and his passengers. The driver left the Afghan passengers to finish their tea and signaled for us to get back into the truck. An armed police officer stood next to him. Where was he taking us? What had we done to cause our arrest? With no other option, we obeyed, and off we drove through the totally darkened village, across the river and through a small wood. We stopped in front of a smiling little man, who having heard the truck coming, was waiting by the side of the road holding an oil lantern. The driver had delivered us, not to the police station and jail but to the doorstep of the local government inn. The driver had decided that we should sleep in warm beds; actually, just beds.

That night our fellow truck passengers slept on the tea-stained and sugar-encrusted carpets in front of the teahouse. They wrapped themselves in the cloth of their turbans against the desert cold. In Afghanistan the tea was usually served with almost half a cup of sugar, just as the coffee was served in Turkey. If someone does not finish his cup of tea, the *batcha* (waiter) would throw the remainder of the highly sweetened tea on to the carpet...thus, stained and sugar-encrusted carpets.

We Americans were the only guests at the inn. According to the register, there had been one guest two nights before.

As the town and the inn obviously had no electricity or running water, it was a little surprising, after posing the automatic and routine question to the French speaking manager, "*Avez-vous une douche?*" ("Do you have a shower?") to be told, "*Oui*" ("Yes"). Certain that we had chosen the wrong noun from our limited vocabulary, we nevertheless followed the still-smiling gentleman and his kerosene lantern to a large semi-outdoor room. There was a hole in the floor, a plank to stand on over the hole, a fifty-gallon drum containing some water, a small valve (faucet) at the base of the drum, and an eight-ounce tin cup to transport water from faucet to soapy body; *voila, une douche.* It was a very cold shower but, nevertheless, a shower. We used it with pleasure by the light of the stars that shone through the drafty, incomplete walls and roof of the room.

The beds in this part of the world are very comfortable, especially after a dozen hours of bouncing in a truck with a Russian suspension system that was not designed for the luxury of human cargo. These Afghan beds consist of a wooden rectangular frame of tree branches with four short legs. A tight grid of heavy rope has been woven back and forth across the frame to make a soft, pliable mattress. On this was placed a feather bed, quilt and a blanket for the cold nights; simple but effective and almost cozy. Sheets are unheard of.

Earlier, as I walked into the inn, the lantern had shown on a wooden door that had two big white letters painted across its panel…WC. If this were true, it would have been the first inside toilet that we found since leaving Herat. When I later went to use the facilities, I discovered that it was in fact not a "water closet" but a door to a path that took you fifty feet from the inn to another hole in the ground—this one to straddle—surrounded by a low fence, for privacy.

The truck driver said he would return to the inn for us at 6:00 a.m. And he did! We were dressed, ready, and amazed. This was perhaps the one time in the entire journey that we departed from anywhere within two hours of the appointed time.

The road from Bala Murghab to Maimana did not start off as a road, but a visible trail across the wilderness, corrugated and horrible. It was mid-afternoon when we reached Maimana. Not a living creature was in the streets, but dozens of schoolboy faces appeared at the windows of a one-room schoolhouse across the road from where the truck had stopped. We got out and unloaded our backpacks and water containers and food bags. As we shook hands with the driver and the remaining passengers, the schoolmaster joined his gawking, waving students at the windows. We waved back and entertained our audience by slicing and eating our final pink melon on the spot before striding off to the hotel we had seen a few hundred yards back.

Time and again, from Maryland to Afghanistan, we listened to words of warning about the dangers to travelers, particularly non-Muslim travelers, in this part of the world. None of the dire predictions seemed to have anything to do with the cordial, smiling, even protective treatment we received from the kind people we met each day.

Nevertheless, we assumed the warnings must have some foundation. Several times during the journey to Maimana, the driver could push his truck no farther over the fine, loose sand of the steep dunes of this desert. He had to stop and ask the passengers to get out and walk (once for more than an hour) so that the emptier, lighter truck could climb up and over the dunes. At the first such stop at a steep dune we jumped out of the cab and started to strike off uphill with our fellow traveler, but the driver wouldn't allow us to leave the vehicle, then or later. He first yelled, "No, no, no." and then gave us his orders in eloquent pantomime, pointing first to the lonely, desolate landscape and to the other passengers up ahead, then tracing an unmistakable throat-cutting, head removing gesture between his ears. Decapitation was not on our itinerary.

That evening we asked the innkeeper in Maimana, why was a man with a shotgun following us around town, through the market and wherever we walked? This gunman was not wearing a uniform and did look a little sinister. He told us that a couple of German tourists had literally lost their heads a few days earlier. The bandits also took their money. The local police thought it best to keep an eye on us, and they assigned a deputy to do the job. We accepted the explanation.

There wasn't a lot to do here. I went to watch some local women weave carpets (or, more correctly, hand-knot carpets). On the way back from the carpet factory I bought a melon, of course. Joanne had a vague fever as an excuse to sleep the morning away; however, on my return she did leap up to admire the carpet I bought. We then gorged on the honeydew-tasting, cantaloupe-colored meat of the Hami melon. It was this part of Afghanistan that Marco Polo said that he found "the very best melons in the world." This statement was made in his book after he had traveled throughout Asia and around the entire known world. And once again, we had to agree with Marco.

The carpet I purchased was the first one made by a thirteen-year-old girl. At first they said it was so poorly made that they did not want to sell it. They finally agreed to a price of thirteen dollars for the young lady's three-by-five-foot handiwork.

Maimana was a quiet, isolated town. We thought it unlikely that we would meet other tourists there. But there they were. There was a constant stream of people flowing past and through our room at the inn. An English cyclist stopped in to ask for some shampoo and rested on the edge of a bed while he talked of his travels and his mysteriously ebbing strength. He omitted until the end of his story the fact that he had been living for two months on bread and water, so he could save money. A German couple who lived in Kabul visited us, and a middle-aged ex-Afghan government official sat with us, on the carpet, at teatime. He told us that he was jobless and wandering through the country and preparing to resume the play writing he had begun and given up years before. I bought a few ancient coins from him that he said were from the time before Marco Polo. I later found

Above: The Friday Mosque of Herat

them to be authentic but not of great value. The "house boy" popped in and out, sometimes merely smiling and speaking words we couldn't understand, sometimes bringing a tray of tea and rice that we ate sitting on the floor. A distraught lady strolled through the halls and at intervals called-out, fruitlessly it seemed, for "Waaalter." We wonder still, who—and where—Walter was. This was another of those surrealistic plays in which we played a part. It reminded me of an old vaudeville routine where every few minutes a man dressed in a page's costume would walk across the stage shouting, "Paging Mrs. Pendergrass." On his first appearance he was carrying a small green plant. On each successive walk his plant had grown in size. About the tenth time he ambled across the stage with the other performers totally oblivious to his presence, he was struggling with a fifteen-foot tree, still paging Mrs. Pendergrass.

There wasn't much to do in the sleepy town except drink tea, walk through the empty bazaar, visit with the hotel guests, and watch a group of local women make carpets at the carpet school/factory. After a few days, it was time to move on.

Ramadan was now over, and the post-Ramadan festivities began. After we had been told that there would be no transportation in any direction for awhile, because of the holidays, an eastbound truck pulled up to the inn early one morning with a driver looking for passengers. After a mere ninety minutes of fare and destination discussions, then the loading and fueling of the truck, we drove out of Maimana. We were his only passengers.

This driver was older and not so spotless, and he drove with less enthusiasm than the green-clad youth from Herat. There was more than an occasional mashing of gears, but he was congenial and, holiday or not, he was going our way, to Mazar-i-Sharif.

Only a short distance from Maimana, we entered a village where the streets were filled with people and color; a procession was just leaving the mosque. Little girls, looking like Oriental princesses, wore quilted jackets over pink and red dresses. Beaded and tasseled hats sat on their shiny black hair. Little boys were dressed in bright blue, long shirts and full pants and brighter, blue-beaded skull caps, and their parents were no less brightly attired in purple and red and green as they celebrated the end of Ramadan. We stopped to buy the inevitable melons and crossed a rickety wooden bridge that led us away from town.

In the early hours of the journey we rode past camel train after camel train. Winter was approaching, and the nomads had begun to move to warmer grazing areas. Some of the camels carried enormous water containers to settlements we couldn't see. Others had been loaded with folded tents, cooking pots, jars, and babies in dirty but colorful clothes. A camel can carry up to 500 pounds for a day's journey.

At the sides of the caravans walked huge and disorderly herds of sheep led by an imperious-looking "king" goat, while not far distant marched the goat herd itself, with an occasional loner posing elegantly, goat-fashion, at the top of a bare cliff. A fat eagle soared overhead.

Over the centuries foreign countries have tried to conquer Afghanistan. The British tried in the later part of the nineteenth century, the Russians came in 1979 and left after a half dozen fruitless years, The Americans arrived in the twenty-first century. This is a very difficult country to dominate, mainly because of its nomadic lifestyle. Outside a few major cities, the countryside is inhabited by nomads who cannot be controlled by foreigners since they and their livelihood are totally mobile and they are mostly subject to the local warlords.

Soon there was nothing. We left all landmarks and all signs of life, animal or vegetable, behind. This part of the desert was absolutely unmarked. Ruts from the truck tires were erased as if the sand was water that filled them in as quickly as they were formed. We felt we were traveling across a lake, vast and flat and almost white beige, without waves or even ripples. Nothing could be seen in any direction as a reference. There were no dunes, trees or mountains on the horizon and at high noon hardly a shadow from our truck—no signs, abandoned vehicles, nothing. It was eerie. We wondered aloud if the driver really knew where the hell he was going, with nothing but the blazing, lemon-colored noontime sun directly overhead. As far as we could tell, he had only his instincts to guide him.

Reassurance came when our driver pointed at a small dark spot on the wavering, glittering horizon, exactly in line with the direction we were heading. He said "Mazar." Our driver was telling us that what we saw was a truck coming from Mazar-i-Sharif. The two vehicles passed as closely as if we had been traveling on a well-marked highway with lanes and outside barriers. I consider myself a good sea-going navigator but without a compass, GPS, or any visible navigational references, how could this guy find his way to Mazar-I-Sharif? I was baffled.

We paused for lunch in Shebergan, a town Marco Polo described as "plentifully stocked with everything needful." The oasis, to all appearances, had fallen on hard times during the last 700 years. This also can be attributed to Marco's book: it offered an alternative route to the East by sea and was a major factor in the demise of the overland trade routes. Although we were accustomed to food prepared and served in a fashion not remarkably hygienic, this teahouse in Shebergan looked dangerously less than clean. Perhaps our impression was biased because several men sprawled on the carpets, obviously in the grips of some debilitating disease. Or maybe it was just one of those days when we couldn't have faced yet another mountain of rice—the only food available on the menu. We ordered tea and finished the fruit-filled cake from Herat.

Not many hours after lunch the truck tugged itself out of the sand and onto a paved road that took us, after dark, into Mazar-i-Sharif.

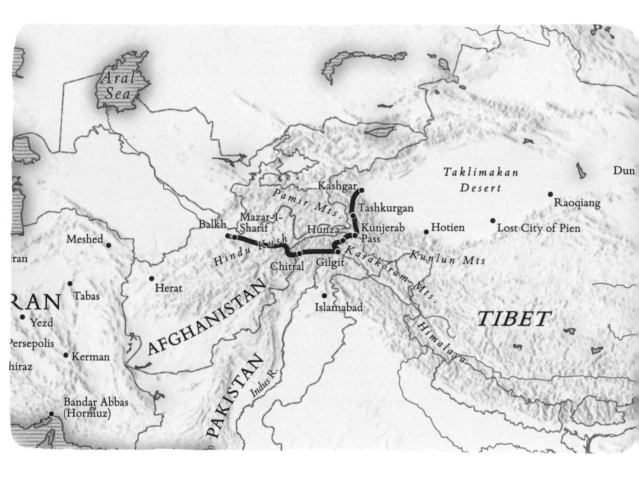

CHAPTER 13

The Ancient City of Balkh
Mazar-I-Sharif, October 6 to 24, 1975

alkh is a noble city and great, though it was much greater in former days. But the Tartars and other nations have greatly ravaged and destroyed it. There were formerly many fine palaces and buildings of marble, and the ruins of them still remain. Since that time Balkh has been little more than a village bordered by cultivated fields and enormous slowly eroding ramparts. The walls are so high and extensive that it is impossible to examine easily only limited sections of them.

The people of the city tell that it was here that Alexander took to wife the daughter of Darius.

Here, you should be told is the end of the empire of the Tartar Lord of the Levant. And this city is also the limit of Persia in the direction between east and northeast.
MARCO POLO, 1298

As we unloaded our *almost* yellow backpacks on a street corner, the helpful driver told us where to find the hotel. "*Bale,*" we replied, "Yes." And he repeated his directions. "*Bale,*" again. And we repeated this verbal exchange another two or three times. Was it that we didn't look bright to this gentleman? Or maybe he was afraid we would lose our way in the night. This wasn't too likely, since for ten minutes we had been looking at the lights of the highly visible hotel only several hundred yards from where we stood.

At the hotel the young man in the brown turban who cleaned rooms and ran errands immediately turned his broad grin in our direction and adopted us—in fact, almost pounced on us. "Do you want a drink? Maybe a beer? A soda? Coffee? Tea? Are you hungry? Do you want to eat?" He recited the entire dinner menu of rice, rice and chicken, or rice and lamb. "Shall I wash your clothes in the djub? Anything?" He would take care of it, as he said every time we met, which was often during the following few days.

This dynamic gentleman was always available to help us find our way around Mazar. He began his food and beverage recitations before we had even brushed our teeth in the morning, and became our local tour guide the rest of the day.

Instead of the winding, narrow streets bordered by mud-brick walls typical in other Afghan towns, in Mazar-I-Sharif (Tomb of the Exalted) we found straight, broad avenues carefully engineered into squares and rectangles. The normal bedlam of bazaars had been replaced by the tranquility of glass-fronted stores. Old Mazar had been sacrificed to modern city planners. Well, modernization was the intent.

As the name suggests in its translation, the town was the site of the tomb and shrine of Hazat Ali, the cousin and son-in-law of the Prophet Mohammad. The disputes over his assumption of the title of Caliph after the Prophet's death led

109

to his assassination in 658 C.E. Originally buried in Kufa, Iraq, his body was surreptitiously carried to this site near the ancient city of Balkh.

It was in the year 1136 C.E. that the Sultan Sanjar commanded that a shrine be built over this grave. Genghis Khan destroyed the first shrine, but it was rebuilt in 1481. It was this shrine—with its many expansions and restorations—that we saw that day. The tile work that covers its many domes and minarets was predominantly a heavenly blue and lavishly speckled with thousands of pure white pigeons. They say that if a gray or brown pigeon joins the flock it will turn white within forty days. Banding the brown pigeons and finding these same birds later with white feathers confirmed this phenomenon. No one knows why.

Mazar-I-Sharif was by far the most beautiful edifice we saw in all of Afghanistan.

Our hotel had another western guest, a young man from Holland who had traveled there by bike on his way to Australia. He had just graduated college and before he started work back home, he wanted to get a job in an Australian salt mine. I asked the inevitable question…why? He proudly answered "Wouldn't that be impressive to have on a resume?"

Our houseboy and concierge from the hotel told us which bus to take for the twelve-mile ride to Balkh, just south of the River Oxus and west of Mazar.

Balkh, ghostlike, was surrounded by what was left of its ancient and massive four-mile long wall. Here was where time had stopped and the past is present today.

Balkh, called Baktra or Zariaspa in ancient times, became the great center of commerce and culture about 2500 B.C.E. It was the "mother of cities" and birthplace of Zoroaster almost four thousand years ago, as well as the place where he was murdered. Balkh fell to the Persians in the sixth century B.C.E. and grew again, to be seized by Alexander the Great. It was in Balkh that Alexander married "the most beautiful woman in the Persian Empire," Roxana, daughter of Darius II. A thousand years later Balkh was again overthrown, this time by Islam. Balkh had lived in peace for centuries as an important part of the caravan route and a focus of Islamic culture with universities and libraries. The warriors of Genghis Khan devastated this historic city some fifty years before the Polos arrived. Marco Polo told a fascinating story of this important moment in history:

In 1222 C.E., Genghis Kahn had conquered most of China. He wanted to start trade with his new neighbors to the west. A thousand camels were assembled and loaded with wares of the East to be bartered in Balkh, the western capital of Persia. However, a captain of the border guard stopped the caravan before it arrived in Balkh. He confiscated all the goods and camels, and the merchants and camel handlers were killed—except for one camel boy who hid in the chimney of a bathhouse. In the dark the boy escaped and made his way back to China to tell this story to the Great Khan. In an atypical move for this infamously ruthless leader, the Khan sent a diplomatic mission to the ruler in Balkh to ask for apologies, compensation, and justice for the greedy captain. Instead of bending to the wishes of Genghis Kahn, the King in Balkh sent these messengers back with singed beards, the ultimate statement of an insolent reply.

Genghis Kahn was a bit miffed, and more to his character, sent 100,000 soldier horsemen to Balkh to besiege this magnificent city of one million residents. The fortifications were quickly bypassed and all its citizens were forced outside the city walls, supposedly so the horsemen could count the population and determine the amount of retribution that the Khan would demand. They were divided into groups of ten…and then summarily slaughtered by the 100,000 Tartar horsemen. Not one living inhabitant of Balkh survived, not even a dog.

Marco Polo arrived in Balkh in 1272, and in his book he comments on the size and the grandeur of this ruined center of commerce and learning.

The most gratifying part of our visit to Balkh was a social call. An elderly gentleman with a wonderful, deep laugh called to us as we passed his shop. He was a metalworker and samovar craftsman, and he invited us in to share, naturally, the Hami melon he had just sliced. We entered the cluttered room, removed our boots, and squatted on the spread carpets to begin our visit. At once the doorway—and soon the entire tiny shop—was filled with beaming neighbors, all men. The novelty of our visit was not only that we were two foreigners but that one of us was a woman.

Wearing a dusty white turban, our host, who was born on the other side of the River Oxus (now Amur) in Uzbekistan, demonstrated his ability to write our names with both Roman and Cyrillic letters. We all spoke about birthplaces and our homes, the distances between our homes and his, and modes of travel to these places, using the very few words understandable to all of us in Russian, Farsi (Persian), Dari (Afghani), Urdu (Pakistani) and English. A dozen of us did our best to convey information using our hands to sketch pictures in the air and making familiar sounds, such as imitating a truck motor while holding and turning an imaginary steering wheel, or mimicking the whirring sound of an airplane's engines while our arms were extended like wings… Always our conversation was supplemented with lots of laughter. Trucks came to Afghanistan from Russia and planes from the U.S. We learned an interesting hand sign: rubbing your two index fingers side by side and sliding up and down meant friendship. If you hook both index fingers together, like a chain link, it meant marriage. They pointed out that Afghanistan and "Amerika" were married but "Ruska" and Afghanistan were just friends; a very politically correct comment. We were able to speak of politics, economics, geography, and personal histories—and all without a common language. People from any two places on earth, who are at peace, have always been able to communicate.

After posing in the center of the shop with his tools and a friend for an exquisitely dignified photo, our host accepted our thanks for a lovely afternoon. We departed to continue our explorations.

From Balkh and Mazar-i-Sharif, the Polos continued on to the east through the passes of the roof of the world and on to Cathay. We had reached Mazar in mid-October, and the extremely high mountain passes into Pakistan would already be snow-filled and impenetrable. This was just a minor physical obstacle. The challenge of finding a way through the political roadblocks that I was to face were so great that a series of miracles would have to occur before I could gain possession of the elusive "visa"—my permission to enter the back door of China; a door that had closed when the Communist government took over in 1949. Therefore, our Marco Polo journey had come to an end for now. Our next step would be to return during the warmth of a summer to pick up Marco Polo's ancient trail.

One hundred and twenty miles south of Mazar was Bamian, the site of the world's tallest Buddha (175 feet) carved into the wall of a sandstone mountain…separated from the outside world in a silent valley with gigantic cliffs to the north and south. Beyond Bamian are the barren, serrated mountains of the Hindu Kush (which means Hindu Killer). What better place could there be for a Buddhist sanctuary? Alongside the Giant Buddha, monks had carved apartments into the wall. There they studied the Noble Law for a thousand years.

Islam arrived in Bamian. Muslims hostile to the imagery continually desecrated this great historical shrine—and the slightly smaller, standing Buddha nearby—by removing their faces and arms. Over the years it had been pockmarked from gunfire, which is how we viewed it in 1975.

In March 2001, I learned of the total destruction of the Buddhas of Bamian at the hands of the Taliban. Few reports of tragedies along the Marco Polo route hit me with such impact. Here in this peaceful valley, the Taliban—the fundamentalist Islamic rulers of Afghanistan at that time—totally destroyed it and the smaller Buddha (115 feet in height), with cannon fire. The rest of the world trembled with anger at this mockery of world culture. Symbolically it was like blowing up the Sphinx in Egypt. The Bamian Valley was like a chapel of gigantic proportions, and now its holiness has been taken away, emptied; its destiny played out.

The primitive bazaar followed the wall of the two Buddhas for almost a mile. Potters turned clay into water vessels using foot-operated spindles; tinsmiths made pails to carry water from the Bamian and Kalu Rivers; cloth, vegetables—all were available at this bazaar, in proportion to the size of this small, remote village.

In talking with vendors, we discovered that the unfired clay pots could keep water cold enough to hold butter solid and fresh and provide a very cool drink. Since the pots were not fired they were porous: this allowed evaporation at just the right rate to keep the vessel and its contents very cool. Who needs refrigerators?

We had come to Bamian by truck and had made our way fifty additional miles into the mountains. Along the way we rented an old Bushkashi horse to help in our visit to the lakes at Band-I-Amir. I was nearly killed.

It is important to understand the Bushkashi horse. It is trained to play the game of Bushkashi, where a dozen to a hundred horsemen assemble on a field. The object of this lively competition is to (without dismounting) pick up the headless carcass of a goat or sheep dropped in the center of the field, carry it across a goal and back to the pick-up point before one of the other horsemen can wrest it away. All the riders go full speed, heading for the carcass. Each rider has a whip in his mouth and pulls at the reins as a signal to the horse to go faster. When he comes up to the dead goat on the ground, the reins are dropped, signaling the horse to stop; the horseman bends over to grab the goat, tucks it securely under his leg, and off he goes. Therefore, tugging on the reins of a Bushkashi horse makes it go faster and slackening the reins causes the horse to slow and stop. The game originated in Polo's time when the Mongolians came marauding through Afghanistan, taking the chickens, sheep, and goats. To protect their livestock, Afghans developed a technique of picking up an animal on the move and carrying it off, and also passing the animal from one rider to the next. Practicing this way of saving their animals evolved into the game of Bushkashi. It became a favorite sport for the Uzbck and Tadjik men on the Roof of the World.

I had rented such a horse near the lakes in Band-I-Amir. In this area one finds very few motor vehicles. Somehow a Volkswagen mini-bus had made its way up this mountain. My horse—having never seen such a strange, noisy, intimidating object—shied, reared, and bolted at a full gallop towards the lake. I was barely able to stay in the saddle. My instinctive reaction was to pull back on the reins to stop the horse…forgetting for the moment that this was a Bushkashi horse, trained to go faster when its reins were pulled. My life was at stake, and I had only seconds to stop this horse before we both went into the lake. The horse may have known how to swim but on this cold morning, I was wearing every bit of clothes I owned plus heavy hiking boots—and I couldn't swim. If I hit the water, I would go down like an anchor. In desperation, I grabbed the bridle on one side and pulled the horse's head around so it was almost facing me. I had no other choice, and he had no choice but to stop. That was close!

Khamar, Gulaman, Aibat, Panir, and Pudina are the mythological names of the lakes at Band-I-Amir. The fairy-tale story of the origin of these lakes goes back to the time this part of the world turned towards Islam. The king of Balkh tried to convince the people of this area to build a dam to control the Kujruk River that flooded every year…to no avail. It came to pass that Ali, son-in-law of the Prophet, came to Balkh and decided he would help. He went to an appropriate place along the river and with some sort of magic, caused the Kujruk River to be dammed, and the first lake was made. It came to be called Band-I-Khamar, Lake of the Servant. A slave was sent to make another dam, and the second lake was

Top: A butcher in Mazar
Middle: The bakery in Mazar
Bottom: A teahouse in Mazar

named after him, Band-I-Gulaman. The local people made the third lake. Women made cheese for Ali to throw into the waters, which caused the fourth lake to be called Band-I-Panir, Lake of the Cheese. The fifth lake was called Lake of Mint, Band-I-Pudina.

These lakes, at an elevation well over two and a half miles high (13,000 feet) were a dramatic spectacle. Although above the level where trees and vegetation grow, the sunlight, mountains and water make for spectacular shows of color. Joanne and I stayed at a nearby inn, and we were up at daybreak. The morning sun crawled down the mountainside with a broad-brush stroke of beige and rust, the rest of the valley lingering in darkness until the sun set fire to the lake in reds that mixed with blue as the mist drifted away. As daylight took over, the bleak mountains and valleys lost their color, creating a contrast with the deep blue-black of the lake and its sparkling water ripples, so as to make this serene mountain plateau all the more awesome. To be at Lake Band-I-Amir at sunrise was to experience a morning in visual paradise.

We did not have permits to enter China along Marco Polo's path, and the clothing we were wearing was not adequate for the fast approaching snows and artic-like winter. These obstacles could not be dealt with there, in the Hindu Kush Mountains.

Northern Afghanistan was also not a place for me to deal with the stomach sickness that I had contracted in Turkey. I had lost over thirty pounds, and I always felt weak. Carrying a hundred pound pack (adding a heavy carpet plus the entire tent) was getting more and more difficult. I was dejected.

Starting in Venice and ending in Xanadu or Beijing in one continuous expedition as did Marco Polo was my original goal; but in this very area of northeastern Afghanistan, Marco had become ill and gone into the mountains to recuperate. He took a year off to rest from a bout with malaria. I was heading home to take care of my amebic dysentery and regain the weight I lost from this affliction. My journey was continually paralleling Marco's, even though we were born seven centuries apart.

I had been working on obtaining the elusive permit since 1971, by contacting the Chinese delegation to the United Nation in New York. This was before President Nixon went to China in 1972. In a meeting I had with one of the diplomats I was told I would have a much better chance of obtaining a permit to cross the Pakistan-China border after China had established diplomatic relations with the United States, in seven or eight years. That prophetic comment had world shaking importance since it signified that something big was about to happen between the US and China, and it did. Meanwhile, I still did not have the permit; but—just as my Chinese contact at the UN predicted— Leonard Woodcock became the first U.S. Ambassador to the People's Republic of China in February 1979.

Top: Mazar-I-Sharif (Tomb of the Exalted)
Middle: The eroding walls and towers of Balkh
Bottom: A lonely camel ambles with his
master through the now small village of Balkh
where the mud walls fence in vegetable gardens

Top left: The world's tallest Buddha in Bamian   Top right: The smaller Buddha in Bamian
Bottom left: A street side potter   Middle right: Doing business in Bamian
                                                  Bottom right: Bamian's main street

Our first of three adventurous raids upon this ancient world was coming to a close. We had set out to capture its image as Marco Polo may have seen it and to show how important Marco Polo was to the advancement of Europe; out of the Middle Ages and into a period of globalization. The dozens of notebooks we filled, the thousands of photographs we took and the memories we shall always carry with us, became the fruits of our effort and the legacy of our project. After more than three months of traveling, we had begun to feel at home in this unfamiliar and sometimes terrifying environment. When the snows melted and the portals to Xinjiang Province in far western China swung open, we would again head for the Roof of the World, to make our way across the mountains, over thousands of miles of desert and Gobi, and then on to Peking—in the footsteps of Marco Polo.

It was time to find a truck to get us to Kabul and a flight home on the Pan American Airline Clipper Ship to America.

END OF THE FIRST EXPEDITION

Above: Riding to the lakes of Band-i-Amir

119 *The Ancient City of Balkh*

This page: Lakes at Band-I-Amir

PART TWO

CHAPTER 14

Across the Roof of the World
China, November 1975 to August 1981

Obtaining a visa to cross the western border of China was comparable to moving a mountain.

After President Nixon's trip to China in 1972, Liaison Offices were set up in Beijing and Washington, D.C. George H.W. Bush, who was to become Vice-President under President Reagan in 1980 and President in 1984, was head of the U.S. Liaison Office in Beijing in 1975. His experience and interest in China would work in our favor. Later, Vice-President H. W. Bush was to play an important role in our project.

The entire border from Vietnam west and north to the Soviet Union had been closed in 1949. The portal through which I hoped to enter China was the Kunjerab Pass, and it was the first to be opened along these thousands of miles of Western China's border. It is very close to the place in these treacherous mountains where the Polos found their way into China.

After I returned from Afghanistan to the U.S., following the first expedition in the winter of 1975, I started contacting the Chinese Liaison Offices in Washington, D.C. and resumed my visits to the Chinese delegation at the United Nations in New York. Their message was consistent: it was impossible to enter China from Pakistan. After three years of hearing their rejections, I decided to take a different tack. I would go directly to China and make my appeals there. I was certain that I would find some sort of support in China for my truly cultural, non-political project. In 1978 it was not easy to visit China unless they wanted you there. I could easily get a tourist visa, but that would limit me to follow a very strict tourist agenda and being totally under the control of the Chinese authorities. Traveling around China on my own was not acceptable to the government. Obtaining an unrestrictive visa to China was a new test to my perseverance.

I came up with what I thought was a great idea. I would offer China's undeveloped electronics industry the opportunity to buy technologically advanced electronics products from America. This would allow me to visit China for this marketing project and simultaneously devote additional time to pursuing permission and the visa necessary to enter Western China. Another benefit would be the opportunity to establish a profitable business in the process.

For many years I had owned a high-tech electronics marketing company called Dorado, so I knew many key people in that industry. I picked half a dozen American made "state-of-the-art" products not available in China; products I believed would be of interest to China's fledgling electronics industry. These were products and components needed in communications equipment, and instruments for developing computer systems. I contacted the leading U.S. suppliers for this type of equipment and asked if I could be their sales representative in China. They all said, "Why not? We're not doing anything in China, anyway." Remember, this was 1978, and Deng Xiao Ping was just starting to pull China out of the cultural, industrial, and economic abyss into which they were thrown by Mao Zedong and his "Cultural Revolution." The average income in China was less than the equivalent of $200 per year. In 1978, they were about to open an Embassy in Washington, D.C., where I received the names of the factories or research institutes that would be interested in what I had to offer. Just to make certain I received an invitation to come to China, I sent out six letters —not just one—with descriptions of the technology I was offering. An invitation was the first requirement needed before obtaining a commercial business visa. Within two weeks I received six invitations. Now, I could at least open the front door to China. So far it had taken over five years.

My new wife, Nancy, and I left for China and started our new venture by attending China's first electronics conference in Canton (Guangzhou). We soon found out from "an old hand" that we were "in real trouble." The six invitations we had received to visit electronic facilities in Beijing meant that we had six official hosts. When we were to arrive in Beijing, a few days later, there would be six welcoming committees at the train station (no flights from Guangzhou to Beijing), each of whom would have arranged an elaborate banquet that evening in our honor. Each would have a full schedule of meetings and visits to their factories and research institutes. This had been the business protocol for a hundred years in China, before communism. Our "old China hand" whom we met at the conference, told us how we could get out of this embarrassing predicament. We should notify only one of our hosts of our arrival time in Beijing and send telexes to the others, apologizing for a delayed arrival. Business protocols and customs in China are quite different from the Western world. Americans doing business in China were going to find it a major learning experience.

My marketing business prospered. I was also contacting the various Chinese Government departments in my quest to gain admission to the illusive Kunjerab Pass. I talked to key officials at the Ministry of Culture, Ministry of Interior Affairs, and Ministry of Defense, which did not want any Americans traipsing through their nuclear and missile testing grounds in western China. The officials of the Autonomous Region of Xinjiang (the region through which I would be entering China) also considered me "persona non grata." No one encouraged me in any way. The Ministry of Defense said flat out, "Forget it!" The only sign of hope came from the Ministry of Culture. They were supportive of the Marco Polo project.

During this time, we were traveling to China about every six weeks. Nancy, my new daughter, Jane, and I would stay for four to six weeks at a time. In Beijing, we lived at the Yu Ying Binguan, the Friendship Inn, which was built by the Russians when they were helping the newly communist China after 1949. The "foreign experts" and other foreigners who stayed for extended time in Beijing lived there. In Shanghai we lived at the Jin Jiang Hotel where there were even fewer foreigners in residence, and our family was a spectacle when we were out on the streets. Whenever Nancy took Jane out in her stroller, a parade of people would follow them. The local people of Shanghai had never seen a round-eyed baby with light brown hair, wearing diapers, which we did not see on their children. Jane was very popular. The staff in the hotel restaurant, where we usually ate, took her into their kitchen to feed her. We have no idea what she ate, but she apparently liked it: the cases of baby food that we lugged from the States were hardly used.

One evening we were sitting in the dining room of the Jin Jiang Hotel talking to Jon Weller, who had set up a manufacturing operation for Nike shoes. Jon told us about a meeting he had that day at his factory. He said, "Last week I was complaining about the white running shoes that were being shipped with dirty smudges. You won't believe the solution they offered me today. They suggested the smudges would not be seen if we make the shoes gray instead of white." This was obviously a communist factory's resolution to a problem, but in a very competitive world a better correction was needed. Moving China towards a flat world economy would be a learning process.

My efforts at getting the western border visa were stymied. At one of my meetings with the Ministry of Culture, I asked an official, "What is it going to take to get the permits that I need to finish following Marco Polo across China?" He explained that the approach I was taking was not going to work. One Ministry cannot tell other Ministries, who are at the same bureaucratic level, to help the Marco Polo project. He said, "What you need is to have someone very high in your government talk to someone very high in our government, who will direct all of the Chinese Ministries involved to approve your project." This made sense. Now, who would be that high person in the U.S. government to talk on my behalf to top officials in China?

*I*t was the year 1225 that there was a Caliph at Baudas who bore a great hatred to Christians, and was taken up day and night with the thought how he might either bring those that were in his kingdom over to his faith, or might procure them all to be slain,

Now it happened that the Caliph, with those shrewd priests of his, got hold of a passage in our Gospel which says, that if a Christian had faith as a grain of mustard seed, and should bid a mountain to be moved it would be removed...

So all the Christians gathered together, both men and women, for eight days and eight nights. And whilst they were thus engaged in prayer it was revealed in a vision by the Holy Angel of Heaven to a certain Bishop who was a very good Christian, that he should desire a certain Christian Cobbler, who had but one eye, to pray that God in His goodness would grant such prayer because of the Cobbler's holy life.

Now I must tell you what manner of man this Cobbler was. He was one who led a life of great uprightness and chastity, and who fasted and kept from all sin, and went daily to church to hear Mass, and gave daily a portion of his gains to God. And the way how he came to have but one eye was this. It happened one day that a certain woman came to him to have a pair of shoes made, and she showed him her foot that he might take her measure. Now she had a very beautiful foot and leg; and the Cobbler in taking her measure was conscience of having sinful thoughts. And he had often heard it said in the Holy Evangel, that if thine eye offend thee, pluck it out and cast it from thee, rather than sin. So, as soon as the woman departed, he took the awl that he used in stitching, and drove it into his eye and destroyed it. And in this way he came to lose his eye. So you can judge what a holy, just and righteous man he was.

Now when this vision had visited the Bishop several times, he related the whole matter to the Christians, and they agreed with one consent to call the Cobbler before them. And when he had come they told him it was their wish that he should pray, and that God had promised to accomplish the matter by this means. On hearing their request he made many excuses, declaring that he was not as good a man as they represented. But they persisted in their request with so much sweetness, that at last he said he would not tarry, but do what they desired.

And when the appointed time had come, all the Christians got up early, men and women, small and great, more than 100,000 persons, and went to church, and heard the Holy Mass. And after Mass had been sung, they all went forth together in a great procession to the plain in front of the mountain, carrying the precious cross before them loudly singing and greatly weeping as they went. And when they arrived at the spot, there they found the Caliph, with all his Saracen host armed to slay them if they would not change their faith; for the Saracens believed not in the least that God would grant such favour to the Christians. These latter stood in great fear and doubt, but nevertheless they rested their hope on God Jesus Christ.

So the Cobbler received the Bishop's benison, and then threw himself on his knees in front of the Holy Cross, and stretched out his hands towards Heaven and made this prayer: "Blessed Lord God Almighty, I pray Thee by Thy goodness that Thou wilt grant this grace unto Thy people, insomuch that they perish not, nor Thy faith be cast down, nor abused nor flouted. Not that I am the least worthy to prefer such request unto Thee; but for Thy great power and mercy I beseech Thee to hear this prayer from me Thy servant full of sin."

And when he had ended this his prayer to God the Sovereign Father and Giver of all grace , and whilst the Caliph and all the Saracens and other people there, were looking on, the mountain rose out of its place and moved to the spot which the Caliph had pointed out! And when the Caliph and all the Saracens beheld, amazed at the wonderful miracle that God had wrought for the Christians, insomuch that a great number of the Saracens became Christians. And even the Caliph caused himself to be baptized …and became a Christian, but in secret.

MARCO POLO, 1298

Fables such as this hurt Marco Polo's credibility.

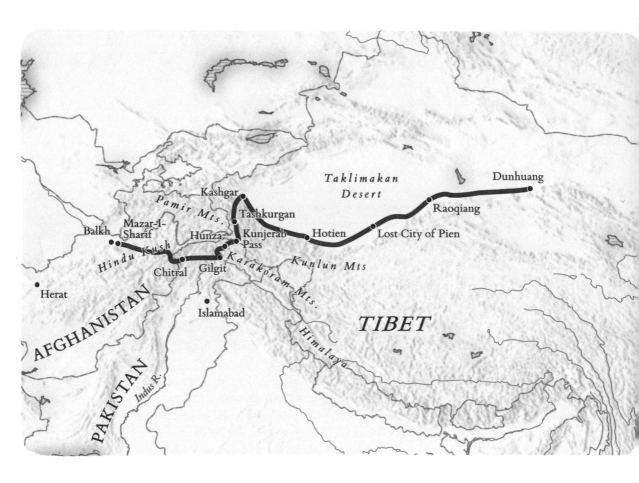

Taklimakan
Desert

Dunhuang

Kashgar

Tashkurgan

Raoqiang

Mazar-I-
Sharif

Pamir Mts.

Balkh

Hunza

Kunjerab
Pass

Hotien

Lost City of Pien

Hindu Kush

Chitral

Gilgit

Kunlun Mts

Herat

Karakoram Mts.

Islamabad

TIBET

AFGHANISTAN

PAKISTAN

Indus R.

Himalaya

With the back door to China closed for now, I decided on an interim project: to produce a TV movie/documentary of our Marco Polo expedition. The 300-mile journey through Pakistan to the border of China would be the most physically demanding part of the entire Marco Polo route. It would cross the highest and most rugged part of the world. Thirty-three of the mountains along this route are over 25,000 feet. The glaciers among these snow-covered mountains are the largest outside of the artic regions. Nature's hand had crushed, crumbled, and thrust this landscape up and out of the earth into one of the most dramatic vistas anywhere on this globe. This would be the ideal venue for a half-hour movie to be used as a "pilot" for a three- to four-hour PBS-TV miniseries of the entire Marco Polo Odyssey.

With the help of George Udell, a documentary movie producer in Baltimore, Maryland, and the genius of Charles Vanderpool, an all-around filmmaker, we started to make plans to produce the Marco Polo movie. We had a shoestring budget and hoped to get adequate funding for the full project using this pilot film to sell the idea. It was a big gamble. A crew of three adventurous souls left Baltimore, Maryland in August 1981 for Islamabad, Pakistan. My teammates were Michael Winn—a photojournalist whose camera had conquered the heart and captured the beauty of some of the most remote places of Africa—and Charles, who was our entire film crew. Charles was the director, cameraman, and soundman and did everything else that was necessary to get the film "in the can." I came along as the executive producer with my 35-mm still camera.

The logistics for this film project defied all reason. We were to travel for a month through territory that provided no access to the electricity needed to charge the batteries used in most modern cameras. Charles' solution to this first challenge was a factory-modified Bolex, a hand-wound 16-mm film camera. No electricity, just muscle power. It was also modified to take 35-mm Nikon camera lenses, which Michael and I were using for our still photography. This gave Charles a wide range of lenses to expand his cinematographic options. Sound was recorded on a book-size, studio-quality Sony tape deck that was battery (dry-cell) operated—we carried lots of cassettes and type AA batteries. We used a small, high-performance stereo microphone and, most importantly, we lugged along over ten hours of the 16-mm film in cans. This was our limit, since all the baggage, including film and film making equipment, couldn't weigh more than the three of us could carry on our backs. Sometimes the only means of moving from place to place was on foot. That weight limitation was not our biggest challenge.

Charles' creativity was exemplified in a remote mountainous area where he found need for an "acoustically isolated mike boom." We were in a place where the most advanced available technology was a box of safety matches. In fact, the microphone we were using was the size of a safety match box. Charles went to a nearby tree and whittled off a six-foot branch with three twigs growing at one end. Charles suspended the mike using a few rubber bands to center it between the twigs. The result was an acoustically isolated mike boom.

If a properly financed Hollywood production company were to have made this movie, they would have had 300 Sherpas schlepping supplies, a motor generator and other equipment along precarious mountain trails.

CHAPTER 15

The Hindu Kush Mountains
Rawlpindi, Pakistan, August 25 to September 8, 1981

*n this kingdom there are many strait and perilous passes so difficult to force
that the people have no fear of invasion. Their towns and villages are on
lofty hills, and in very strong positions. They are excellent archers, and
much given to the chase; indeed most of them are dependent for clothing on
the skins of beasts, for stuffs are very dear to them. The great ladies, however,
are arrayed in stuffs, and I will tell you the style of their dress! They all wear drawers made
of cotton cloth, and into the making of these some will put 60, 80 or even 100 ells of stuff. This
they do to make themselves look large in the hips, for men of these parts think that to be a great
beauty in a woman.*
MARCO POLO, 1298

Three intrepid adventurers had checked into Flashman's Hotel at the Saddar Bazaar,
Rawlpindi, Pakistan. Michael Winn, Charles Vanderpool, and I were about to
travel across four mountain ranges that converge in Northern Pakistan. We started
with the Hindu Kush. Since the time of Alexander the Great, writers have been
overcome by the wonder of its fearsome beauty. Samuel Johnson synopsizes their
sentiments:

*They who have penetrated farthest into the mountain ranges of the Hindu Kush report of the
silent abysses of the midnight sky, with its intensely burning stars and the colossal peaks lift-
ing their white masses beyond storms, impress the imagination with such a sense of fathomless
mystery and eternal repose, as no other region on earth can suggest. Here are splendors and
glooms, unutterable powers, impenetrable reserves.*
SAMUEL JOHNSON

Our first stop was to meet with Madame Begum Noon, the head of the Pakistan
Tourism Development Corporation (PTDC) under the Ministry of Tourism. She
had arranged for a guide to shepherd us through the mountains, canyons, and bureaucracies that we were about to enter. Pervez Khan was not only our guide but
also a published photographer and, soon, a cherished friend. The Nikon camera
he carried also added some lenses from which Charles Vanderpool could choose
in filming this journey. Pervez was a sturdy man in his thirties who wore an appropriate trekking outfit and whose multilingual capabilities were important in
keeping our trek on track.

The flight from Islamabad to Chitral was a little over an hour, flying over and
among many snow-packed mountains. Chitral was not far from where Joanne and
I had ended our travels, on the other side of the Afghanistan border, at the end of

1975. On the north side of town was the Mastuj River, running along the main street and bazaar for more than a mile. The street was full of people. The stalls and shops were bustling, brimming with goods of all kinds—guns, fruits, clothing, and a breathtaking array of precious rubies, sapphires, and other stones found nearby. Gems were the currency of exchange that the Polo family used for trade.

It is in this province that those fine and valuable gems the Balas Rubies are found. They are got in certain rocks among the mountains, and in search for them the people dig great caves underground, just as is done by miners of silver...

There is also in the same country another mountain, in which azure is found; 'tis the finest in the world, and is got in a vein like silver. There are also other mountains that contain a great amount of silver ore, so that this country is a very rich one; but it is also a very cold one.

MARCO POLO, 1298

Many turbaned Afghan refugees milled about, lost in another world without adequate means for survival. They had come across the border to escape the Russians and someday hoped to go home. With the Afghans came the game of Bushkashi (capture the dead goat) played on the playing field when the field was not being used for Pakistan's fiercely competitive national game of polo, a game that was here for centuries before the British adopted it as their own.

Above the valley where Chitral was built, hundreds of stone and wooden homes were stacked one on another, plastered against the hillside. At the very top of the hill was the Government Cottage with an imposing view: a promenade of mountains dominated by Tirich Mir at 25,438 feet. At the bottom of the gorge, the bazaars of Chitral and the white stone Shahi Mosque stood close to the Fort that the British had held for fifty years before Pakistan became a nation. It had become the police headquarters.

To get closer to the Afghanistan border we left Chitral and made our way west, up the Bumberet River to the Kalash valleys—domicile of the non-Islamic Kafir Kalash (or Black Infidels). When the children of Bumberet village saw western strangers arriving, they started yelling "paysar, paysar!" ("money, money") and pelting us with small stones when there wasn't a quick response. We stayed in the area for a few days giving out ballpoint pens, offering Polaroid photos and smiling a lot. We began to win them over. I have always felt that giving a small gift as a token of respect is better than offering money, which serves to recognize their relative poverty.

Most of the original Kafir Kalash tribe lives in Afghanistan, in an area that was once called Kafiristan. The Kafirs are the most dramatically colorful people in this part of the world: this is true of both their clothing and their culture. They still follow their ancient religion, a combination of animism (a belief that all natural things possess souls) and ancestor-and-fire worship. Sajigor is the prime deity to whom they make offerings, along with many lesser gods: Surisan protects the cattle, Goshedoi is worshipped to honor milk products, and other gods are thanked for many of nature's gifts.

During our visit the women and young girls performed one of their ritual dances, arm in arm, snaking around the pasture where we stood. They were dressed in an exotic costume of long black robes; red and white necklaces; and elegant black, flowing headdresses covered in cowry shells and other ornaments. I thought these colorful ensembles were just for the show, but I later found a few women dressed in the same outfits sitting by the river and weaving baskets. A group of the local Kafir men provided the music with drums, tambourines, and a type of Asian flute. They were not as elegantly attired.

The Kafirs live in log cabins and worship in elaborately carved wooden temples. It was very surprising to see that the dead were placed in open wood coffins and left above ground for years, where everyone was able to view their gradual decay.

One of the many reasons that Kafirs do not fit into the surrounding cultures is that most have fair skin, light hair and blue eyes. Because of these Mediterranean features, some historians believe the Kafirs were descended from the Greek troops of Alexander the Great who came this way 2,300 years ago. It is well known that many Greek soldiers left the army and stayed.

You can imagine the fun Charles had filming and recording these colorful people and their music. The more I saw Charles working with his camera, the more I came to see him as a creative, low budget genius. A good example was with his filming of the Kafirs. In one of the film sequences of their dancing he stood on an upside down basket holding the camera high above his head. He rotated around in one direction as they danced around him in the other direction. On a movie studio lot, Charles would have had special equipment like a cherry picker, but all Charles needed here in remote Northern Pakistan was a strong wicker basket, a steady hand and some ingenuity. Charles had a lot of ingenuity.

Marco Polo refers to his travels through this territory as "The great province of Pasciai." According to Leonardo Olschki, one of the leading authorities on Marco Polo, this corresponds to the mountainous district of present-day Kafiristan and the adjoining Chitral, where we now stood.

Bumberet was where our expedition picked up Marco Polo's trail, to follow the Mastuj River north. It took two days, by jeep, to travel the rugged sixty miles up the Yarkund River Valley to the town of Mastuj, about the same travel time it would have taken a camel caravan. The road was not designed for jeep travel.

Mastuj was the home of Prince Sikander Ul-Mulk, whose name means "from the son of Alexander." During our visit he quickly explained that he was Mongol not Greek. He was a descendent of Tamerlane, whose family had ruled this province for five hundred years. He told us that his family's rule ended in 1972 when the government of Pakistan confiscated his lands. His highness looked like a young

movie star playing the part of a prince; he spoke English like an Oxford scholar but dressed like a peasant in baggy but well pressed pants, a long loose shirt, and the rolled-edge wool cap that they call "bakhol." We talked as Charles filmed our conversation. I felt, again, like I was on a back lot at a movie studio in Hollywood. The retired prince told me he now tended to his orchards of apricots and walnuts and coached the local polo team.

"The British discovered polo here in Asia," Sikander Ul-Mulk said, "and turned it into a gentlemen's sport. We used the game for centuries to settle land disputes between villages. It is a much rougher game here, as there are no rules. The same horse and rider must play for the full hour without substitutes, rather exhausting at these altitudes. There is a lot of excitement and noise—each team has its own musicians with drums and flutes and special tunes that provide a play-by-play commentary to help the spectators to keep track of the game. Unfortunately, it can be dangerous. Riders and spectators are often hurt and some have been killed."

The only object of advanced technology in Mastuj was the hand-cranked phone at the police station. When we asked the prince if he would like to bring the modern world into his two-mile-high domain in the Hindu Kush, he answered, "If you have an expert on solar energy or wind generators, send him up. I'll be happy to trade him some land and a house for his services."

It was another two-day jeep trek to reach Shandur Pass, where the Hindu Kush met the Karakoram Mountains. The dominant feature was bigness, combined with desolation: vast mountains sit in silence, carrying a mantle of eternal snow, wild white rivers born in glaciers; brutal precipices, and barren hillside pastures where the goat and sheep find a precarious existence. After crossing the pass, it took time to recover from the depression instilled in us by the stillness and a landscape of somber giants. I felt microscopic and lost in this vast new world of the Karakoram.

This page: Kafir women weaving baskets

Color was purged by the sun's glare, and birds do not sing above 12,000 feet. Life was often limited to an occasional hawk poised in the sky. Somewhere in the gorge below was the dull, unremitting roar of the Ghizar River.

This old Silk Road was once busy with traders and nomads. Local tribes used this abandoned alpine wonderland for their summer migrations. On the first night beyond the pass, our caravanserai turned out to be a shepherd-farmer's stone hut, furnished with red and yellow pillows to make our sleeping bags more comfortable. The farmer gave us a hardy breakfast of hot porridge and whole-wheat nan. He refused money, even when we insisted. Traveling can often offer pleasant surprises.

After a day of trekking along this lost section of the Silk Road we came to a plateau surrounding Lake Handrap. It was twilight as we sat around waiting for Michael to light a fire of dried yak dung, over which we would heat up our dinner. At an altitude of 12,000 feet it was not an easy task. In desperation he poured some purple poison from a can of Sterno. The fire could not produce enough heat to boil water, just as Marco Polo had told us would be the case.

The plain is called Pamir, and you ride across it for twelve days together, finding nothing but a desert without habitation or any green thing, so that travelers are obliged to carry with them whatever they have need of. The region is so lofty and cold that you do not even see any birds flying. And I must notice also that because of the great cold, fire does not burn so brightly, nor give out so much heat as usual, nor does it cook food so effectually.

MARCO POLO, 1298

131 *The Hindu Kush Mountains*

Above: Kafir women dancing in their elegant everyday clothes

Our guide, Pervez, told us that this area was known for its evil spirits. Just as he spoke a strange shadow appeared in the distance coming towards our isolated campsite. Was it one of the evil spirits Pervez predicted? An evil spirit would have been more likely: it was a young Japanese man pushing a bicycle! I invited him to join us for our dinner of roasted sparrows. Here we were at two and a half miles above sea level in one of the most remote parts of the world, far from any human habitation, and we had a guest! We met twenty-one-year-old Keisuke Seto, who had already won acclaim on four continents for his attempt to bicycle around the world. It was so surprising, yet so fitting for adventurers from opposite sides of the earth to meet on the road over which 2,000 years of goods and ideas had been exchanged. We sat around the small fire summarizing our reasons for being there. I asked Keisuke where he was planning to go after he finished visiting so many countries around the world and triumphed in his formidable quest. He answered, "Someplace else." In the morning Keisuke continued west on his bike, and we headed east.

I'd driven over a million miles but never had I seen a single mile of road as terrifying as the stretch between Mastuj and Gilgit in Northern Pakistan. The tires on our jeep were often just inches from the edge of the crumbling dirt track that was carved out of the mountain's vertical wall. A couple of thousand feet below us, the whitewaters of the Ghizar and Gilgit Rivers thrashed their way along the gorge. There were a dozen switchback turns needed to get us over one mountain pass after another. Each hairpin turn was so tight that even a short wheelbase jeep had to back up two or three times to gyrate around these corners. In order to keep close to the inside wall, our side view mirror had to be folded in. I sat helpless with sweaty palms in a jeep piled high with five people, luggage, and movie making equipment. It was quiet except for the groaning of the jeep's engine and the crunching of stones beneath the tires. I was in the front holding my breath in the seat next to the mountain wall. Pervez and Charles sat relaxed in the back, but Michael clung to the rear of the jeep camera in hand, looking for photo opportunities. At one of our stops Michael was standing on the edge of the road overlooking the river a thousand feet below. As he walked back to the jeep a ten-foot section of the road on which he been standing fell into the ravine.

The driver, Hassan Abdul, took us along this trail that has clung to these mountains for more than a thousand years…a path designed for donkeys. When we reached a high plateau to stop for tea, Hassan casually mentioned that five jeeps had fallen into the gorge that year–after improvements had been made.

This trail was part of the ancient Silk Road.

It was the middle of the afternoon, and we stopped to relax at a mud hut that served as a roadside chai hanna (tea house). Charles went to lie down across the seats of the jeep for a nap. As we drank our tea, the earth beneath our feet began to

This page: The Silk Road in the Karakorham Mountains

shudder violently—another earthquake. Standing became difficult. We squatted. The jeep rocked slowly enough that it did not wake Charles. Later we discovered the quake measured at 6.1 on the Richter scale and had demolished a town on the other side of the mountain, killing 300 people and injuring over 2,000. Our journey had taken us to a part of the world that has always been plagued with earthquakes. Hassan savored the last of his tea and said, "It is God's will." Charles slept through it all.

Further along our trail we had to make our way around landslides the earthquake had caused. We stopped to visit a Buddhist shrine on the other side of a river. To do so, I faced the challenge of crossing a 150-foot bridge consisting of three ropes made from twisted vines tied to boulders on either side of a deep gorge. Many of the vines were shredded or broken. I held tightly to the upper two strands and gingerly put one foot in front of the other on the bottom rope, to begin making my way to the other side. My acrophobia (fear of heights), the swinging of the bridge with each step, and its questionable construction made my movement across this deep cleft in the mountains very slow. Over fifty feet below me, I could see the turbulent river and an abundance of rocks. As I inched along, I tried to stabilize myself by pushing out on the two upper ropes. This was a mistake. When I got to the middle of the span my arms were fully extended, and I could move neither forward nor backward. For a moment I was petrified. When my senses returned, I realized that I must pull my arms and the ropes closer to my body so I could release one side and move that arm further along. After losing gallons of sweat I got to the other side, visited the shrine and made the long journey back. It was the longest 150 feet that I ever had to walk—twice.

We had been lucky so far. Retracing Marco Polo's journey meant traveling in areas known for disastrous quakes and dangerous political situations. It was extremely fortunate that we had been able to make our way along the Marco Polo trail without a major mishap—through Turkey, Iran, and Afghanistan—during our first expedition in 1975. Many of the places we had visited during that first trip had been subsequently ravaged, lost or totally destroyed. In 1976, the city of Van—near Lake Van in Eastern Turkey—experienced an earthquake that killed thousands and made thousands more homeless. An earthquake in September 1978 leveled my cherished little oasis of Tabas, in the middle of Iran, and almost all of its 14,000 citizens were killed. Tabas—a city of flowers, palms, and serene beauty—had been abandoned. That year, the revolution in Iran was fermenting. In January of 1979 the Shah was forced out of Iran. Under the new, revolutionary Islamic government, Iran went from being one of the most advanced, industrialized, predominantly Islamic nations to political isolation and economic depression. Meanwhile in Afghanistan, a Soviet-backed coup deposed that government. In the following year the new Islamic government of Iran took 53 Americans hostage from the U.S. Embassy in Teheran. Then, in early 1980 Soviet troops had invaded Afghanistan. All this had happened in the few short years after our first expedi-

tion. As luck would have it, we had traveled this part of the Polos' journey before these events took place. Our project had allowed us to see a part of the world that quickly disappeared or was no longer within the reach of most people. Luck had traveled by my side, and it seemed that the harder I struggled to fulfill my dream of following Marco Polo, the luckier I got.

135 *The Hindu Kush Mountains*

Left: The rock fell away as Michael stepped to safety

Right: Crossing a swinging rope bridge over a white water river

CHAPTER 16

Road to Hunza
September 8 to 20, 1981

*T*hese mountains are so lofty that it is a hard days walk, from morning to evening, to get to the top of them. On getting up, you find an extensive plain,
with great abundance of grass and trees, and copious springs of pure water
running down through the rocks and ravines. In these brooks are found
trout and many other fish of a dainty kind; and the air in those regions is
so pure, residence is so healthful, that when the men who dwell below the towns, and in the
valleys and the plains, find themselves attacked by any kind of fever or other ailment that may
hap, they lose no time in going to the hills; and abiding there three or four days, they will quite
recover their health through the excellence of the air. And Messer Marco he had proved this
by experience: for when in these parts he had been ill for about a year, but as soon as he was
advised to visit the mountains, he did so and got well at once.

MARCO POLO, 1298

As we descended from the 12,000-foot barren plateau to lower altitudes, the stark
landscape gradually transformed to lush strips in many shades of green. We were
still in the vertical world of the Karakoram and strip farming was the name that
came to mind: each terraced strip was carved out of the mountainside. I saw vegetables growing on a 60-degree mountain slope, with the retaining wall almost
twice as high as the terrace was wide.

White frothy water, from mineral-filled glacial runoff, drains into irrigations
ditches to feed these fruits and vegetables that grow in this verdant environment;
a true cornucopia of farm products: apples, cucumbers, melons, potatoes, onions,
peppers, beans, endive, lettuce, radishes, turnips, spinach, Brussels sprouts, parsley
and more. Most of these plants have been growing here for centuries. The practice
of grafting apricot trees has gone on for 1,600 years. Grapes and mulberries are
made into wine or dried for the winter, plus a wide variety of grains are grown.
The quality of what I saw grown along these mountainsides, I'm certain, would
win blue ribbons in any county fair.

We stopped to talk to a farmer who was loading a giant basket with hay. He told
us about his family—a wife and four young children—plus his greatest material
asset, the family's goats and sheep. He said he could only afford to kill one or two
of their animals when they returned from "pasture." The meat from each animal
would last for a week or two. Now his goats and sheep were in the high summer
pasturelands at altitudes up to 15,000 feet, being tended by the community's shepherds. They milked the sheep and goats every evening. Our new friend explained
to us the process the shepherds use to make butter. You simply strain the milk
through a leafy Juniper branch then shake it in a gourd until butter forms. The
shepherds then wrap twenty-pound slabs of the butter in Birch bark and bury it

in sheep dung to protect it from rats. Later someone packs it down the mountain on donkeys to the village, along with a large accumulation of dung needed for fertilizer and winter fuel. Using dung is far more cost effective and environmentally friendly than cutting down trees.

Our farmer friend filled his giant, conical reed basket with hay, slung its leather straps over his shoulders, and carried the 150-pound load more than a quarter of a mile to the roof of his house, where he would store the hay as winter food for his animals to eat when they returned home. Our farmer was living what we as modern city dwellers would call an oppressive lifestyle, but somehow farmers have survived this way of life for thousands of years.

Charles and Michael were photographing the farmer as he did his chores. Charles was on the roof of the farmer's house pointing his camera down as the farmer was lugging his load of hay up the ladder. A white chicken ran under the ladder and across the scene as if on cue. For a cinematographer this was a perfect photo opportunity and not easily repeated.

An ancient ferry system—the same type Marco Polo described 700 years before—would help us cross the Ghizar River not far from the town of Gupis. The raft was made of eight inflated goatskins tied to a rectangular frame of tree branches. Michael, an experienced white water kayaker, asked the boatman for permission to row the raft. Charles was going to film our river crossing, but it would require two takes—one from each riverbank. He stayed on shore as the boatman, Michael and I made our way downstream. Everything went well until one of the skins deflated in the middle of the river on the first run. The other skins held up, and we made it across.

After weeks of traveling through a part of the world that was barely out of the Middle Ages, we arrived at the "almost" twentieth-century town of Gilgit: electric lights, a few paved streets, and blaring boom-boxes. The market was full of everything from Willie Nelson cassettes to Willys Jeeps to plastic buckets and T-shirts—a potpourri of goods showcasing Gilgit's perspective of the Western world. Silks, porcelain, china, and grilled mutton on a stick were also available, as they were in Polo's time.

Gilgit has always been the hub of trade. Trails and new roads radiate in all directions...west to Chitral, east along the Indus River, north to Hunza and China, and south, along the Karakoram Highway, to Islamabad. The Karakoram Highway has been the primary agent of change, impacting the character of Gilgit and all of Northern Pakistan as well as Western China. By the time of our arrival, this part of the Silk Road had been covered in asphalt. Now, former farmers have been "enriched" by the introduction of Western commerce, and the area will never turn back. Our expedition across Asia gave us a chance to look through a window that modern technology—or so-called progress—will darken; hopefully, the record that our project made will offer a glimpse of this part of the world the way Marco Polo experienced it.

The Karakoram Highway was a Chinese-Pakistani joint project that took twenty years and tens of thousands of workers to build, and in the process took the lives of four hundred. It was one of the biggest Asian public works projects since the building of the Great Wall. This two-lane, 720-mile road cuts its way through the highest and most treacherous mountains in the world—from Islamabad, Pakistan, to Kashgar, China. Earthquakes, encroaching glaciers, and crumbling slopes had a big impact on its construction and made travel along this road both dangerous and unpredictable, as we would soon see.

Not everyone was happy with the progress the road brought. Our Hunzakut friend, Gulum Mohammed Beg, who owned a bookshop along the main street in Gilgit, had this to say: "Yes, we are getting rich, but this new road is ruining our society. It has brought new diseases and unhealthy food from cans. In the old days we were like a big family—we climbed the mountains; we danced together every day in the winter. The winter solstice was the time we all shared a huge feast for

Above: The lush terraced farms of Hunza

a full week. Now everyone is lazy and wants to get money for himself. But what can we do? The road is more important than our village."

Still, there were also positive signs of change. Schools had been set up all through Northern Pakistan with both religious and secular teachers. Most of the classes we saw were outside, nestled within the walls of white-capped mountains. Boys were the only students except for a few classes of girls in Hunza Province. Still this was progress; up until the 1960's, education was exclusively for the royal family and even then only religious books were permitted.

Most of the Pakistani people have been followers of Mohammed for more than 1,200 years, but followers of Buddha have also played an important part in the history of these crossroads between the Eastern and Western worlds. Buddhist monks made their way from India to China through this part of the Silk Road. These Buddhists originally used objects to symbolize their faith: a wheel, a tree, the stupa, or other decorative objects. But here in these mountains Buddha took on the human shape—with Grecian facial features and wearing a tunic, as expressed in the art left by the army of Alexander the Great. A new Buddhist art form had emerged.

Not far from Gilgit we found a rare, sixth century, twenty-foot-high female image of Buddha carved into the face of a mountain. In a clearing below the Buddha, we stumbled upon the camp of Professor Carl Jettmar from Heidelberg University, one of the leading researchers studying the history and culture of the people in the Karakoram Mountains. "Little is known about the history of the early Himalayan kingdoms," the professor told us as we sat drinking tea. "The artifacts have been destroyed by flash floods, landslides, glaciers, and earthquakes. The elements are very severe here. Yet a wealth of fascinating evidence has survived in rock carvings; there are more first-millennium rock carvings here than in any other place in Asia. My team has located thousands of sites. The inscriptions in early Sanskrit languages offer the first solid proof that there was a kingdom called Lesser Bolor at the crossroads of trade between India, Central Asia, and China."

In the 1960's, a trip from Gilgit to Hunza would have taken two or three days. Then a jeep trail was built, which reduced the travel time to seven hours. The Karakoram Highway could have gotten us to Hunza in less than a couple of hours; however, we stopped along the way to examine ancient sketches chiseled on the stone outcroppings by hunters. We found a giant boulder with dozens of line drawings of ibex and deer, each about the size of a handprint. Those who killed the animals carved these pictures into the rock to help preserve the creatures' souls.

A ring of four-mile-high, snow-covered peaks, like a circle of dragon teeth, protect the ancient valley of Hunza. Rakaposhi, the dominant peak at 25,550 feet, soars majestically in a multitude of colors that change hour by hour, reflecting the pigments painted in the sky by the setting sun. For twelve miles the Karakoram Highway and Hunza River cut through these mountains, which appear cleaved by a galactic ax. We crossed a beautiful Chinese-built bridge protected at each end by stone lions. This was our turnoff to climb to the entrance of Hunza Valley. The landscape opened into a sweeping panorama, wondrous in comparison to the stark vertical cliffs through which we had just passed. Eric Shipton, the British Himalayan explorer, called Hunza "the ultimate manifestation of mountain grandeur" and at 8,000 feet (2,400 meters) above sea level it appeared to us an enchanted world, "rich, fecund, and of ethereal beauty." The mountain wall was landscaped with emerald green terraces supported by dry stone walls and punctuated with slim, Lombardy Poplar trees, which visually held together this vertical world.

The same family ruled the Kingdom of Hunza and its 30,000 Hunzakuts since the eleventh century. They believe they were descended from some of Alexander the Great's soldiers, and this was somewhat confirmed by the blue-green eyes and lighter complexion of many of the people we saw throughout Hunza. It became part of Pakistan in 1974, but their mir (king) still retains some political importance.

The most memorable part of my visit to Hunza was the conversation I had with the 75-year-old wazir of Hunza. The wazir was the advisor to the mir. We talked as we sat on the wall supporting a farming terrace. He wore the traditional bakhol, a beige, long, slit-sided shirt, and matching Pakistani pants. He looked my age and yet he was twenty-four years my senior. Hunza is famous for having more of the oldest living people per capita, than any other place on earth. I asked the inevitable question "Why do people in Hunza live longer?" A wide smile spread quickly across his face, and he answered in British-accented English, "Scientists have come here from all over, to find the answer to this profound question. Some have said it was the high mineral content of the water. The water we drink and feed to our plants and animals comes from the run-off of the glaciers. You can see it flows and foams white with minerals…but there is more.

"Some say it is the robust physical condition of our people since they live on the side of a mountain. In order to do anything or go from one place to another, you are continually climbing up and down the terraces. This keeps your heart, lungs, and the limbs of your body in excellent condition from the time you first learn to crawl and walk…but there is more.

"Other scientists have come to find the secret of our longevity and measured the character of the air. They found that our air has a high content of negative ions because of the altitude…but there is more.

"Most of the researchers believe it is because of our food. You know that our sheep and goats are taken higher into the mountains during the summer and early fall for the better pasturelands. The animals are milked there and the cheese and butter are packed down to our villages during the warm season, for the additional nourishments they offer. Of course, during this warmer season, we have no meat and therefore live off the many vegetables and fruits that we grow on our terraces. There is an ample variety, which provides every kind of nutrition needed for a healthy life. Some of this produce is preserved. You know, winters in Hunza are rather cold with continuous snow. This is the time of year that we require the meat and fats that come from our goats and sheep to keep us warm; with further warmth provided from their skins and wool. There are researchers that believe this is the explanation for long life in Hunza…but there is more.

"We Hunzakuts feel the real answer, in addition to all the other justifications to explain our long life, lies in the fact that we have a lack of stress. This was an important part of our lifestyle in Hunza before the building of the Karakoram Highway. Let me explain. Unlike all other parts of the world, we were never concerned about survival. Hunza was a totally self-sufficient kingdom. Our fruits, nuts, vegetables, and animal products were guaranteed each year. We were not dependent on the weather. The glaciers water our crops. There has never been a drought. There was very little disease in both our community and animals because of our isolation. Very few people could enter our valley. Mountains isolate Hunza, and outsiders were prevented from entering without our permission. The few trails that wound their way into our valley could be easily cut off, preventing unwanted warriors from entering Hunza. As a result we were not under the stress of being invaded.

"In the summers we work hard to prepare for the next winter but hard work is good to minimize stress. Winter is the time of year that we really relax. The many older people of the community offer council to solve the personal problems of the young, helping to reduce the stress of growing up and old. Our greatest celebration is at the time of the winter solstice at the end of December. All weddings are held on that day and the party lasts for a week. Even the stress the parents of the wedding couple often suffer in trying to decide whom to invite and whom not to invite is eliminated. Everybody in Hunza comes!"

Marco Polo knew of Hunza's reputation as a healthy place. He had developed a fever in nearby Afghanistan in the province of Badakshan. It lasted a year and is assumed to have been malaria. When he heard about Hunza, as he tells in his book, he went there to recuperate. From Hunza, Marco went a few miles north to the Mintake Pass and then as he says "northeast by east" on the main Silk Road to Kashgar, China. I was unable to enter China at this point: without a visa my journey to Xanadu was temporarily postponed…but my will to complete it was as healthy as a Hunzakut.

On returning to Baltimore at the completion of the film project, Charles put in months of eighteen-hour days doing all the post-production work, including editing and synchronizing the independently recorded non-synchronous sound. This was truly a one-man show with me peeking over Charles' shoulder. Finally, the movie had its premiere at the Metropolitan Museum of Art in New York in April 1982. The title was "On the Roof of the World with Marco Polo."

After completing this pilot film, we started to seek financing to produce a full-length documentary called *The Marco Polo Odyssey*. The possibility for funding disappeared when we discovered that RAI (Italian TV) and NBC had a $25-million, eight-hour docudrama of the Marco Polo story, to be shown on prime time NBC-TV in the fall of 1982. Our film project ended, and I was devastated. Tens of thousands of dollars and over a full year of effort by a lot of dedicated, financially uncompensated people…forfeited!

END OF THE SECOND EXPEDITION

PART THREE

CHAPTER 17

The Long Road to the Kunjerab Pass
Pakistan, August 5 to 15, 1985

S o the Two Brothers and Marco along with them, proceeded on their way, *and journeying on, summer and winter, came at length to the Great Khan, who was then at a certain rich and great city, called Kemenfu (now called Shangtu and "Xanadu"). As to what they met with on the road, whether in going or coming, we shall give no particulars at present, because we are going to tell you all those details in regular order in the after part of this Book. Their journey back to the Khan occupied a good three years and a half, owing to bad weather and severe cold that they encountered. And let me tell you in good sooth that when the Great Khan heard that Messers Nicolo and Maffeo Polo were on their way back, he sent people a journey of forty days to meet them; and on this journey, as on their former one, they were honourably entertained upon the road, and supplied with all that they required*

MARCO POLO, 1298

On a cool summer evening in Seattle, I boarded British Air Flight 84 to begin the final segment of the greatest adventure of my life—becoming the first person to retrace the entire route of that intrepid explorer who traveled overland from Venice to Beijing in the thirteenth century, Marco Polo.

As I flew the polar route to London, my thoughts soared back and forth between the experiences of the past two expeditions and anticipation of the months to come. I was excited to be returning to the spectacular, mountainous landscape of Northern Pakistan. The expedition would revisit a portion of our previous route, from Gilgit to Hunza, only this time we would continue across the snow-sheathed mountains into China. Marco Polo had crossed at the Mintake Pass, on what was then the main Silk Road. We would echo his footsteps a short distance south at the Khunjerab Pass, the only border crossing in all of western China and the highest border crossing in the world with a paved road. And we would be the first Westerners to bridge this passage in nearly four decades.

Michael Winn was waiting for me at Heathrow Airport at 10:00 a.m. He was joining me again on this odyssey, flying in from New York. He was easy to spot, with his flaming red hair and a matching beard. I knew I wouldn't lose track of him on our expedition; he wouldn't be able hide in any part of China.

It was a rousing reunion, as if we were two, long-lost brothers. Both of us were elated over the accomplishments of the last expedition and really excited about this next one. Mike's story and photographs of our escapades in Northern Pakistan had been published as a ten-page feature article in *Smithsonian* magazine.

Adventure Travel had featured his story, with a photo of me riding a horse on its cover. Photo stories of the project had also appeared in other publications. We were famous.

I hadn't seen Michael in more than a year, but over the next few months we would rarely be more than a few yards apart. He looked great. He was now the owner of two Ethiopian restaurants in New York City, and he must have been sampling a lot of his own, exotic dishes. The extra weight looked good on him, and (considering what we expected to find for food in Western China and the continuous threat of dysentery) it couldn't hurt to have a few extra pounds as a backup.

British Airways generously forgave the overweight charges on our luggage, as a gesture to what they felt was a worthwhile project. We took off on our fifteen-hour flight for Islamabad. As Michael slept, I sat with my carry-on bag in my lap: a blue cloth bag with a thin, frayed shoulder strap and the Pan Am trademark on its side. It contained documents and papers that had taken a dozen years to amass—a visa plastered into my passport giving permission to enter China from Pakistan at the Khunjerab Pass, copies of correspondence from officials in both countries, an officially signed contract with the China News Service (CNS), plus maps made by the early twentieth-century explorer, Auriel Stein. The bag had been given to me in 1975 by our sponsor, Pan Am, who provided free round-trip flight tickets for the first expedition. During the first expedition it had rarely been detached from my body. On the back cover of my book describing the first expedition, *In the Footsteps of Marco Polo,* was a photo of me on a horse, high in the mountains of Afghanistan, with the same Pan Am bag over my shoulder. Ten years later, this simple cloth bag once again contained the lifeblood for the Marco Polo Project. That's why it sat on my lap instead of the overhead compartment. If I had to abandon the plane, it would stay with me.

In the hold of the plane were two huge backpacks and a gigantic, overweight, blue duffel bag, all stuffed with the gear we would need to survive the next few months in the deserts, mountains, and cold northern gritty grasslands of China. We also had a two-cubic-foot car-battery-operated refrigerator, needed to protect hundreds of rolls of 35-mm film as we crossed the terrible Taklamakan—one of the world's largest, and most formidable deserts, where nothing lives. Temperatures were expected to reach above 130 degrees Fahrenheit during the day and almost freezing at night. This film would be far more comfortable than the six photographers who would use it. The word "Taklamakan" translates to, "desert from which one never returns."

I touched the toiletries kit in my carry-on bag and smiled, feeling the dinky case of dental floss. I'd long before concluded that dental floss was the most indispensable item needed for back-country traveling: it takes up almost no space and has a thousand uses—as a spare shoestring, for tying packages, as a fishing line or clothesline. You can attach a stone to a stick with it for a makeshift hammer; tied around the bottom of your trousers, it keeps small biting animals from crawling up your legs. While filming our second expedition in Pakistan, we once created a makeshift camera-boom by tying the 16-mm Bolex movie camera to a tree branch with dental floss. Our cinematographer, Charles Vanderpool, clearly had full confidence in the strength of the floss. You can even use dental floss to cut cheese and clean between your teeth.

Also indispensable were the gifts we carried for people we met along the way. Doris Crawford, an anthropologist who had spent a great deal of time in Afghanistan, suggested safety pins, which were a big hit in 1975. This time I packed 1,000 balloons to entertain the children; they were imprinted with "The Marco Polo Expedition" in both English and Chinese.

We were ready to go.

Among the hundreds of Pakistanis greeting the crushing throng of arriving passengers on the early morning flight, a small stocky man held a sign saying "Rutstein and Winn." He drove us to Flashman's Hotel in the ancient city of Rawalpindi, on the southern outskirts of Pakistan's modern capital, Islamabad. These arrangements had been made with the help of Gulum Beg, whom we had met during the 1981 Marco Polo project in Gilgit, Northern Pakistan. Gulum was a big, gregarious guy with a bushy mustache and a knack for getting tough things done. Gulum owned the "Mohammad Book Stall" where Michael and I had drunk a lot of tea while solving all the problems of Northern Pakistan and philosophizing on life.

A few hours before I'd left Seattle, Mr. Mohamed Salim from the Pakistani Embassy in Washington D.C. had called to tell me he'd received a telex from Islamabad saying that the Pakistan Tourism Development Corporation (PTDC) would provide us with transportation, accommodations, and facilities all along the route to the border with China. This was welcome news! Soon, however, we would learn foreboding news that he had not mentioned.

Our first morning in Pakistan, Islamabad's daily newspaper, *The Muslim*, blazoned the front-page banner headline, "KHUNJERAB PASS TO BE OPENED FOR TOURISTS." We learned that the Pakistan Federal Cabinet, in their meeting three days earlier, had approved a modification of the Pakistan-China Protocol of 1972, allowing the use of the Khunjerab Pass for nationals of third countries—including the United States. This news shocked us. We'd been led to believe that our visas from China were all we needed to travel through Northern Pakistan and cross the Khunjerab Pass. If the Cabinet hadn't changed the protocol, our adventure would have ended before it began. That border had been closed to everyone but locals for over 36 years and on August 5, 1985 the government decided to open it. We didn't know whether to consider this a miracle, good luck, or another example of accidental good timing, but relief flooded us once we recovered from this astonishing news. Not long before, I'd opened a fortune cookie at my favorite Chinese restaurant in Seattle. It said, "Luck is what happens when preparation meets opportunity." Amen.

Mr. Salim of the Pakistan Embassy had told us to contact Assad Naqvi, team director for promotion at PTDC, as soon as we arrived in Pakistan. We met with him at Flashman's Hotel. He was a short, bushy-haired man with a toothy, shy smile. For many years, he'd worked for newspapers in England and Pakistan before taking his current position.

Mr. Naqvi confirmed that the Cabinet's decision was very good news for us, then proceeded to give us the bad news. The tourism division of the Ministry of Tourism and Culture had not set up the procedures that would allow us to obtain permits to travel from the Batura Bridge to and over the Khunjerab Pass into China. Once again, we were dumbfounded, but this time with no relief in sight. On our previous expedition we hadn't traveled past the bridge and hadn't needed permits. No one had mentioned that permits were required this time, especially when they informed us they were providing us with transportation and accommodations to the border... Was this expedition going to be haunted by the "no problem" mantra that followed us from the beginning of our journey?

After reviewing our situation, Mr. Naqvi took us immediately to the Ministry of Tourism and Culture, and we talked to Mr. Muneeruddin, Deputy Chief of the tourism division. This was Thursday, August 8, a week before our scheduled crossing into China. Everything in Pakistan would be closed Friday and Saturday, the Muslim weekend; we only had a few precious hours to determine what steps were needed to resolve our predicament. Mr. Muneeruddin said an expedition application was required from the Marco Polo Foundation. As one of its directors I composed a handwritten letter requesting special permission for our passage to the border. He submitted my request, along with other documents proving that we had the necessary visas and approval from the Chinese government, to cross the border from Pakistan.

Approval from the Chinese government had been very long in coming. I had first contacted the Chinese delegation to the U.N. in 1971. In 1980, my politically-connected friend George Udell and I had made a presentation to U.S. Senator Paul Sarbanes from Maryland, and he'd agreed to send letters on my behalf to key officials in the Chinese government. This had little impact within the Chinese bureaucracy. My contact at the Ministry of Culture, in typical logical Chinese fashion had advised me, "What you need is someone very high in your government to talk to someone very high in our government, who will direct all the authorities involved to approve your project." It was that simple.

In 1982, through my wife Nancy's political contacts, I was able to approach Seattle Congressman Joel Pritchard. In his offices in Washington, D.C., I showed him and his staff our movie *On the Roof of the World with Marco Polo,* documenting the second leg of the Marco Polo Odyssey and describing our project. The congressman was impressed and communicated our dilemma to Vice-President George H.W. Bush. This was the "high person" in my government I sought; someone who could talk to his counterparts in China. George H.W. Bush decided to help our project.

At my suggestion, the Vice-President wrote letters to the Chinese government's top bureaucrats. More importantly, he arranged for the U.S. State Department to assign a representative from the Beijing Embassy to work with me. My new embassy contact was a Chinese national who knew his way around the Chinese bureaucracy. He knew all the political "back doors" and how to contact key officials. Every six to eight weeks during my visits to China, he and I sat down to plan whom to see and what to do. After three years of frustrating effort, we had no tangible results.

Finally, in early 1985, we had a breakthrough. My embassy contact introduced me to a young photographer, Jin Bo Hong, who had just published a three-volume photo journal of the Silk Roads of China. Many of the places he covered in his books were along the Marco Polo trail. I met with Jin, who spoke excellent English, and he promised to help. On my next visit to China in the spring of 1985, he introduced me to a young female photographer, Luo Xiao Yun. She worked for the China News Service (CNS) and was very interested in photographing the Marco Polo Expedition as we traveled across China. She felt this would give her photographic work the international exposure it deserved. Since she was the daughter of a very, very high official—her father was the number-three person under Deng Xiao Ping—she could not get permission to leave China, but she could move mountains *within* China. Xiao Yun was the final key needed to open the country's back door at the Pakistan border and complete the Marco Polo Odyssey. Once she asked her father, all the permits started to fall into place.

In an amazingly short period, Xiao Yun obtained the authorizations we needed to go wherever Marco Polo had gone in China. In addition, we would have the support of her employer, the politically powerful CNS, the voice of the Communist Party. The Chinese team would include three of the leading photographers of the CNS, Xiao Yun included. Jin would travel with us as an interpreter, adding to our crew of top-level photographers. In addition, we would be accompanied by a band of Chinese officials—to make local arrangements and keep us out of trouble and away from sensitive military facilities. It was really going to happen! Or so I believed.

Back in Pakistan we put the bureaucratic ball in motion, requesting the crucial permits; then all we could do was wait. Our original plan had been to travel three days overland to Gilgit, then two more to the border. Unless the permits came through early on Sunday, we would have to revise that plan and rely on air service to Gilgit, which was always as undependable as good weather. I was more than a little concerned.

The Chinese contingent would be waiting for us on Thursday, according to the agreement we'd signed with CNS. We had no easy way to contact our fellow travelers on the Chinese side. If the delay lasted more than a few days, the Chinese might cancel the whole project because I would have defaulted on the agreement to meet them at the appointed time. In that nightmarish scenario, both the CNS and the Marco Polo Foundation would forfeit a great deal of money. Abandoning the dream of a lifetime and going home embarrassed with my tail between my legs was not an option I could consider!

Two days passed agonizingly in the summer heat. We tried to find a way to contact the CNS, to no avail. They would be at the border on August 15 at "high noon," a colorful term used because all of China had only one time zone, whereas by world standards it should have at least three. Twelve o'clock noon on the Pakistani side of the border was 3:00 p.m. on the Chinese side. We were to meet when the sun was directly overhead. John Wayne would understand this.

First thing Sunday morning we arrived at Assad Naqvi's office. We had hoped to meet immediately with his boss, Madame Begum Noon, Chairwoman of the PTDC, who had been so helpful on our previous expedition. We were told she would not be available for several hours, so we met instead with Mr. Kabir-Shaikh at the Ministry of Tourism and Culture. In true bureaucratic fashion, he explained the procedure for the permission we sought. He said it would take at least until the first of September, maybe the first of October. I was devastated. I could see the whole project colliding head-on with a wall of bureaucratic inefficiency. I tried to think of alternatives. *Perhaps we could fly to Beijing, then backtrack to Kashgar in far western China, and then pick up the route on the other side of the border.* But how were we to reach the CNS crew waiting in the most remote area in all of China? *Could we possibly slip away from the PTDC and find someone to drive us to the Khunjerab Pass, no questions asked?* If we were caught, that type of illegal maneuver would destroy our project and give us experience in a Pakistani jail. My stomach churned from anxiety. The sword of Damocles swayed over my head, ready to drop and sever me from my Marco Polo dream.

Mr. Kabir-Shaikh suggested we ask the U.S. ambassador to contact Pakistan's President Muhammad Zia-ul-Haq. My gut feeling was "fat chance," but we returned to Naqvi's office and placed some calls to the U.S. Embassy. The ambassador would be out of the country until the first of September. His Deputy Chief of the Mission would be leaving his post on Monday. The third person in line was in a meeting. Things did not look good.

At that point, Begum Noon stepped into the office. What a great lady. She was draped in a vibrant sari, red-with-gold-thread. A few traces of gray were sprinkled throughout what we could see of her scarf-covered black hair. She always had a regal air about her.

When we had met in 1981, Madame Noon had told me of her experience hosting our precursors—Franc and Jean Shor, in 1949, as well as the author Gary Jennings (*The Journeyer*) many years later—all unsuccessful followers of Marco Polo's route. Franc and Jean Shor had stayed with Begun Noon and her husband, a former governor, in Lahore, Pakistan.

In 1949, on their journey following Marco Polo, Franc Shor had fallen seriously ill with a fever while traveling in the same area where Marco Polo had developed malaria. By the time Franc recovered, the Communist Chinese government had taken over the country, and the new government had closed off all of China from the rest of the world. Franc and Jean Shor never completed their Marco Polo journey. Jean wrote a book entitled *After You, Marco Polo* and Franc became Associate Editor of *National Geographic*. I had met often with this colorful world traveler, at his Washington office. Franc Shor was the only person I knew who had been to every country of the world and every place that was not a country. The day I met him he was wearing riding britches, boots, and a safari jacket. It would not have been out of character for him to be slicing the air with a riding crop. Franc had taken me under his wing and helped with the many preliminary arrangements with the governments of Turkey and Iran. I can compare Franc Shor's assistance to Kublai Khan's support of Marco Polo. I am forever indebted to him for his help and the sessions he arranged for me to consult with his staff on exploration and photography. Begun Noon, who had helped Franc Shore thirty-six years earlier, was now committed to helping us reach the border the Shors had been unable to cross.

Our discussion with Madame Noon gave us hope. Whenever Naqvi presented a problem, Begum Noon shot back, "We'll have none of that negative talk." She suggested we contact the new Secretary for the Ministry of Tourism and Culture, Lieutenant General Mujah-ur-Rehman. She said he had been very interested in our project in 1981 when he was Information Secretary at the Ministry. After a few attempts, Naqvi was unable to track him down, so Madame Noon took Michael and me to her own office. The towel she was using to wipe perspiration from her face was now dripping wet; air conditioning in Islamabad's hot humid August heat was intermittent at best.

Begum Noon sat down at her desk, dialed the home of the Secretary of the Ministry of Tourism, and spoke to his wife. Within minutes, Madame Noon knew the whereabouts of Mujah-ur-Rehman and had arranged an appointment for us through his personal secretary. She said, "Go over to his office and sit there until you talk to him." She really knew how to get things done. She added that she would telephone the secretary herself on our behalf and asked him to help us even if it meant a call to President Zia.

During the hour and a half that we waited in a quiet, wood-paneled, outer office, my concerns about our project grew. At 3:30 p.m., I looked at the secretary's ancient, mahogany grandfather clock, which stood on the other side of the room, mocking me. My heart felt as if it were in my stomach. I was making every effort to pull my emotional self up, and nothing was working. Then a very tall, stately man with understanding eyes walked in. He was immaculately dressed in gray Pakistani pants and the traditional long, slit-sided shirt (the *shalwar-camise*). He walked in and introduced himself. Both Michael and I felt a positive force radiating from this very powerful person. We instinctively knew something good was about to happen.

A few minutes later, we were in the secretary's office explaining our problems. He made some calls to the Secretary of the Interior, another to Mr. Kabir-Shaikh, with whom we'd spoken earlier, and the ball was rolling. He told us about his interest in the project four years before and how he recognized its importance to Pakistan. He said we would receive the necessary papers for travel in one or two days. I was flying...or at least hoping to fly!

We were now getting close. I could almost see the gate at the border over the next ridge. Then, Monday morning, the Secretary of Interior changed his mind, stating that *seven* ministries and agencies would need to sign off on our request for approval to travel to the border. The noon flight on Tuesday would be the last flight we could catch to Gilgit with enough time remaining for the overland trek to the border: getting the necessary signatures in time seemed impossible.

Michael and I worked out a contingency plan. The next morning, he would take the 8:30 a.m. flight for Gilgit. If I were unable to join him via the noon flight, at least he would be closer to China and might be able to find some way to contact the CNS; possibly he could find a Pakistani citizen who would make the 350-mile round trip as a courier. Meanwhile, I would stay in Islamabad doing whatever I could to expedite the permit.

At 7:30 a.m. on Tuesday, two days before we were to meet with the China News Service, I dropped Michael at the airport and headed for the office of Mr. Muneeruddin, Deputy Chief of the Tourism Division. He was a giant of a man in his early forties who had once lived in Queens; experience that most certainly prepared him for this job in Pakistan. Towering behind an ancient wooden desk, he simultaneously dialed people on two phones, in an effort to get the final approval for our project. The Office of the Ministry of Foreign Affairs promised to call back in an hour. Other people were not answering their phones, and some lines were busy. He showed me the actual permit: he had completed it the previous day so that as soon as the okay came through I could leave with Taleh Mohammed, the Assistant Chief of Tourism Division. If we had verbal approval, Taleh would accompany Michael and me to the border, and Mr. Muneeruddin would collect the signatures later.

There was no question we were being supported by everyone involved. The world looked a little brighter, but my ten o'clock deadline for heading to the airport was creeping up. At 9:55, the phone rang. *We could go!*

Taleh Mohammed was a quiet guy about five-foot-six with a slightly receding hairline. Behind that demure façade was a very efficient bureaucrat and an excellent traveling companion. On our way to the airport we concluded that what had just happened could only be classified as a miracle; the miracle for which I had prayed. The new law allowing foreigners through the Khunjerab Pass was approved on August 5. The recently appointed Secretary of Tourism, who knew and supported our project, managed to compress the bureaucratic permit-processing time from two months to two days, without a minute to spare. Madam Begum Noon played a big role, as well. The amount of politicking going on behind the scenes was mind boggling; the heads of seven ministries and departments were signing documents to allow some insignificant Americans to walk across a remote border crossing in their country. But I was on my way to China, and I was euphoric. I had to remind myself that the Khunjerab Pass was still 130 miles by jeep from Gilgit, through challenging mountains and numerous checkpoints. We weren't home free.

Michael was waiting for us at the hotel in Gilgit. Our plan was to waste no time, but first we needed to clear our papers with the immigration officer in Gilgit. A young Englishman named Nicholas Danziger had crossed the border illegally the previous November—he hadn't received the permission that we'd just received to travel the sixty miles from the Batura Bridge to the Chinese border. He had worn Pakistani clothing—a turban and *shalwar-camise*—as a disguise. (I later saw his photo in this outfit in the *China Daily*.) A Pakistani immigration officer had been fired because of Danziger's illegal passage, and an investigation of the incident was still in process. Even though we had a legal permit, the immigration officer at Gilgit refused to stamp our passports, claiming that our papers were from the Ministry of Tourism, and he worked for the Ministry of Interior. Taleh Mohammed produced photocopies of supporting documents stamped "Secret," but the officer still wasn't satisfied. It took a phone call back to Islamabad to convince him that our papers were in order. He notified the checkpoints at Hunza and Batura Bridge. We spent the night in Gilgit.

We were finally on our way: Wednesday morning, four of us—Michael, Taleh, the driver, and I—plus two hundred pounds of gear packed into an army jeep. We passed quickly through a region we had lingered in four years before. The landscape was spectacular: above the tree line, a gray stone world with snow and glaciers in every direction, totally barren. Gilgit is situated in the center of the most mountainous region of all the Himalayas. Nowhere else in the world are there so great a number of deep valleys and lofty mountains in such a small area. Within a sixty-five mile radius from Gilgit, amidst innumerable smaller peaks are eleven mountains soaring from 18,000 to 20,000 feet, thirteen from 20,000 to 24,000 feet, and eight from 24,000 to above 26,000 feet, including K2, the second highest mountain in the world. Before the Karakoram Highway was built, people, donkeys, and the occasional goat herd moved between villages on shelf roads. These roads, built on the sides of vertical mountain walls hundreds of feet above raging rivers, were made by forcing tree limbs into mountainside cracks, holding the limbs up with wooden braces and paving the road with thin, flat stones. Having navigated a few of these precarious shelf roads in 1981, we were thankful to be on the highway.

Our first crucial checkpoint was at Hunza. Despite the call from Gilgit, the official there also doubted our papers. He insisted on calling back to confirm our right to travel. After another agonizing delay, we were again on our way. It wasn't easy being pioneers.

A few hours later, along the side of a remote stretch of the Karakoram Highway, a large billboard suddenly loomed in the fading light of a long day; the first sign of any sort we'd seen since Gilgit. Three-foot-high yellow letters blasted forth on a bright blue background: MARCO POLO. This was the sign for the Marco Polo Inn, our home for the night. What could be more appropriate? I felt it was a good omen and another crazy coincidence.

The owner of the Marco Polo Inn was a descendent of the local Mir. His name was appropriately Rojah Bader Khan, (Khan means king) and he was also the curator of the Gulmit Folk Museum. The bones of a "dragon" from a nearby dry lakebed were the main attraction at the museum. Mr. Khan told us the story of the seven-headed dragon that had lived in the lake. The story involved an orphan girl left by the side of the lake as a sacrifice to the dragon, and a hunter who said he would help her but fell asleep, and the girl's fearful tears that awakened the hunter, who killed the dragon.

"After that," Mr. Khan told us, "a great flood destroyed the village. All that remained were the ruins of the village and the bones of the dragon."

We also met the regional police chief at the Marco Polo Inn. He gave us a personal note for the officer at the Batura Bridge, our next crucial checkpoint, beyond which we would need our hard-won permits to enter China. With the note from the chief, and every possible supporting document the guard at the checkpoint could possibly require, plus a high official from the Ministry of Tourism as our guide, surely things would go smoothly at the bridge. I was exhausted from the challenges that I'd overcome during the past week and fell asleep quickly. The next day I would follow Marco Polo into China.

We got an early start in the morning, to be certain we could reach the Khunjerab Pass by noon. At the Batura Bridge, ten miles up the highway, we confidently showed the police guard our papers. Rather than waving us through, he commandeered our jeep, leaving us stranded in the middle of the empty road. We had no choice but to sit by the side of the road and sulk.

Assuming we could get our jeep back and be allowed to pass, only the Sust Immigration and Customs Station would stand between us and our rendezvous with the Chinese. However, the drive from the station to the actual border would take several hours on a challenging road. Similarly, on the Chinese side the Pirali Immigration and Customs Station was located nineteen miles down the mountain from the inhospitable Khunjerab Pass.

The minutes crept by—eight-thirty, nine o'clock, nine-thirty—we'd be late, if we reached the meeting place at all! Where was our jeep? Had the team from the CNS already begun the drive to the pass? Finally, after two anxious hours, the police officer returned with another officer who, after further deliberation, allowed us to move on.

The road descended into a valley where yaks and wild donkeys quietly grazed on the few small patches of grass. Glaciers inched their way to the edge of the road, embraced by snow-mantled mountains tickling the heavens. Within a hundred miles of this stretch of the Karakoram Highway rose thirty-six of the world's one hundred highest mountains; mind boggling.

The Sust Border Station was the first place that anticipated our arrival. The immigration officer, a big burly man with the mandatory mustache covering a large part of his round face, used his direct line to call the China border post in Pirali and tell his Chinese counterpart that we had arrived. The phone was a black handset, of the type popular in the early 1930's. Instead of a dial it had a paper disk with large hand-printed letters: "CHINA." Seeing that word on the phone, I shuddered with excitement. I was almost there.

We learned that our delegation from the CNS was waiting at the Pirali station. Thank goodness they hadn't started for the pass! Now, though we'd clearly be late for our high-noon date, we were finally in contact. Another burden of worry dropped from my shoulders.

The formalities were completed with a brief ceremony. Our names were the first names to be recorded in the new immigration book at this remote border post, the only gate to western China and—for foreigners from Pakistan—the sole access to its Xinjiang Province. The borders with India, Afghanistan, and the Soviet Union were still closed. We sat and chatted over some tea as the immigration officer inspected our baggage. He then stamped our passports "EXIT AT KHUNJERAB PASS," and climbed in the jeep to accompany us the rest of the way to the border.

The jeep was doing switchbacks up the serpentine road, going higher and higher, following the Khunjerab River. I still had one major concern. Would I be able to handle the high altitude? In just a few hours we were escalating from 10,000 feet above sea level to over 16,000 feet. Would I get mountain sickness, like so many others? Even Sir Edmund Hillary, the first to top Mt. Everest, could not go up past 12,000 feet when he was my age. Would I have to be taken back to Islamabad and not complete the journey? I rubbed the small river stone that I carried as good luck. On Father's Day, 1984, my two-year-old daughter Jane had found this small smooth river stone while we were on a picnic and presented it to me as her Father's Day gift. I guess it worked. We reached the top of Khunjerab Pass.

When the twenty-year-old Marco Polo came to this point in his journey, he had been traveling over two years, including the year he had spent recuperating from malaria. At the top of Khunjerab Pass I thought about how the young man

from Venice must have felt. He, who had never before traveled beyond the city of Venice, had voyaged to the ends of the known world. I, inspired by his journey, had pursued his path along the well-worn Silk Road. In the year 1985, I was alive in the same soaring mountains that he had crossed in 1273. He had been about to descend into a different world. I was about to do the same. It is ironic that in order to get to this point in my journey I had to bring western technology to China and it was to be Marco Polo's mission to take Chinese technology to the West.

During our travels from the Marco Polo Inn to the border, an extraordinary geological transformation occurred. The rugged landscape and jagged peaks gave way to smooth rolling hills. The newer Karakoram mountains (only 20 to 60 million years old) and the rugged ranges along the Northern Pakistan border seemed to have pushed themselves up through the even more primitive (some 200 million years old), smoother high altitude landscape like a two-mile-high, monstrous, ragged, stone fence protecting vast pasturelands. The change in landscape attested to our transference from one world into another. We were about to arrive in China. It was 2:00 p.m. Pakistan time and 5:00 p.m. China time, so we were two hours late. Not bad, considering the chaos of the last ten days.

I felt both giddy from the altitude and elated about reaching this high point in my life. We parked the jeep and walked the final yards to the border, passing the official stone marker at the spot where Pakistan and China met. It looked like a six-foot-high tombstone; a smaller stone with a hand-painted sign read, "Foreigners not permitted."

About ten people waited on the Chinese side. The only person I recognized was Mrs. Luo Xiao Yun, the young photographer who had arranged for support from the CNS and authorization for the previously unobtainable visas to cross into China. I soon learned that Jin Bo Hong—our photographer friend from

Beijing—and a number of others had been unable to tolerate the altitude and had returned to the Pirali Immigration and Customs Station to wait for us there.

We must have looked like a motley crew, wearing much of our cold-weather gear in this chilly three-mile-high world. Michael was carrying the Explorers Club flag (the Explorer's Club was one of our sponsors). Taleh Mohammed was waving the Pakistan flag. The Pakistani immigration officer from Sust carried the flag of China, and I was flying the Marco Polo Expedition banner as we paraded those last few steps across the border to China.

The Chinese delegation—including Foreign Affairs Officer Mr. Sukow and several regional representatives—made warm welcoming speeches, and I expressed my thanks to all who had made this historical moment possible. In my heart I was also thanking Marco Polo for inspiring me to pursue such a cockamamie idea. It had taken more than ten years of my life to follow a trail seven centuries old; however, the way I felt at that moment provided total compensation for all the time, money, energy, and heartache it had cost.

Michael and I were the first foreigners to cross officially into China from the West since the border was closed in 1949. My dream was finally fulfilled after a lifetime of fantasizing. I was flying, and I was also a little high from the altitude. It was very cold, cloudy, and windy at 16,350 feet. I gave a Gore-Tex jacket and my old Hunza cap to Taleh Mohammed for his cold journey back to Islamabad, plus a big hug as thanks for all the tough spots he had gotten us through. I really appreciated his efforts.

In the course of my travels, I had overcome one adversity after another. I'd reached many milestones and experienced strong feelings of accomplishment. This was different. This was extraordinary. This time it felt as if I were on the top of the world. And I *was*—on "The Roof of the World."

Left and right page: Border markers between Pakistan and China

CHAPTER 18

Khunjerab Pass to Tashkurgan
August 15 to 20, 1985

To say I was jubilant after crossing the border would be an enormous under-statement. For more than a decade, my path to China had been strewn with im-passable policies and unassailable bureaucracies. I'd faced every type of cultural, economic, and physical obstacle; but I had finally made it—the hard way. Now a new journey was beginning as we set out to follow Polo's path the last 3,500 miles to Beijing.

As soon as the welcoming ceremony ended, the Chinese delegation began pushing to return to the lower elevations. The altitude was more than most of them could handle. Michael and I were more acclimated to the lower oxygen level of the air because we'd climbed to the pass more gradually. Xiao Yun, the only woman, was also doing fine. She had a round, attractive face that always broke out in a smile; but she was also a tough lady. I learned later not to cross her.

After loading our gear into three army jeeps that would be our transportation for the next few days, we said our goodbyes to our Pakistani friends and headed downhill. On the way to the customs station, Xiao Yun told me about the problems encountered by the Chinese photographers.

To support the project, the CNS had obtained three Toyota Land Cruisers in Urumqi, the capital of the western Xinjiang Province. They had driven more than 1,100 miles on their way to meet us at the border. The previous week, a gigantic avalanche had blocked the path from Kashgar to Tashkurgan, which would be our first stop in China. The avalanche had stopped the photographers just a hundred miles from their destination. The drivers had no choice but to take the vehicles back the sixty miles to Kashgar and wait for instructions. Rather than return-ing with the vehicles, the other members of the expedition literally crawled and dragged their luggage across the rocks and mountain debris that covered a few hundred yards of the road. They had managed to hitchhike to Tashkurgan and then had commandeered the jeeps that had brought them to the border. The Chinese contingent of the project had experienced almost as much trouble getting to the Khunjerab Pass as we had from the Pakistani side.

I greeted Jin Bo Hong with pleasure. He had played a huge role in making our expedition possible.

Our customs inspection went smoothly, which was remarkable since we were the first foreigners to go through this Chinese immigration station. The Khun-jerab Pass had never been a crossing point into China—even before 1949 when the Communist party took over and the Nationalists fled to Taiwan. Before 1949, all that existed was a small path in the cleavage of giant mountains. The Mintake Pass, thirty miles northwest along the border from the Khunjerab Pass, had been for centuries the Silk Road crossing point from Gilgit to China.

Our research had convinced us that Polo traveled through the Mintake Pass, the ancient gateway to China. Polo does not mention the pass, but his description of the area where he spent a year recovering from malaria could have only been Hunza. From Hunza, it's just a short hike to China over the pass on the way to Kashgar. To keep us on Polo's trail, our hosts took us to the Mintake Pass.

This is the area where the Hindu Kush, Pamir, Kun Lun, and Karakoram mountain ranges collide with one another, creating the highest and most formidable region of the world. These mountains' dark ridges rise along China's border like a monstrous, craggy palisade protecting the country's western and southern boundaries. Among them are treacherous granite walls, towering thousands of feet over raging rivers: all at an elevation above the range of trees, birds, and adequate oxygen.

We visited a small village at the border near Mintake Pass. Just outside the village, a nomadic family provided us with a scene that could have taken place at any time over the past 2,000 years. The father, mother, and two young sons traveled with all their worldly possessions as they moved to a new homestead: clothing stuffed in sacks, colorful blankets, cooking gear, all roped and girded to the backs of their greatest asset: two horses. For this part of the world, the horses were exceptionally large. They meandered down a precipitous trail with a slow lumbering gait. Each boy held a halter as their parents trailed behind.

An extraordinarily photogenic landscape enveloped us. We could point our cameras in almost any direction and capture something wonderful: unending vistas or beautiful people, dark from the sun and rugged because of their lifestyle. It was dreamlike.

So much of what we saw seemed untouched by time. It was like walking through a looking glass 800 years ago. I knew that it would not last. The world, even this world, was becoming homogenized. I was delighted to be able to visit these isolated societies that had been developed and sustained for a few millennia and be there before they were absorbed into a modern culture replete with cell phones, motor vehicles, and frozen foods.

Sixty miles down the mountainside, we arrived at the town of Tashkurgan, home to the Tajik people—one of the many minorities of western China. Like most of the ethnic groups of Xinjiang Province, the Tajik are Muslims. Polo called them "Saracens." The majority of the population in the largest province in China is Islamic, and they have continually sought independence. To discourage both independence and the influence of Islam, the Communist government encouraged and sometimes forced many ethnic Han Chinese to migrate west. We saw little evidence of this migration in the high mountain towns and were lucky enough to witness their ancient Muslim traditions. Since our visit, the railroad

has stretched across Xinjiang province to Kashgar, and the Han population has exploded in Western China.

A grand reception and the first of many banquets awaited us. In China, a banquet is a meal at which you are served portions of food that exceed your consumption capacity by at least a factor of four. The local director of the Tashkurgan and Tajik Autonomous Region was there along with other local authorities. A brief welcoming ceremony preceded our meal, which started with a gallon bowl of goat yogurt and was followed by piles of cut-up mutton and other parts of sheep. We sat cross-legged, with bowls all over the floor in front of us. It was almost dark inside the windowless, one-room, mud-brick cabin, so every bite was a surprise in taste and texture. Illumination came solely from an eerie column of sunlight mixing with smoke from the cooking fire: the light coming in through a hole cut in the center of the roof. Because of the one time zone in all of China, dinner in Tashkurgan was served at 9:30 p.m. while according to the summertime sun; it was only 6:30.

About a third of the world's people eat with their hands, a third use chopsticks, and the last third, forks. I have always felt that using chopsticks is the most civilized way to eat. Cutting is done in the kitchen so the food arrives in bite-sized, digestible morsels that are easy to maneuver with wooden chopsticks. Wood, not metal, is said to be used so as not to interfere with the energy that surrounds nature's victuals. When Polo entertained guests after his return, he served meals with chopsticks; but in doing so, he may have been responsible for the use of forks. His Venetian friends did not easily master chopsticks, so they used their knives to sharpen one of the wooden sticks to skewer the food. They then found that if they held two sharpened chopsticks side by side, picking up small morsels became

Above: A banquet in Tashkurgan

easier. *Voila*, the wooden fork! Much later, in the sixteenth century, forks made of metal gained wider use in Northern Italy. When the Italian daughter of a French princess, Catherine de Medici, married the King of France in 1533, she brought this utensil to the Parisian upper classes. Within a hundred years, England and the rest of the Western world began using forks.

After the banquet, we were taken to the Tashkurgan Inn, where we stayed for the next five nights. Not yet finished, the hotel had twenty rooms, each with two single beds. Michael and I got the VIP suite of two rooms with two windows, out of which we could empty our washbasins. In place of running water, 50-gallon drums of non-potable water were stationed in the hall for communal use. Hot-water thermoses embellished with bright flowers arrived daily for tea: loose green tea and cups were always available. The hotel would eventually have toilets. On morning walks, Michael and I would visit the cesspool construction site to check out the progress: workers used shovels, picks, and a traditional bucket hoist—the prevailing method of construction in most of China—to dig and remove soil from a twelve-foot hole. A motorized backhoe could have done the job in a fraction of the time. In thinking about this, I was reminded that ten years earlier, in 1975, a massive earthquake had ravaged Northeastern China. There had been very little earthmoving equipment available, but Chairman Mao would not accept foreign help. Removing debris to find survivors had been done by hand. A quarter of a million people had died.

Lunch at the hotel was simple but again overwhelming. We ate *nan* (flat bread), mutton, and vegetable dishes that included rice brought in from Kashgar, 170 miles to the northeast. The ground in Tashkurgan was free of frost only seventy days a year: their soil could support only a few, fast-growing crops. Of the 15,000 square miles of land in this region, only 2% is suited to cultivation. We had arrived in Tashkurgan on one of the hottest days of the year, a comfortable 68 degrees. The average temperature is below freezing, and temperatures go down to minus 40 degrees. The region is at the same latitude as Southern Spain and Las Vegas, but the 12,000-foot elevation keeps it frigid. The Mongols call this region "Sarikol," which means "the top of the mountain."

Tashkurgan means "stone city" in Turkic. In the afternoon, we climbed to the ruins of the original Stone City, perched on a hilltop not far from the center of town. From its crumbling battlements, we could see most of Tashkurgan and the surrounding pastures and farmland. It was built at a perfect vantage point for spotting approaching enemies. The walls of Stone City offered its inhabitants protection, as did the snow-crested mountains that engulfed the valley.

To own and control the area of Tashkurgan was like owning the tollbooth for trade between East and West. The Stone City citadel was built before the Han Dynasty in the second century B.C.E. The Hans treasured its dominance over the region. In the centuries that followed Russia, England, China, the Mongols, and local warlords fought to the death trying to capture this remote real estate. The victors kept rebuilding the city.

Tajiks, who make up more than eighty percent of the local population, have lived for centuries at the crossroads, with Persians to the west and the Uighur to the north and east. As a result, their language is not fully their own. Our conversations sometimes required multiple translations: from Tajik or Uighur-to Mandarin Chinese-to English, then the reverse. We had no idea how much was lost or modified in the laborious translations. There were fascinating descriptions of local traditions (such as weddings) and wonderful insights about living—no—*surviving* at an altitude higher then most of the mountains in America.

At the Tashkurgan Museum and Exhibition Hall, within the same compound as the hotel, we found a cylindrical yurt, the ubiquitous home for nomads throughout Central Asia, with the standard trappings: carpets, wall tapestries, and other nomadic household goods. A single low-wattage bulb dangling from the ceiling was all that illuminated the yurt and the entire room. The museum walls were drab green. Dozens of barely visible glass cabinets displayed stuffed fowl and other fauna plus many examples of primitive textile handiwork in silk, wool, and cotton. Much has surely changed since the opening of the Khunjerab Pass, so I hope that the museum is now illuminated enough to do justice to its collections.

The CNS and local officials arranged our first outing, north over vast, flat stretches of rich grasslands. We visited a family in their mud house, about a mile from their village compound. Along two walls of their one, large room they had built raised mud-brick platforms *(kang),* wide enough to sleep on and spread with small pads and carpets. Beneath these platforms, accessible only from outside the house, small fires were lit during the winter to heat the platform. This was safer and kept the smoke outside.

For our meal, a silk cloth was spread across the rug-covered floor. Everyone sat cross-legged. Mike, who had been a yoga practitioner for many years, was far more comfortable than me. It was 10:30 a.m., China time, 7:30 sun time. Our host said it was teatime. A fat-tailed sheep had been killed in our honor and was boiling outside in a huge iron wok, about three feet in diameter, over a fire pit next to the front door. For morning tea our hosts served a simple meal of salted-milk tea, thick pieces of *nan,* and a delicious goat yogurt. It's astonishing how much flavor pasteurization has taken away from milk, cheese, and yogurt.

here are numbers of wild beasts of all sorts in this region. And when you leave this little country and ride three days north-east, always among the mountains, you get to such a height that 'tis said to be the highest place in the world! And when you have got to this height you find a fine river running through a plain clothed with the finest pasture in the world; insomuch that a lean beast there will fatten to your hearts content in ten days. There are great numbers of wild beasts; among others, wild sheep of great size, whose horns are a good six palms in length.
MARCO POLO, 1298

The big horned sheep that Marco Polo described in his book became known as the Marco Polo sheep with the Latin name of *Ovis Poli*.

We walked a quarter of a mile to another house for a demonstration of herding sheep on horseback. Michael and some of the Chinese photographers tried their hand at riding the horses. No sooner were the new cowboys in their saddles than the herding turned to chaos as sheep stampeded in every direction. Local shepherds mounted their horses quickly to round up and corral the sheep back onto their grazing area.

The neighbor invited us for tea, again served with goat milk and salt. Central Asians add salt as Westerners add sugar. In addition to nan and yogurt, we ate what Michael and I called "hush puppies." They resembled the fried balls of cornmeal dough found in the Southern United States, but these were much crispier.

Dancing followed teatime, and I took part. Musicians accompanied the dancers, playing a bongo-like drum, two-foot diameter tambourine-type drums, and a flute carved from the leg bone of an eagle. In style and rhythm, the sound was Middle Eastern or Turkish. They called this "the dance of the eagles." My movements were more like those of a chicken, but I loved dancing on the roof of the world.

The head of the household apologized for not preparing a sheep for our visit. We thanked him for his hospitality, and Michael offered Polaroid photos as gifts.

Left: Musicians at the outdoor dance performance

Right: A Tajik dancer from Tashkurgan

People were amazed at the process and excited with the results. I gave Marco Polo balloons to the kids. After filling our stomachs twice within two hours, we went back to the first house for a "simple lunch." Another gross understatement—and I'd been worried about Michael and me losing weight.

It was a Tajik tradition to serve the guest of honor the ear of the sheep, which I gratefully accepted. Large hunks of fat from the tail were also served. The Foreign Affairs Officer of Xinjiang Province, Mr. Pamir, sliced the fat and the sheep's liver with his giant pocketknife. A sandwich of boiled fat between two slices of liver was surprisingly tasty. The fat was amazingly sweet and had the consistency of a slightly warm Brie cheese, the perfect contrast to the liver but a blow to my low-cholesterol diet. Westerners might turn up their noses at fresh-cooked fat, but they would be missing a treat. The side dishes were sheep brains, mutton burgers, nan, hush puppies, and a delicious mutton soup with globs of fat floating on top. The only part of the sheep we didn't see was the hooves.

We used our fingers or the nan to pick up the food. We slurped the soup out of bowls. In parts of Asia, soup was sucked from the bowl, sometimes without the lips touching the side. The slurping, gurgling, guttural sounds heard around the room when soup was consumed were loud and strange to a western ear.

The following morning, Michael and I took a quick tour of the hot baths tucked into the side of a nearby mountain. The water gushed out of the mountain wall at 185 degrees, but by the time it flowed through the stone aqueducts to the bathhouse, it had cooled to a tolerable temperature. People traveled great distances to cure themselves of skin diseases and other maladies. The admission was 40 fen (15 cents), including a towel and a bed to rest in afterwards.

The community used a pasture outside of town for parties and entertainment. To reach it, we forded a river in bare feet with rolled-up trousers. The glacial water was refreshing. A colorful band of musicians and dancers had been waiting for us all afternoon. This ensemble consisted of a violin, a few drums, tambourines, and a couple of bone flutes. At 5:30 p.m. the band struck up a melody and the dancing began, another "dance of the eagles."

Tajik people claim their ancestors were descendents of the eagle. With their very dark brown skin, high cheekbones, sharp eyes, and strong nose like the eagle's beak some of the Tajik men do bear a resemblance to their winged antecedent.

Two dancers, young women, dazzled us with their orange vests, and their green-and-vibrant-yellow flowing gowns, adorned with beautiful golden jewelry that jingled to the beat of the tambourine. Atop their dark hair were jewel-encrusted pillbox caps attached to flowing, yellow shawls that reached to their feet and spread out like the wings of an eagle as they danced.

The men—wearing bright, sky-blue jackets, black wool pants and caps trimmed in a black karakul—moved to the music around the women, but they never touched. It wasn't long before Michael and I got carried away by the enticing rhythm and joined the dancing. This time I found myself doing an Israeli "Hora" to the Islamic music.

The next day we visited what the locals called an urban home, since it was located in Tashkurgan, a town of about 2,000 people. To reach it, we forded (or jumped across) irrigation ditches and sewage troughs, then walked through fields of wheat for about half a mile. The owner of the house was a retired judge from the local court. He wore traditional Tajik clothes and a hat trimmed in black karakul wool, but he didn't look Tajik. With his ruddy complexion and round pudgy nose, he looked more like a rotund Irish pub owner. He had a self-assured, vivacious air about him.

The judge's four beautiful daughters wore traditional clothing that made them alluring. The youngest was a teenager and the eldest in her twenties. Two of them were the dancers from the previous evening. They were ready for the photo fest that followed. It must have taken them hours to apply their elaborate makeup, including a modern touch—glitter on their eyelids. The four Chinese and two American photographers shot hundreds of photographs of these Tajik beauties.

The oldest daughter attended Beijing University and was studying Urdu, the language of Northern Pakistan. She was home on her summer break. I was impressed that this relatively poor family from the most remote corner of China was able to send a daughter to one of the most prestigious universities in China, and that the young woman had the self-confidence to leave her family and travel two weeks by bus to a far-off place to pursue an advanced education.

This was a good sign for the future of the country's poor. Since Deng Xiao Ping had taken over the reigns of the Chinese government, the economy had grown at an average of ten percent a year, the highest rate of any country in the world. When asked by reporters to explain this phenomenal economic expansion in a communist country that condemned capitalism, Deng replied, "It doesn't matter whether the cat is black or white, as long as it catches mice."

Left: Wedding guests dancing for the groom   Right: The groom arrives at the Tajik wedding on horseback

That evening, we had a fascinating conversation with the tall, handsome Yuen Jian, Vice Director of Administration for Tashkurgan County. He was one of the officials who had braved the high altitude to greet us at the Khunjerab Pass. Yuen had come to the Tashkurgan Commune in 1975 from the eastern Chinese province of Jiangsu. His first three years had been spent working with shepherds and farmers, and he had quickly learned the Tajik language. Yuen had traveled the entire Tashkurgan region—mostly by horseback—learning their culture, and he planned to write a book about these people.

Top: Flutists follow the groom throughout the ceremonies
Bottom: The bride and groom listening to the marriage prayers

We were going to attend a Tajik wedding the following day, and he gave us a detailed description of what we could expect. Through our interpreter, Jin Bo Hong, we asked, "How do you know the wedding traditions so well?" Yuen said that even though he had married a Han Chinese girl from the East, their ceremony had been performed in the Tajik tradition.

During Tajik courtship, Yuen told us, young people exchange small, embroidered bags containing small gifts. Yellow stones, apricot pits wrapped with the bride's hair, salt, broken matchsticks—each gift has a romantic significance. Mutual

165 *Khunjerab Pass to Tashkurgan*

Top: A Bushkashi game played during the wedding
Bottom: The bride and groom leave the ceremony on a horse

friends deliver the bags. A bent sewing needle with a blue thread means that the romance is over. We learned that, in this culture, blue also represents death and is used for funerals and dance costumes.

Tajik weddings in Tashkurgan have two ceremonies, the engagement ceremony and the marriage, with fifteen to thirty days between them. The groom's family goes to the bride's parents' home to ask permission for the marriage. If the parents agree, the groom's family offers the bride a beautiful scarf, a *Ray Mole*. If accepted, the groom presents gifts of sheep, cattle, and jewelry to the bride's family. This dowry has been part of the tradition for many Islamic cultures. In Afghanistan we met many young men who could not marry because they could not afford the gifts.

For three days before the wedding, the parents of the bride visit with and invite guests to the ceremony. For close relatives and friends, festivities start the day before the wedding. On the morning of the wedding we attended, we drove a grueling three hours east to the village of Bendar. Our entourage of three Army jeeps crawled through streams, with water up to the floorboards, and along tracks that would have been easier for horses to navigate. As we approached our destination, we passed many of the wedding guests traveling by horseback, dressed in their finest with red-and-white scarves, symbolic colors worn for good luck and happiness.

When we reached Bendar, we watched the groom ride his horse to the bride's house. He was wearing a black, cylindrical, sheepskin cap; its top wrapped in a flowing red-and-white silk scarf. The bride's friends used brooms to produce a dust storm along the groom's path, as he tried to find his way to the bride's house. This was yet another challenge in his quest to win the heart of his soon to be bride. A band followed him: two drummers, a cymbalist, and two flutists, playing as loudly as possible. The groom dismounted and stepped onto a red silk rug that led into the bride's house, where the religious service would take place.

Inside was bedlam. About a hundred people crowded into a room that may have comfortably handled ten. The musicians continued to play full blast. Each guest seemed to have his or her own idea of how everything should be done—where the bride and groom should stand, who should and shouldn't be there—which led to endless shouted disputes. Six of the ten members of our group toted cameras, and every few seconds a camera would flash in the semi-darkened room. The only other light was that same eerie, solid smoky shaft from the hole in the roof over the cooking fire. In the middle of all this chaos, the diminutive imam sat calmly on the floor, totally oblivious to the madhouse around him. He was reading quietly from a small copy of the Koran, which looked hundreds of years old.

The wedding was a two-ring ceremony: a red silk thread hung from each ring as another symbol of good luck. The couple drank from a ceremonial bowl of salt water, followed by a bowl of milk and butter. The bride wore a bright red shawl over her head and an opaque white veil, discretely lifted each time she ate or drank. The ear-splitting music continued as the imam softly chanted prayers.

We traveled back and forth between the groom's house and the bride's house, to photograph each stage of the wedding—including the slaughtering of a lamb, a gift from the groom. The ceremonies lasted all day. Between rituals, the male guests escaped outside for exuberant games of Bushkashi on horseback. I assumed they were trying to get away from the noise of the band and the yelling guests.

Wherever the stoic groom went, flour was thrown over his shoulder to assure fertility. He was very nervous. Most of the action centered on the groom. Not once did I see the slightest hint of a smile. You would think that he was being led to his execution. Having half-dozen paparazzi popping flashes in his face probably did not help.

According to tradition, no one should see the face of the bride on her wedding day, but as special guests, we were allowed to peek under her veils and take pictures. She was pretty, shy, and very scared, as any fourteen-year-old would be on her wedding day. When her mother coaxed her to smile for the photographers, a small smile crept across her young face.

As the first foreigners to travel in these areas, the advantages we had were extremely valuable. Since 1985, a parade of tourists has no doubt romped through these mountains, and I'm certain that the attitude towards and the reception of foreigners have changed. All along the trail we found people open and hospitable. They allowed us to intrude on their lives with just our warm thanks, a few red balloons for the children, and a Polaroid photograph as compensation.

Left and right page: People of the Xinjiang
province

CHAPTER 19

A Muslim World
Kashgar, August 20 to 26, 1985

Kashgar is a region lying between north-east and east, and constituted a kingdom in former days, but now is subject to the Great Khan. The people worship Mahommet. There are a good number of towns and villages, but the greatest and finest is Kashgar itself. The inhabitants live by trade and handicrafts; they have beautiful gardens and vineyards, and fine estates, and grow a great deal of cotton. From this country many merchants go forth about the world on trading journeys. The natives are a wretched, niggardly set of people; they eat and drink in miserable fashion. There are in the country many Nestorian Christians, who have churches of their own. The people of the country have a peculiar language and the territory extends for five days' journey.

MARCO POLO, 1298

Marco Polo defines the direction to Kashgar as north-east by east, which is the direction we were to travel after crossing the Kunjerab Pass. We were on the path of my medieval wayfarer.

The road from Kashgar (closed earlier by an avalanche) was finally reopened, and the five buses headed southwest for Pakistan got through. Two of our three vehicles, which had been waiting for word from us, also made it. These were large Toyota Land Cruisers: they could carry nine or ten passengers plus gear, were fully enclosed and air-conditioned, and had an AM/FM radio—useless in this part of the world, where no radio stations exist. Marco Polo may have appreciated the use of a Land Cruiser; however, some of the places we attempted to visit were beyond its capability. Marco Polo's travel style was our alternative…camels, horses, donkeys, and an occasional farm tractor with massive wheels. The road we took, along the Taklamakan Desert's southern border, was the Old Silk Road. It had been abandoned in about the fifteenth century and replaced by the New Silk Road, on the north side of the desert. The Taklamakan Desert had expanded since then, and sand overran the old trader's thoroughfare and the towns along the way. Since Marco and company had traveled the Old Silk Road we chose to follow this old abandoned trail as best we could and visit the remains of the deserted towns and villages. This was not always doable by modern vehicles.

We set a 9:30 a.m. departure time for the 200-mile trip to Kashgar; without stops it would be a seven-hour drive, on a trail where there are no stop signs or stop lights. I awoke at 8:00 a.m. local time to finish packing. Since the bedroom had thick, hand-knotted carpets and a relatively clean sitting room with new concrete floors, I felt it would be okay to go barefoot, but as I crossed the bedroom, a sharp pain shot up my right leg. I had unwarily stepped with my full weight on a rusty,

one-inch nail that was pointing straight up through the red carpet. My foot bled a little, but not enough to cleanse the wound that must have penetrated the center of my heel up to the bone. I immediately put on some antibiotic ointment, but I worried because there was no way to clean inside such a deep puncture. I remembered, from my Boy Scout days, that stepping on rusty nails in farm and horse country was bad news: there was a possibility of tetanus or, more likely, an infection. One important thing in traveling, overland explorers need two good legs. I finished packing and managed to get the crippled leg and myself into the Land Cruiser. The pain in my leg worsened as we drove north. I tried to ignore it.

An hour and a half out of Tashkurgan, we came to our first mountain pass at 13,000 feet. There was a small Kirghis encampment, a few yurts on the grass plain just beyond the Pass. They had their flock of goats, sheep, and yaks nearby, nibbling the brown ground cover. An old, white-bearded man in a long black wool coat, tied closed with a white sash, came out to greet us. He insisted we meet his family. I hobbled over to meet this quiet old gentleman with the long pointy beard, and the many children who surrounded him. I gave balloons to everyone, bright red balloons with "Marco Polo" imprinted in both English and Chinese.

In back of one of the yurts I found a young girl bent over a small loom, her long black hair covering her face as she wove a distinctive, multicolored band about the width of a hand span and about twenty yards long. These bands are used to encircle the inside of the yurt by covering the wooden, horizontal framework. The

171

Above: A nomadic family with camels outside their yurt

old man's daughter-in-law had given birth to a baby girl a few weeks earlier, and we were taken inside the yurt to see the infant. She was bundled in fluffy quilted blankets, lying on the ground in the center of the yurt, her round rosy face bathed in the sunlight from the vent hole above. It seemed strange to me that she was not kept in a crib or cradle or something elevated off the cold floor. During our travels in isolated places around the world we continually found local mores and cultural priorities different from our own. However, in the eyes of this young mother, as she picked up her daughter, was an expression of love that was truly universal. I was bothered all day about the baby lying on the ground until I realized that was where she would sleep every night for the rest of her life.

Inside the yurt we found a small metal cook stove as the only source of heat, a few colorfully painted wooden boxes for clothes, and a cotton curtain covering the area where food and tools were stored. The earthen floor was matted with red, yellow, and black felt rugs and blankets that were made by sewing various fabric pieces to a felt backing, like a patchwork quilt. A few knotted Turkoman carpets were spread across the floor as well. Hanging on the walls were block-printed cotton fabrics in a rainbow of colors. (In the home of a wealthier shepherd carpets would be on the walls as well, to help with insulation.) A stack of neatly folded blankets and quilts lay to one side. The outside flap over the round opening at the top of the yurt was pulled back to allow in a lot of warm sunshine for the baby. By modern standards, a yurt may be considered a very primitive place to live, but this one looked very cheerful and homey.

We waved good-bye to our new friend and his family. No one in our group was fluent in his language. It is amazing how much can be communicated without a common language.

At lunchtime we stopped along the road, next to a lake. Here was another shepherd family's yurt, overlooking the lake and the snowcapped mountains beyond. As any real estate professional will tell you, the three most important factors in determining a home site are "location, location, and location." This shepherd family had set up their home in a pastoral paradise. There were two camels parked in their front yard and plenty of run-around room for the kids. In the Western world this location would be the site for a millionaire's estate.

When Mr. Zheng, of our party, heard about the hole in my foot, he gave me some Chinese herbal remedy that he said was used for soldiers when wounded by bullets or shrapnel. It was supposed to prevent infection. I put some on the hole in my heel. My foot began to throb. I hoped something beneficial was happening.

For lunch, we opened a few cans of sardines and chicken curry. This, with nan, was delicious. Our entrée was washed down with mouth-watering watermelons and Hami melons. The Hami melon's meat is the color and consistency of a cantaloupe and its flavor is sweet, similar to a ripe honeydew melon. It is rarely sold in the U.S. but is a popular delicacy in China. The mayor of Shanghai, when asked what the biggest problem he faced was, replied "How to get rid of the Hami melon rinds in the late summer."

A few hours after lunch we came to the place where the avalanche had covered the road. It looked like the mountain had exploded. The Chinese had carved and blasted their way along the Kashgar River to create this roadbed, but the mountain wanted to either take sections of the road away or add to it, making it almost impossible to navigate most of the time. Keeping the road open required constant attention from the authorities, and navigating the road required constant attention from the drivers. None of the road was paved except for a few miles outside of Kashgar. Along the way, segments of the old shelf road were still used by local people.

Just across the river from a police checkpoint, we saw the green mountainside village of Gez. Horsemen were making their way up the treacherous switchback trail that was less than a goat track along the sheer rock wall—hundreds of feet above the valley. Marco Polo, Genghis Kahn, and many merchants, warriors and travelers who traveled the Silk Road between India, China, and Afghanistan, had stayed in Gez. By this point, I was anxious to get medical attention for my heel, so this time we took note of this way station of history and moved on.

Kashgar was just as Polo wrote about it 700 years earlier; nothing had changed, except most of the people we met were not as wretched as he said they were. As a traveler I can understand finding the people of one particular city as unbearable. I feel the same way about Paris.

After dinner at a Kashgar restaurant that served traditional Chinese cuisine with chopsticks, we were taken to the Kashgar Hotel. It had been six days since we entered China and this was our first Chinese meal.

In the morning I visited a clinic. Following a brief discussion, it was decided I should be taken to the hospital. The outside of the hospital building looked quite modern and clean. It had a wide, sweeping driveway leading up to a four-story polychrome, aggregate concrete-surfaced building; but as soon as I crossed the threshold, the picture changed. Each of the rooms I visited or peeked into, from the reception room to the examination room, resembled a Civil War Army hospital's set up. I saw unpainted walls, bare floors, archaic medical equipment, and scenes that made me think cleanliness was not a high priority. The only thing that was reasonably up to date was the Terramycin medication they offered for the possible infection. I met with the surgeon on duty, and after a brief review of my story and an examination of the foot, he said I should get a "TAT" shot of 1500 mg. I assumed this stood for "tetanus and typhoid." First, they performed a skin test on my forearm to check for any allergic reaction. This seemed to be a sign of good medical practice. The reaction was negative, so I dropped my pants and was administered the fastest, most painless shot I've ever received. I was given a painkiller, some relaxant pills, and the supply of Terramycin with instructions to take two pills every four hours, until they ran out. My first impressions of this hospital melted away and I saw it as a competent medical operation with a very low budget.

Even though I had a great deal of pain, there was no swelling or discoloration of the area around the wound and most important, in my self-diagnosis, I didn't have a fever. According to doctors I consulted before I left, and my local medical consultant, Michael Wynn, I should not take antibiotics unless there was a definite sign of serious infection throughout the body, i.e., fever. I held off taking the Terramycin. Would an infection develop? Would taking this shot after I got the germ, be a mechanism for treating the disease? How long would the pain last? These were questions for which answers would have to wait. So I waited. The far end of the earth was not a place for paranoia.

As we ate dinner, the dishes, the chair and the floor beneath me began violently shuddering. The epicenter of a major earthquake was within a hundred miles from where we were eating at the government inn just outside Kashgar. The severity was 7.6 on the Richter scale. Michael rushed and I stumbled to the open windows, and we jumped the six feet to the ground. The tremors were so violent that standing on the lawn was impossible. We squatted on the grass until the shaking subsided. A forty-foot flagpole in front of the building was whipping back and forth as if a semaphore signalman on an ancient frigate was waving it. The earth stopped moving and the building survived. Our meal was now cold.

The next morning, I stayed in bed checking my temperature every four hours… 98.8°F. In the afternoon, I went to the bazaar and hobbled around using Michael's lightweight camera tripod as a cane. I tied the tripod legs together with dental floss, and it really helped. I was able to keep weight off my right foot.

Kashgar's bazaar was brilliant, exciting and loud. Haggling is never quiet in this part of China. Negotiating prices is an art form that is learned by the child at his father's side. The bazaar is a cornucopia of foodstuff, entertainment and every product a nomadic shepherd may need or want. Dozens of soup kitchens, noodle bars, and "Uighur bagel" bakeries dominated the hundreds of stalls at the bazaar. "Uighur bagels" is the name I gave the bagel-shaped nan found throughout Xinjiang Province. These were very similar to a New York style "bialy"—but without the garlic.

There were hundreds of all types of nan and miles of fried noodles stacked on tables for sale all over the bazaar. Nan is a local dietary mainstay in Xinjiang Province, as is rice in the rest China. Classic Frisbee-shaped bread, also called nan, was baked in the traditional hole-in-the-ground oven. We found these tandoor-type ovens in every market across Afghanistan and Xinjiang Province, China. They were cylindrical clay ovens located below ground, their top flush with the floor and a fire below. Discs of dough were squashed against the side of the oven, baked, and removed with wooden tongs. One of the "bialy" stalls was run by four young

175 *A Muslim World*

Top left: A vendor at the bazaar
Middle left: A mountain of fried noodles
Bottom left: Preparing lunch

Top right: Melons for sale
Middle right: A nan bakery
Bottom right: Negotiating a price

teenagers in tattered clothes: one kneaded the dough, the second shaped the rolls, the third slapped the dough to the inside of the oven, and the fourth pulled out the finished piece. I took their photos as they continued their work, able to face the camera with bright, white-toothed smiles spreading from ear to ear, and not miss a beat in their work. This was the closest to a production line for a manufactured product, other than the silk factories, that I had seen in all of Western China.

In the middle of this eclectic market I discovered about twenty red, little girl dresses hanging on a pole across the front of a stall. One was just about the right size for my four-year-old daughter, Jane. Jane had been very specific: she wanted a bright red dress, and this one looked perfect. I bought it. It was as bright a red as could be dyed and had a very feminine ruffle around the neck. I was certain she would love it.

As I walked around the market, I saw an ancient world at work. People were still weighing their merchandise with primitive balance scales using stones for weights; they wove cotton and silk on hand looms then made their clothing from it; they ground spices using a mortar and pestle; and the abacus, designed two or three thousand years ago, was still used to compute the price. Drinking and cooking water was carried in buckets at both ends of long poles on the shoulders of women and barefoot children. We have all seen the paintings of "coolies" walking with these same poles across the rice patties of old China. It may have been viewed as a pastoral scene of the past, but these people were just poor: the prosperity that was developing in Eastern China had not yet reached far, far Western China.

We went to visit some handicraft factories where ornate Uighur caps were made for the local Islamic men. Uighur caps are cylindrical- or square-shaped skull caps made with silks, metallic threads, spangles, and beads, each cap individually decorated with all manner of geometric designs. (In Islamic cultures, animals and all other forms of living things are never shown in any form of art, especially on something that is worn.) Lines of girls sat dutifully at foot-powered sewing machines, adding colorful embroidery and other artistic embellishments to the caps. These young women were all dressed in vivid colors, with scarves wrapped around their heads. Some were wearing dresses made of the soft patterned Atlas (Ikat) silks that come from Hotien (Khotan), 300 miles further along the Marco Polo trail.

In another part of the building, a group of young men were hand carving musical instruments: single reed clarinets (Eastern style) and a two-stringed instrument called a "Do-Tar," plus their cases. Next door a group of giggly girls sat in front of huge vertical looms knotting carpets. Only young girls are hired for this work because small fingers are needed to tie the smaller knots. The more knots per inch, the greater the value. Their fingers move so fast, an observer cannot distinguish each movement. The number of square meters of threaded lines of wool or silk they had knotted determined their pay.

Things were much better during our visit to Kashgar than they had been during the Cultural Revolution. At that time, all of the 100 mosques had been closed except the Jamie (Friday) mosque. An Islamic believer prays five times per day: at sunrise, noon, in the afternoon, after sunset, and finally in the early part of the night. We asked a local Uighur farmer if he prayed at the mosque. His answer was "no" because the "cadre" (local political leaders) required him to get up early for political meetings, and this did not give him time to go to the mosque. He told us he did his praying at home.

I spent the following morning in bed to rest my leg. It seemed to be getting better, and there was no sign of infection. Everything was starting to look better again.

At the next 9:00 a.m. hotel breakfast, we met a group on an American Lindblad tour. Most of the people were from the East Coast, except for the tall, blond tour guide, Michael Edwards, who was from Oregon. I asked if he would carry back video and audiotapes and forward them to our publicity agent, Don McConnell, in Seattle. He would. The material Edwards got to McConnell was then widely distributed for broadcast on TV stations across the country.

Soon it was our day to make the obligatory visit to a commune. Every tour group is mandated to visit a commune, and to the local government we were just another tour group. In our case, the visit was a special one: Yosup Simayel, our man from the Kashgar Foreign Affairs Office, had grown up in this commune. The whole gang went; including Michael, Jin Bo Hong, the three CNS photographers, the interpreters (Uighur and Chinese), and the local government representatives. In the traditional manner, we met with the commune's director, and the party secretary. There would be a short "warm-welcoming speech" by the director and a brief reply by the guests. Usually this meeting is held in a reception room, with soft armchairs and sofas lined up around the walls and in front of each sofa a low table for tea. The guest of honor sits in the chair furthest from, but facing the door. This ritual, the standard procedure in all of China, was carried out, but because of the heat, we were moved outside under a very cool grape arbor in the vineyard, like the one Marco had mentioned. The sofas, chairs, and tables were also moved outside. While we were waiting, we tried the grapes; they needed a little more ripening. As with each visit to a Chinese commune we listened to a half hour of statistics including the exact numbers of the workers, facts about the facilities, and details on every product produced.

At the Kashgar kindergarten, children ranged from three-and-a-half to seven years old. Tucked behind the bazaar, it probably offered a convenient location for working mothers and fathers. The children put on a fantastic show for us. Their dancing, singing, costumes, and musical ability were superb. It was obvious that they were very well rehearsed. It takes a great deal of effort by the teacher, and

personal discipline by the children, to produce the type of performance that we watched. A cute little Uighur girl, no more than six years and fully outfitted in a colorful Uighur costume of reds and gold, introduced each new number of the performance in a voice that projected throughout the school yard without amplification. Ethel Merman would have been envious. All the little girls' and boys' faces were covered, in the appropriate places, with rouge, lipstick, and eyebrow pencil in an exaggerated style, creating very animated painted dolls.

Their music was totally unfamiliar but played on a trio of very familiar instruments. A small thin man, wearing a white shirt and a long belt cinched tight to hold up his oversized pants, played the violin. (I think during the Cultural Revolution, to be efficient, they only made one size pants and belts for men, all over China.) A young woman wore a flowery cotton dress with a matching bandana around her head. She pumped the accordion. The third member of the trio was a middle-aged woman percussionist playing a tambourine/drum. We saw the same instruments used at all the wedding parties.

Dozens of wooden chairs had been set up in the front play yard, and our group was soon joined by a hoard of Japanese tourists. The children sang in a single voice while they danced and moved as one, perfectly synchronized. I felt I was watch-

This page: A singing and dancing recital at a Kashgar kindergarten

ing a younger edition of the "Rockets" at Radio City Music Hall in New York. The musicians and students performed in the manner of professionals. I loved it.

Following the entertainment, which lasted for about an hour, we visited a classroom where one teacher and her assistant presented material that seemed appropriate for the six-year-olds. There was just one blackboard at the front and no student work; nothing on the walls—not even a flag or picture of Mao Tse Tung. The children sat quietly with hands folded on their laps; boys were on a long, single bench along one side and the girls sat across the room on the other bench. This austere environment was common to most of the schools, mud-brick buildings, and local homes we visited.

This school had over 400 children and a staff of sixty. According to our host, things were improving. Since officials from the local government were with us, I do not believe he could have said anything else. Based on my personal observations, I believed he was telling the truth.

Just before we left, I looked out a second-floor window of the schoolhouse. There was the accordionist, playing an American song of the 1930's, "Fascination," while sitting on a chair in an empty courtyard. China was full of surprises.

My heel was feeling better. I had passed the crisis point, and I felt confident that within a week I could be running without pain. We decided to leave Kashgar early and head for Yarkand in the morning.

From Kashgar one can cross almost 1500-miles of Xinjiang Province, to Gansu Province, by one of two roads. For the past 500 years merchants, soldiers and travelers had taken what is now known as the "New Silk Road." It follows the northern border of the Taklamakan to Urumiqi and winds up about 1500 miles to the east at Dun Huang, where it continues on to Beijing. The "Old Silk Road" leaves Kashgar to the southeast on the south side of the Taklamakan and also finds its way to Dun Huang. As I mentioned earlier, the old route had been abandoned a couple of hundred years after Marco Polo because the desert kept expanding and overtaking the communities and caravansaries (way stations). These old cities and towns were removed to the northern edge of the desert. We followed Marco Polo, who traveled to the southeast along the Old Silk Road, most of which is no longer there, as we soon discovered.

Kashgar was about the halfway point of my odyssey in Marco Polo's footstep. It is the place where the Chinese and Muslim cultures merge. The Chinese were attempting to alter this ancient community and bring it into the modern world, yet it remained as Marco described it. Kashgar is Kashgar and not easily changed.

arkand a province five days journey in extent. The people follow the Law of Mahommet but there are also Nestorian and Jacobite Christians. They are subject to the same Prince that I mentioned The Great Khan's nephew. They have plenty of everything, (particularly of cotton. The inhabitants are also great craftsmen, but a large proportion of them have swollen legs and great crops at the throat, which arises from some quality in their drinking water.) As there is nothing else worth telling we may pass on.

MARCO POLO, 1298

The road to Yarkand was mostly through farmlands of rice, corn, cotton, and millions of tall, slender Lombardy Poplar trees planted along the roads and outlining every farm patch and pasture. Without these fast-growing, tall barrier trees, the desert would soon take over and the Taklamakan would quickly become an even larger desert. In this stretch of desert called Yarkand Prefecture we found the capital city of Yarkand, home to 45,000 people. Very few of the residents of this area had ever seen a Western person. This explains why a walk through one of the local bazaars would create an immediate stir. Whenever Michael or I stopped, even to take a photo, within a few seconds, dozens of local people would quickly encircle us. Taking photographs became quite a chore. Everyone mugged for and tried to get in front of the camera. This was quite the opposite of most other Islamic nations. In many other places I had to resort to using a right angle lens that looked like a regular camera but had a built-in mirror to take pictures at right-angles to the normal direction of the camera. The unsuspecting subject never knew their picture was being taken.

Jin Bo Hong had an interesting experience in the Yarkand village bazaar. He was trying to photograph a shop as a teenager kept persistently pulling on his arm. Jin did not speak Uighur so the young man tried to convince Jin to take his picture by waving a one-Yuan note (about $0.25) in his face. Jin complied and in a short period of time another teenager approached him with a five-Yuan note. Jin was wondering how high the price would go, but there were no more offers. These photos were developed many months later. Jin could tell us nothing about the subjects, other than the fact they wanted to be photographed.

The oldest mosque in Yarkand had been around for 572 years. At the entrance stood a well with an ancient bucket and rope, operated by a smiling, gaunt-faced Uighur with a sparse black beard. He would fetch the water required for the washing of hands and feet before entering the mosque. A few men knelt and bowed in the far corner of the nearly empty mosque. All mosques were devoid of furnishings and decoration, except a few wall inscriptions of Arabic quotations from the Koran and a small niche where the imam stands for prayer leading and sermons. The imam's place directs the worshipers to face Mecca. Everyone goes barefoot (shoes are left outside) and the floors are usually covered with rugs and carpets. Before entering this mosque, as I have always done before entering these sacred

181 *A Muslim World*

Top: Selling skull caps at the Yarkand bazaar
Bottom: Cooking at the bazaar

places, I removed my boots. The keeper of the well, thinking I had come to pray, came over with water to allow me to wash my hands.

The Jami (Friday) mosque in Yarkand was a couple of hundred years old, and the state was providing funds for refurbishing. The covered sanctuary was being totally rebuilt and repainted in garish colors, but according to our local guide, Yosup, it was to be in accordance to the original design.

The Yarkand bazaar was fabulous. There were hat bazaars and produce bazaars, fabric bazaars, *chai hannas* (teahouses) galore, and food stalls everywhere. Services of all sorts were available: from knife sharpening to barbering. I watched the barber, who served his customers on a chair out in the sun, shaving their heads with a six-inch straight razor. He noticed me observing his actions and continued to shave a man's head while looking at me rather than the head over which the blade traveled. He must have been pretty good at what he did since I didn't notice any blood.

At the herb stand, I watched the proprietor process his products using a primitive mortar with pestle then pour them into the pan of a balance scale to be weighed. He then rolled the product up in a piece of newspaper, for the customer to take home. If the vendor had used a small cloth or straw bag instead of a newspaper, the scene might have been just what Marco Polo would have observed.

The colors were vivid, but either my sensitivity to smells had changed or the pungent odors of drying urine and decaying shit were not as prevalent here as they were in the bazaars of the Middle East and Afghanistan.

I really enjoyed being a pioneer traveler. We were so warmly received. There was no hassling by shopkeepers to buy their wares. No turning away of heads when the camera was brought up to the eye, plus we had the secure feeling of knowing we had been traveling with complete safety. All of this made the process of walking the corridors of these exotic marketplaces a complete joy; however, danger would have made it a little more thrilling. To all this I added the thought that few foreigners had come this way in almost forty years: I was on another one of those roads "less traveled."

Lombardy Poplar trees were everywhere. No matter how small the thoroughfare, poplar trees were planted to protect this ancient city from wind, sand, and sun. I remember a place on the outskirts of town where six tree-shaded dirt roads converged. From this one spot at the intersection of the roads you could see a few donkey carts and about a dozen bicycles meandering along. It was rush hour in Yarkand.

The evening we arrived at the Government Inn at Yarkand, I was in my room discussing the region's cultural history with Abdul Kadear, head of the Cultural Center of Yarkand. This stocky middle-aged man was dressed in standard, government-issued, dark blue pants and jacket, worn by most of the Cadre of the Chinese Communist Party. This was also the uniform of many of the people who helped us throughout China. As he talked about the 2,300-year history of this caravan crossroad, I was distracted by what I heard outside. I excused myself and left to find out the source of some very familiar music. I followed the sound outside the compound of the Inn and into the village center. It was coming from the trumpet speakers mounted on electric poles up and down the street. A few years before, their normal function had been to continually spew out communist propaganda to "control the minds of the people." These sound systems were leftovers from the Cultural Revolution and could be found in every city and hamlet throughout China. However, what was oozing from these horns was the moving, melancholy "Love Duet" from the opera "Madama Butterfly" followed by excerpts from "La Boheme." It was Puccini night in Yarkand. I stood in the street a little mesmerized by the music I've always loved and now totally surrounded by it. A curious crowd started to surround me, so I headed back to the compound. To add to this emotional experience, a second strange occurrence immediately followed. I passed an open courtyard with a recently built brick wall that housed a 17-inch TV on a shelf. I joined the people squatting on the ground in front of this color TV. It was a program of western ballet dancers in tutus doing tour-jeters and pirouettes to Spanish music. A modern dance group followed, performing to the music of the Pink Panther. I remember when TV first came to America; people would sit in front of a TV set operating in the window of an appliance store watching it, no matter what was being presented; just as this group was doing.

There were a few very low power TV stations in Western China with all programming provided by VHS videotapes. News programs mailed about once every week or two, from Beijing, so the news could not be called new. I was astonished to find that here I was, in the most remote and primitive part of a Third World Nation, finding myself immersed in Western culture. I loved being a pioneer, yet Puccini still holds an important part of my heart and made me feel a little homesick. I thought this project had forced me to abandon Western music and dance but through the magic of electronics, the world was beginning to compress. Satellite reception would soon follow.

Breakfast at the Yarkand Inn started with the Uighur version of hot, freshly baked Russian style "pirogui" (a small pie filled with meat), bowls of hot goat milk, fried dough, fried Uighur potato slices, and a few standard breakfast dishes of sliced lamb, green peppers, and boiled eggs. So far, I hadn't walked away hungry from a meal in China.

As any tourist would do, I went to the larger and main Yarkand bazaar. A lamb was meandering in front of the stall that was selling traditional caps and hats for Uighurs, Kirghiz, Tajik, and the other minorities of Xinjiang Province. The Islamic tradition requires men to always have their head covered. Next door to the hat shop, a short chubby man sat yoga-style behind his stack of folded Atlas silks, velvet and cotton fabric in every color of the rainbow plus gold and silver. The bulbous proprietor looked as if he were a statue just removed from a Buddhist Temple. Further along, butchers wielded their hand axes and sharp knives, taking apart the carcasses hanging on racks in front of their stalls. The market was filled with every imaginable kind of spice, nuts, herbs and dozens of unidentifiable foodstuffs sitting on the ground in open bags to be weighed on the antiquated balance scales and then sold at a negotiated price. The amount was determined by the shopkeeper's evaluation of his customer.

There was no electricity in the bazaar so the men who sharpened the knives and axes pedaled a bicycle wheel to which a cylindrical grinding stone was attached by pulleys. Again, it was easy to believe that the bazaars of western China in 1985 were just as they were when Marco Polo came this way. The food, the wood burning stoves and style of cooking, the products being sold and primitive facilities and structures were all timeless remnants of an ancient past; the time of Marco Polo and before.

It was almost lunchtime, and the cooking fires were heating up the iron woks. Ladies with bright-colored scarves around their head sat chopping vegetables, garlic, and meat for the meals soon to be sold and served. Some of the women wore dresses of the Atlas raw silks made in Hotien, the next stop on our journey. Not like the machine-made silks from factories, this material had the strength of iron in order to sustain the tough wear needed by these hard-working women. There were tons of every type of Asian dish cooked in the dozens of kitchens and pushcarts serving the thousands of people who shopped and worked at this bazaar. This open-air supermarket stretched out for almost a mile. Everything that the residents of this part of the world wanted was available, as it had been for a couple thousands years.

We packed our Toyotas and left Yarkand to follow the perimeters of farmlands fed by the Yarkand River and irrigation system. As we traveled along the banks of this river, we saw where the water was partially diverted to feed small hydroelectric plants. The modern world of electric power was about to convert the pedal-powered knife sharpeners in the bazaars to electric and the people of Yarkand will say, "What is this world coming to?"

CHAPTER 20

Ancient Khotan
Hotien, August 26 to September 2, 1985

ollowing a course between southeast and east (from Yarkand), you next come to the province of Khotan, the extent of which is eight days journey. It is under the dominion of the Great Khan, and the people are Moham-medans. It contains many cities and fortified places but the principal city and the one that gives its name to the province, is Khotan. Everything neces-sary for human life is here in the greatest plenty. It likewise yields cotton, flax, hemp, grain, wine, and other articles. The inhabitants cultivate farms and vineyards and have numerous gardens. They support themselves also by trade and manufactures (silk and jade), but they are not good soldiers...through this flows a river and in its bed are found many of those stones called chalcedony and jasper (varieties of Chinese jade)...The people are generally afflicted with swellings in the legs and tumors in the throat resulting from the water they drink).
MARCO POLO, 1298

The road to Hotien was straight as a giant billiard cue laid across a perfectly flat desert and both seemed to go on forever. Oil-drilling rigs speckled the bleak landscape, as another modern industry was about to destroy a way of life and environment that had been sustained for hundreds of generations. The truck, tractor, and motorbike had already started to replace the horse, donkey, and camel but we saw very few passenger cars. They couldn't be far behind.

It was 200 miles or a six-hour drive but a couple of stops for the Hami melons made the long trip that much more pleasurable. Auriel Stein traveled this same route in 1906, and it took him a "fortnight." Auriel Stein was an archeologist and historian working for the British Museum who essentially stole—or paid little money for—tons of artifacts that he took from western China and that can now be seen in museums and private collections all over the world.

I have previously mentioned the Hami melon. Marco Polo had an interesting story about the town of Hami for which this sweet melon was named. Hami was an ancient city that Marco's father and uncle had visited on their first voyage to the East. It is located on the north side of the Taklamakan where Marco never traveled. The people of Hami followed a very unusual custom. His father related the following story of this strange lifestyle to Marco:

ami is a province, formerly a kingdom containing cities and castles, with a capital of the same name. It stands between two deserts, the great one already described (Taklamakan) and a smaller one, extending three days journey. The people are all idolaters (Buddhists) and have a peculiar language; they live by the fruits of the earth, having enough to eat, and also sell to the traveler. They are men of great gaiety, thinking of nothing but to sound musical instru-ments, to sing, dance, and delight their hearts. When a stranger comes to lodge in his house, the master is highly pleased and leaves him with his wife, desiring her to treat him in every respect as a husband, while he goes to spend two or three days elsewhere. All the men of this province proceed in this manner, and do not account it any disgrace. The women are handsome, gay and fond of diversion. Now, when Mangou Khan reigned as sire of the Tartars, it was reported to him how the men of Hami gave over their wives to strangers. He sent orders, that under a severe penalty, travelers should not henceforth be entertained in this manner. When they received this injunction, they were greatly grieved, held a council, and did what I will now tell you. They made up a large present, and sent it to Mangou, praying that he would allow them to treat their wives according to the custom handed down to them by their ances-tors, who, for the kindness to strangers, had gained the favor of their idols, and their corn and other crops greatly multiplied.

When he heard this message, he said, "Since you are so bent on your own shame, let it be so." He allowed them to do as they pleased and hence they have always maintained this custom.

MARCO POLO, 1298

Just west of Hotien is the town of Yotkan, situated on the west bank of the Kara-kash (Black Jade) River. As we approached the town, we found it more and more difficult to sneak our way through the hoard of donkey carts. Most towns and villages had only one passable road for motorized vehicles and many donkey trails but no alternate route. Off to one side of this road was what we could call a parking lot. It was crammed full of two-wheeled donkey carts, laid back with their harness poles pointing straight up. This lot looked like the back of a gigantic porcupine with wooden quills. The cart owners from the market, as well as out-of-town visitors, kept their donkeys munching hay in an adjacent corral. Our procession made its way past the donkey carts only to be confronted with a hoard of people totally blanketing the road, and we were forced to stop. Michael got out on top of one of the Land Cruisers to shoot pictures of the massive crowd. It was a strange sensation to see such a vast array of faces with all eyes quietly star-ing, waiting for something to happen. I now know how the animals in a zoo feel. We estimated more than twenty thousand people were jammed into that road for almost a mile. Mr. Lu, Mr. Zhang, the government escorts, and Luo Xiao Yun, our mighty lady photographer, went out in front of the lead vehicle to shoo the people away so we could make our way through town and on to our next stop. Luckily, in Hotien we were able to bypass the market street. It had been eight hours of driving before we finally arrived at the Hotien *Binguan* (Inn). This was to be our headquarters for the next week, making side trips to villages, archeological sites, and other places of interest

Mr. Matnur, whom I had originally contacted by mail from the U.S. regarding our visit, came to the inn to greet us and take us on a tour of the bazaar. He was a quiet, friendly man with a round face and a bulky body, rarely seen without his black-and-white pot-shaped skull cap perched on his head. The Hotien bazaar was not quite as primitive as the other markets we visited in Western China. The local government rented many of the shops to individual vendors, as would be normal in a capitalistic world. The shops and stalls were made of mud-brick and some even had glass windows and doors. We found the commodities being sold were much the same as in Yarkand and Kashgar. Since silk was a major local industry in Hotien, there were many stalls for both the modern factory-made silk and the locally-made raw Atlas silk. Venders of tools and other hand-crafted products were scattered among the dozens of specialty food shops: nuts, spices, tandoor baked nan, vegetables, and putrid-looking carcasses attracting flies in front of the butchers stall. Scattered amongst the mundane necessities of daily life were the stalls selling the scull-caps worn by every Uighur man. These short cylindrical head coverings were beautiful. Each was uniquely embroidered in every conceivable geometric pattern as we saw at the factory in Kashgar.

We immediately recognized a higher standard of living for the people of Hotien. It was very obvious in the clothes they wore. Here, the men were dressed in the standard-issue, western-style pants with the six-button blue Mao-type jacket. The houses were of a higher quality. There was a wider distribution of electricity. This was most likely due to the silk industry that flourished successfully in this area. The daily pay at the local silk factory averaged $3.00 a day, which was much more than the nation's average in 1985.

The head of the Cultural Center had not returned from Urumqi. Our meeting was postponed. Instead we went to the Friday Mosque to plan an early morning photo assault on this house of worship by five still photographers and me as a videographer. We planned to cover a very special service that every male Muslim in the area would make every effort to attend.

At 6:00 a.m., my radio alarm sounded off with the Voice of America. It was not a strong voice but even mixed in with static, it still woke me up. Today was the big festival day, "Kuerban." It would start at the mosque before sunrise. Please remember 6:00 a.m. in Hotien was more like 3:00 a.m. for the sun. We each took our camera positions like riflemen waiting for the attack. Jin Bo Hong and I were perched high on the minaret about 80 feet above the mosque. Luo Xiao Yun, Lao Lu (the senior photographer from CNS) and his associate Jin Tie Lu were all on the wall and balconies over and around the main entrance to the mosque. In the pre-dawn darkness, I lost track of Michael. As the sky started to lighten before the sunrise, I saw Michael outside, on top of a large truck. Every worshiper would undoubtedly be recorded on film.

The men started to file in. An imam stood at an entrance greeting the worshippers. Inside as the services begin, the imam led the prayers and set the timing for each prayer movement. The entire congregation would move as one. We had already learned that there are seven movements, each with their appropriate recitations. The first is the recitation of the phrase "God is Great" with the hands open on each side of the face. The second is the opening passage of the Koran while standing upright; the third is the bowing from the hips; the fourth is straightening up then gliding to the knees; the fifth is a prostration with the face to the ground; the sixth is to sit back on the haunches. The final movement is a second prostration.

The inner sanctuary filled up first with more than a thousand men. The outer courtyard was next to be occupied by at least 4,000 men. It was easy to take a tally of the people in attendance since the rows of worshippers were uniform and tightly spaced. I could see from my perch that thousands more were on their way to the mosque from every direction. Vehicular traffic was not a problem since everyone walked. Where would these newcomers pray? As soon as the mosque was full, long muslin sheets were rolled out across the street in front of the Mosque. Before too long Michael had estimated the outside crowd had reached 5,000 or 6,000. The 11,000 worshippers represented about one person from every Uighur household in the area.

The people were led in prayer by a highly distorted sound system that only operated intermittently. In the inner courtyard, a man in a white turban and a powerful voice got up to lead the worshippers by calling out the prayers in unison with the faulty PA system. Worshippers did not have a problem since I'm certain they each knew all the ritual movements and prayers by rote.

It was one of those magic sunrises where the sun makes a slow hazy appearance painting the heavens in purple, pink, and vague yellow brush strokes as it tries to push itself through the clouds that hold back its brilliance. As the sun made its journey across the sky, the services were over. Four drums and two Asian clarinets blasted forth, heralding in the sun and providing a cadence to the men as they slowly marched to their homes. The musicians were ensconced on a narrow wall over a small exit door as the thousands of devout Muslims slowly left their house of worship.

On this holy day, it is the tradition for every Uighur family that can afford it to slaughter a sheep. We were invited to the house of a physician who had three grown sons. They were going to kill three sheep. By the time we arrived, one of the sheep had already been dispatched, and they were in the process of skinning the animal. The other two sheep were tethered in the courtyard nervously waiting their turn for execution. One was brown and the other pure white with sad black eyes that made me melt. Their bleats were heart rending but no one seemed to pay any attention to these pleas for mercy. We all just sat around waiting for the next killing. A small hole was dug in the dirt courtyard. The oldest son was given a special ritual knife to slit the sheep's throat. It was the brown sheep's turn. His legs were tied together and the poor lamb was placed on its side with the neck over the hole in the ground. The father pointed to the correct artery. The long curved

blade easily slit through the skin and the artery beneath it. The blood gushed out. The knife continued through the neck as it was snapped back with the butcher's other hand. The lamb wiggled for a few seconds but soon it was all over. A small cut was made across the right rear leg. The skin was pulled back and the doctor's oldest son put his mouth to this opening and blew very hard. The intention was to blow air into the lamb, thereby separating the skin from the muscle. This makes the next step of skinning that much easier. This stage of the carnage was over; it was not my favorite type of entertainment, so we left. As we walked down the street we could see into the courtyards of the other families as they also slaughtered their sheep. We estimated 10,000 sheep were killed in Hotien that day and maybe a million in Xin Jiang Province.

Matnur invited us this day to visit his house. He and his wife lived in a two-story apartment with the living room upstairs. The room was crowded with a couple of sofas, chairs, and a polished wooden breakfront. The apartment was similar to what I found in Eastern China except that many of the walls were covered with traditional red and black Uighur carpets. On the living room cocktail table were mounds of cookies, nan, and fried noodles, a staple in this part of the province. Matnur brought out a dish of mutton, which he sliced for us to have with the nan.

Visiting friends and relatives is carried on for three days during the Kuerban festival. We too carried on this tradition. The next person we visited was a local celebrity, the beautiful Uighur film star Fatima. She was home for a holiday visit with her father and mother, who were professors at the Hotien Normal School (Teacher's College). This was also where Matnur's wife taught Philosophy, History, and Sociology. Fatima was twenty-one years old and beautiful beyond words, with those deep dark penetrating eyes that have appeared on the cover of

Left: A mass exodus from the mosque   Right: The inner sanctuary of the mosque during services

National Geographic. She too had a problem walking down streets. Crowds would immediately gather to gawk and examine this lovely creature as closely as possible. Fatima's parents provided us with another big spread of now familiar food. To this they added Beijing wrapped candies. Being a movie actress was just Fatima's part-time job; she also taught at the Arts College in Urumqi.

The ancient city of Malekawat was about 15 miles southeast of Hotien along the White Jade River. The Black Jade River is on the west side of Hotien. Obviously, they were named for the type of jade that washed down from the mountains. We crossed the grass/dirt runway of the Hotien airport to get to Malekawat. Our driver got lost, and we had to backtrack a few times before we found the bridge that crossed the recently-built canal. A long series of switchback roads led us down to the level of the river and then through an oasis of verdant groundcover, bushes, and trees. The ancient city of Malekawat stood just on the other side of the oasis. This was the original capital of the Uighur nation—from 206 B.C.E., during the Han Dynasty, to 906 C.E., during the Tang Dynasty. Our visit was like browsing in an open-air flea market of antiquities. It was surprising so much was left in a place that was abandoned for 1100-years. The ground was littered with potshards from two to three millennia ago. As we scoured the ground, we each found pieces of rock containing jade. We were disappointed to find that nothing could be removed from this historic site without permission of the government in Beijing. Eighty years earlier, Auriel Stein had visited Malekawat and wrote in his

Left: Sacrificing a lamb   Right: Removing the skin of the lamb

book that he found "fragments of pottery, terracotta figurines, chiefly of monkeys, engraved stones and coins."

After dinner at our inn in Hotien, the sun was low and we drove about twenty-miles to the northwest where the Taklamakan had not yet been tamed. Here the desert sands were soft and wind-sculptured into soothing shapes. The wind sang through the sand in many voices as nature's organ invited the naïve traveler to seek the source of the celestial music like a beautiful woman beacons a man to her bosom. While walking through the sand in bare feet with each step plunging just below the surface, I felt the millions of miniscule round particles rolling between my toes, caressing my feet, yet not restricting their movement. Curiosity drew me to the top of the next dune to see if the view was even more breathtaking. The winds were calm and the desert slept, the unmoving sands and soft air were refreshing and soothing to the soul. The Taklamakan was mesmerizing. As Marco Polo said, do not listen to its calling, for you will go there but never return. The following is part of his understated description of the "Great Desert":

he truth is this. When a man is riding by night through this desert and something happens to make him loiter and lose touch with his companions, by dropping asleep or for some other reason, and afterwards he wants to rejoin them, he then hears spirits talking in such a way that they seem to be his companions. Sometimes, indeed, they even hail him by name. Often these voices make him stray from the path so that he never finds it again. And in this way many travelers have been lost and have perished. And sometimes in the night they are conscious of a noise like the clatter of a great cavalcade of riders away from the road; and believing that these are some of their own company, they go where they hear the noise and, when day breaks, find they are victims of an illusion and in an awkward plight. And there are some who, in crossing the desert, have seen a host of men coming towards them and, suspecting that they are robbers, have taken to flight; so, having left the beaten track and not knowing how to return to it, they have gone hopelessly astray. Yes, and even by daylight men hear the spirit voices, and often you fancy you are listening to the strains of many instruments, especially drums, and the clash of arms. For this reason bands of travelers make a point of keeping very close together. Before they go to sleep they set up a sign pointing in the direction in which they have to travel. And round the necks of all their beasts they fasten little bells, so that by listening to the sound they may prevent them from straying off the path.

MARCO POLO, 1298

This is how the Polos crossed the desert and this story is the origin of the children's swimming pool game of Marco Polo. The game mimics this story by having one player in the swimming pool close his eyes and call out "Marco" and his comrades in the pool respond with "Polo." It is the object of the game for the person with closed eyes to tag those who have called out "Polo" by swimming to the source of the sound.

The following morning after breakfast we left on another desert excursion. Before you reach the desert, the area between the Yurung-Kash (White Jade River) and the Kara-kash (Black Jade River) is the town of Yangi-arik. It is much larger than it was when Auriel Stein came to these jade rivers. A little at a time, irrigation canals were built, and trees planted; the sands are now covered by rich fertilized soil, and gradually vegetation is starting to stabilize the land. The battle was won but the war against the desert is never ending.

Outside the main building of Yangi-arik, under the grape arbor of the commune, a map showed about 200 farm units growing a wide variety of grains, fruits, and vegetables. The place was quiet and eerie. It was still a holiday, and no one was around.

Nearby was another sleepy village called Bozak. On Auriel Stein's map, Bozak is about 10 miles southwest of Hotien's bazaar. Since the town looked abandoned, we went on to another small village high on a ridge overlooking the Kara-kash River basin. It was called Layki. The town was famous in this area for a cave that was the tomb of an Islamic hero. It is said that birds would follow him wherever he went, even now. This cave was a sacred place and many Muslims came there to pray. At the entrance to the cave are eight, tall, thin sticks woven together starting to form a picket fence with prayer flags on each picket. The keepers of the shrine were a seventy-six-year-old man and his 110-year-old father who still got around fairly well with only a cane. The father's eyesight was starting to fail, but otherwise he seemed to be in remarkably good health. The family made its living catering to worshippers who came to visit the shrine. The Chinese government published the statistic that Xinjiang Province, with only a few percent of the total population of China, has over 20 percent of the people over 100 years old.

The local Hotien Museum had as its "piece de resistance" two corpses, each about 1,400-years old. One had long brown hair and the other black hair. They were not mummified but were well preserved by the dry desert. The balance of the exhibit consisted of artifacts taken from the nearby ancient cities through which Marco Polo traveled along the old Silk Road: jade carvings and wood tablets in ancient Hotien script, and samples of silk, wool, and other household articles, some thousands of years old. These were similar to the objects Auriel Stein and other "foreign devils" (a term used by modern Chinese archeologists) had taken by hundreds of camel loads from sites all around the Taklamakan.

Down the street from the museum was the Arts and Crafts Showroom, featuring lots of local handicrafts made of jade and the famous Atlas silk. In the evening we sat around and discussed trade and history as Marco Polo may have done here some seven centuries before. On previous trips to Urumqi and Turpan in Northern Xinjiang Province, I saw women wearing the Atlas silk. It is truly an exotic material, worn by women all over Central Asia, but very little is of the homemade Hotien variety. The colors with the strange fuzzy design patterns resulting from the Ikat process of weaving gives this silk fabric its unique character. Mr. Mammet Kasun of the Cultural Center told us the technique of weaving silk in Khotan goes back fifteen hundred years. In Eastern China silk cocoons were found in tombs from the Late Stone Age of five thousand years ago. Making silk was a state secret in Eastern China and the people of Hotien knew nothing of mulberry leaves or silk worms except that they existed in the East. To maintain secrecy, the Emperor of China directed the border stations to watch for and prevent mulberry seeds or silkworm eggs from leaving the country. A seventh-century monk, Huan Tsang, wrote this story:

In the fifth century A.D. the King of Hotien asked to marry a princess of the Emperor's house. The Emperor agreed. An envoy from Hotien was sent to meet the princess. In the process of telling her about her new home, he mentioned that the kingdom to which she was going had neither mulberry trees nor silkworms. If she wanted to wear silk, she would have to bring some mulberry tree seeds and eggs for the people of Hotien to make beautiful clothing. She secretly obtained the mulberry seeds and silkworm eggs and hid them in her superabundant hairdo. When she arrived at the border gates they searched her thoroughly but would never touch her hair. This was the beginning of the silk industry in Hotien.

The Atlas silk is mainly produced in the village of Geeya across the White Jade River. It is located about fifteen-miles to the northeast of Hotien at the edge of the desert. The silk-making complex that we visited was run by a seventy-year-old man with an enlarged neck goiter. His wife was a very frail person, also suffering from a goiter, who squatted on the ground putting the silk thread on bobbins. She had what to me were two ugly sacks around her neck the size of grapefruits. Matnur told us that before "Liberation" (1949), 60 percent of the people had this malady, locally called "Hotien Buh Hak." It was so prevalent in this area, a woman was considered more attractive if she had a goiter sack hanging from her neck. In some rare cases the goiter grew to be as much as a yard in length and had to be thrown over the shoulder and strapped to the back when working. After Liberation, a major attempt was launched by the central government to wipe out goiter. All store-bought salt was iodized, and they added chemicals (iodine) to the wells in the villages. The original problem was that poor people went to the mountains to gather rock salt, which did not contain iodine as sea salt did. Hotien is further from the sea than any other place in China. No one in Hotien under the age of forty had this affliction.

The old farmer had a complete production facility for making Atlas silk. They bought the cocoons from nearby farmers who specialized in growing the mulberry trees and raising the silk worms. The cocoons were first heated in boiling water for a short period of time to kill the worms. This was done in a large vat of hot water some three feet across located outside over a fire pit. It must be kept hot enough to loosen the threads but not too hot or the cocoons would fall apart. A young woman was churning the pot with a stick that allowed the outside threads

Top left: A baby in its cradle
Middle and bottom left: Washing the raw silk
in boiling water

Top right: The knife sharoener
Middle right: A seventy-year old woman at
Atlas silk factory with a goiter

to float off. She would pull a dozen or more strands together and feed these over a rack directly to another woman who wound the twisted multi-stranded silk thread onto a large wooden slated cylinder about a yard across. A single thread from one cocoon could be from 1,000 to 3,000 feet in length. The little worms had been very busy inside these cocoons. Factory silk made with automatic machinery draws only seven strands to make a silk thread. This explains why the homemade Atlas silk is so much more robust than the commercial fabric.

The next step in the process was to take the silk threads from many spindles and combine them into a rope bundle less than an inch in diameter and 600 feet long. These bundles of loose silk rope were washed three times in boiling soapy water to remove the sticky resin. The silk was then dried on long racks set up inside the house.

After drying, the bundles were untwisted from the rope of silk threads and spread out on two, 18-inch-wide horizontal racks about 20 feet long. The designs were painted with dye on the warp before weaving. During the weaving process, the unwoven dyed threads were slightly shifted by variable stretching, and this random position of the threads before weaving results in blurry outlines of the patterns between adjacent colors. It is this special quality that makes the Atlas silks so special and beautiful. The result will be a section of silk some 15 inches wide and 18 feet long in about a dozen different dazzling designs with the indistinct colorful patterns.

The work was hard, tedious, and smelly. During the course of a year this family may produce about 120 sections of silk. The cost of the cocoons, dyes, soap, wood for the fire, and other materials amounted to about half the selling price. I bought one 22-foot length of Atlas silk for ten dollars. I was told that a half dozen people at a home silk production shop earn a total yearly income of $1200 (in U.S. dollars).

That evening we were standing in the lobby of the Hotien Inn when, to our surprise, a young American appeared with a group of photographers from the eastern city of Jianguo. It was Justin Rudelson of Beverly Hills, California. I had heard of and had been part of many "small world" stories but this one took the cake. Sitting around drinking a few cups of tea at the inn, Michael and Justin discovered that not only had they gone to the same school, Dartmouth, and had been traveling in Israel at the same time, but by weird and uncanny coincidence they had both lent money to the same guy, David Bedeal, in Swat, Israel. To top it off, neither had ever been paid back. It was easy to like and admire this amiable young man whose light hair and good looks would easily allow him to play the movie role of a California beach boy… and maybe he was. Justin and I had some connections also. I had known his uncle, Irvin Gross, who worked at a Long Island, New York, electronics company, and we had another mutual friend, Geoffrey Newman, from Beijing. It is amazing how much people can learn from one another when there is no TV, radio, movies, beer, or hard liquor and all there is to do is talk. What really endeared me to this young man of twenty-five was his project to unite China and Israel for a joint effort to win in their battle with the desert. His plan was to first learn the language and culture of the Uighur people. He would then go to Israel to study the Israeli methods for dedesertification and bring this technology to Xinjiang Province.

While studying Uighur at Beijing University, he convinced Professor Chen Jia Hou of the Eastern Language department to start a program of Hebrew and Judaic Studies. A four-year Hebrew Language program was to start in 1985. Justin recruited Ilana Bougardier from Israel as their first Hebrew instructor. Accomplishments like this in the very structured Chinese educational system, under a communist government, are rare. For a young Jewish man from Southern California to have achieved this without support from the Chinese and U.S. government had to be an unparalleled feat.

Luo Xiao Yun and Mr. Matnur went out to find a wedding for us to photograph, which resulted in an invitation to attend a wedding on the edge of town in a peach orchard. It was quite a setting. On one side—behind a fence made of bright-red, block-printed fabric draped over a rope tied between the trees—sat women in four rows. All were colorfully dressed in silks. They wore either the locally hand-woven Atlas silks or garments made from fabric produced by Hotien's giant silk factory. This must have been a very special occasion, since everything looked newly made. By contrast the men on the other side of this fabric fence were a seedy bunch. They all looked like they had slept in their jackets and pants.

Before the ceremony started, only men were dancing to the music of the local Uighur band. This was the same musical group we saw perform at the mosque earlier in the week. Huge woks of "polo" (rice, turnips, and mutton) were being cooked over holes in the ground in which fires were blazing. Large farming spades were used to mix the food in these king-size woks. Giant pots of vegetables were simultaneously being prepared. The men were doing the cooking. The wedding service would take place only after everyone had been fed. The white-robed, white-turbaned giant of an imam finally came and sat in the middle of the men's section. The groom stood at one end of a carpeted area lined up with a group of his best friends. The imam recited some excerpts from the Koran, and offered the prayers to sanctify the marriage. Only the groom was present, but a representative of the bride stood in her place next to the groom. The bride with her family and friends stood nearby. When the vows were completed the best man took some nan, dipped it into salt water, and gave half to the groom and the other half to the bride's representative who rushed it over to the bride for her to eat. Whoever consumed the salted bread first would be the head of the household. It was about four yards for the best man to get the nan to the groom and the bride was some twenty yards away. Even an Olympic runner could not have helped the bride. There was no question of the dominant sex in this society.

We visited the largest silk factory of the five northwest provinces located in Hotien. In 1953, a number of local Uighur people were sent east to Suchou in Jiangsu Province to learn modern silk making skills. Suchou is the major center for silk production in all of China. A year later the factory was opened. The present manager, Mr. Hua Zu Rong, came from Eastern China to Hotien when the factory first opened. In 1985 there were 1,520 employees with an equal number of Uighur and Han (people from Eastern China). Two days earlier we had seen how silk had been produced for thousands of years in a long, complex and tedious process. By 1985, through modern technology, electrically operated machinery had been designed to replicate each step of the process to produce a more uniform silk thread and cloth in less than one-thousandth the time.

Sunday, in the big towns such as Hotien, is Bazaar Day. In order to be less conspicuous we decided to split up our team of six photographers; each would go separately though the bazaar. This was only a partial solution since we found we had to walk fast to keep ahead of the curiosity seekers who may have never seen foreigners. If you stop, within minutes a crowd surrounds you. One must develop special techniques to overcome this distraction to picture taking. If you are photographing with a still camera you plan your shot in advance, aim your camera away from the true subject because all the young people will jump in front of the camera, then quickly turn around and shoot. Working with the video camera was an even greater challenge.

The Sunday bazaar was typical of others we had visited in Western China…outdoor barbers shaving heads, lots of chai hannas (tea houses), hardware dealers, spice vendors grinding away with mortar and pestles, mothers feeding their children on their bosoms or with chopsticks, parking lots for the donkeys and separate lots for the carts all standing upright on their ends with harness poles in the air. In a grove of trees, I came across a crowd of people listening to what may have been a political speaker, an Islamic evangelist, or a traveling entertainer/musician. I did not have anyone with me to explain his intent. He played a Dotar (a two-stringed instrument with a long neck) and sang what sounded like Uighur "Rap." He then told a story, and everyone sang a chant with him. I wished I could have understood the language. Later that evening Justin told me he came across a similar person in Kashgar who was explaining "Kuerban," which is the celebration commemorating the bible story of Abraham taking Isaac to sacrifice him to God. The story was being told in the Islamic version where Ishmael replaces Isaac. Justin understood Uighur and he knew the story, making the experience all the more interesting.

Large bazaars, such as the one in Hotien, were broken down into specialty areas. There would be a fabric bazaar, a carpet bazaar, and a hardware bazaar where nails, tractor parts, tools, locks, and every form of metal object used by the local people could be found. The mutton bazaars offered meat butchered in many different cuts of every part of the animal. There were produce bazaars with dozens of vendors spreading open cotton bags of spices lying side by side on the ground with the legumes, root vegetables, and a wide variety of unidentifiable plants—unidentifiable to me. I was told there were over 500 vendors at the Hotien bazaar. Some of the vendors installed makeshift cloth canopies over a few square yards of dirt. The canopies were moved with the sun to protect their wares. Those who could not afford to rent a stall simply sat on the ground and spread a cloth to hold their merchandise. Their theme for a successful business was to keep it simple.

There were no rowdies or hawkers shouting to promote their efforts. There was, however, a new, noisy, high-tech area where cassette players were blasting. All the marketers of electronic products were competing to have the loudest tape players in the Bazaar.

On my way back to the hotel, I saw what looked like a gigantic tapered peach basket about 60 feet wide at the top, some 30 feet high and 30 feet wide at the base. A yard-wide platform around the outside top held some 200 people standing and cheering a daredevil motorcyclist who was whirling his bike around the inside of the basket. The whole structure was made of rickety wooden vertical struts on a thin metal frame held together with bailing wire and a prayer to Allah. While I was looking around between shows I was invited to go inside the basket. They also gave me a ticket for the next show. The ladder used as an entrance and exit to the viewing platform, had broken rungs but somehow held together. Every fourth board of the thin planks that made up the viewing platform was missing. However, it was perfectly safe because the opening between planks was six inches wide, which would allow only one foot to fall through.

The platform was full and it was SHOWTIME! The cyclist was a thin Chinese man wearing a Hong Kong (printed in English) T-shirt and jeans. His dirt bike was powered by a small engine that looked like it would have trouble getting up the hills of Seattle. He mounted, kicked it over one time and with one giant "whrrrrrooomm" he was circling the inside of the basket spiraling up to the top and down again. The crowd cheered and yelled, urging him to go faster and faster. Each time he rotated, the entire structure synchronously swayed a good two or three feet, adding additional excitement to the event. This dirt-bike racing basket seemed as if it was heading for a catastrophe. I did want to finish my Marco Polo project, so I didn't stay for the next show.

Rajap Yusaf was the Director of the Cultural Center of Hotien and Administrator of Antiquities. He spent the morning telling us about the history of this area. Hotien's first kingdom started in 260 B.C.E. and lasted a thousand years. Then Islam came in the tenth century to last until the time of communism when religious restrictions were put in place.

He told us a fascinating Uighur fable:

A long time ago there was a beautiful girl with eyelashes so long they were like a roof shading her face. When she turned eighteen, many sons of kings and other rich men asked for her hand in marriage and she refused them all. Her father was the king and one day he and his advisors came to her room and told her that since she had not chosen a husband she must marry the sun. Being an obedient daughter she asked the sun if he would marry her. The sun replied "I am warm and beautiful but sometimes I am blocked by the clouds therefore you should marry the clouds." The cloud said "I am very strong and I can block the sun but the wind can move me across the sky, therefore you should marry the wind." Because he could not move a stone wall, he refused. The wall was only there because a stonemason brought the stones together and made the wall. Since the stonemason was more powerful than the sun, she married the stonemason.

Mr. Yusaf told us the moral of the story was when a woman is choosing a husband she doesn't have to reach for the sun. She may find her best choice in her own back yard.

When Marco Polo came to Hotien he was warmly received. His descriptions of Hotien were too accurate not to be true, especially his accounts of finding jade in the White Jade River. The day we arrived in Hotien a farmer found a 60-kilo white jade for which he received 4,500 yuan, almost four years' earnings.

Marco Polo's words about Hotien were as valid in 1985 as they were in the fall of 1273.

CHAPTER 21

The Deserted City of Pien
Taklamakan, September 2 to 15, 1985

P *ien is a province five days in length, lying between east and north-east. The people are worshippers of Mahommet, and subjects of the Great Kahn. There are a good number of towns and villages, but the most noble is Pien, the capital of the kingdom. There are rivers in this country, in which Jasper and Chalcedony are found. The people have plenty of all products, including cotton. They live by manufactures and trade. But they have a custom that I must relate. If the husband of any woman go away upon a journey and remain away for more than 20 days, as soon as that term is past the woman may marry another man, and the husband also then may marry whom he pleases.*

I should tell you that I have been speaking of from Kashgar forward, and those I am going to mention (as far as the city of Lop) belong to great Turkey.
MARCO POLO, 1298

After arriving in Domoko, China, we found that farm tractors had been hired for us to visit the ancient sites of "Pien." In the fifteenth century, when the desert sands had overwhelmed Pien, the town was moved beyond the edge of the desert and became Domoko. This was the region and the city that Marco traveled to after he left Hotien (Khotan). Today, Domoko is not just a town. It is a giant commune with some 15,000 people living and working together. Yusaf Khan, the director of the commune, was a relatively young, thirty-something guy, tall, dark, and Uighur-handsome. After a few years as principal of the middle school he was sent to Urumqi to study agriculture. Yusaf then came back to run the commune and lived in what would be called by local standards a palatial house. The entrance was off the main road not far from the commune headquarters and guesthouse. The path, approximately twenty yards long, led to the front door and was totally covered with a grape arbor ready for picking. On either side, he grew onions, eggplant, tomatoes, carrots, and fruit trees. A half dozen pheasants and a few geese had the run of the grounds. On the roof, the director kept about 150 caged pigeons. On occasion, a few became their evening meal. Yuma's house was built in the early eighties for 5,000 yuan (less than $2,000 U.S. dollars), which was a good way to assess the level of the local economy. The front porch had a carpeted floor. Inside, all walls and floors were covered in carpets. There were many large rooms and through the kitchen door we found the path to the latrine, past the animal pens. The toilet facility was again an old wooden shed with the standard two wooden slats for your feet and a hole above a hole in the ground. This arrangement was designed for squatting, the traditional position used throughout Asia. In 1985 even five-star hotels in China had a ceramic version of this design.

Dinner was mutton and veggies from the garden.

Somehow our local "handlers" in Domoko found two giant Tienjin Type 55 tractors with five-foot-diameter rear wheels to help us to explore the soft sand desert. The local nickname for these vehicles is "wu shi wu" which translates into "55." Their cabs had enough room for the driver and possibly a second person. I was to be given the privilege of riding in the cab. Four other men, plus our desert guide, found that they could squeeze into the cab with the driver and me. It was a bit crowded. The second tractor, with Michael, was to pull a farm trailer that had a large tarpaulin over a pipe frame to provide protection from the 110-degree sun. The unusual thing about the trailer was that it was outfitted with three large overstuffed living-room-type sofas to provide comfort for the "delicate" Americans. This did provide us with a very cozy environment in which to travel across this foreboding desert terrain. The trailer looked more comfortable, so we left the cramped tractors, boarded our motorized parlor and drove off into the desert.

As we headed across the sand dunes, our photographic team sat in the covered trailer comfortably eating Hami melons and watermelons, spitting the seeds on the floor. Spitting is a common trait all through China. I saw it often in the streets and in worker's restaurants in the Eastern China. Spitting on city streets of the major cities of China is misdemeanor. The melon seeds were periodically propelled with the passengers towards the overhead tarp as the springless trailer bounced its way through the undulating dunes on our way to Old Domoko, a.k.a. Pien in Marco Polo's time. We went to the site of the "Ulugh Mazar" (Tomb of Ulugh) outside of Pien, which was quite easy to find since there were many donkey and camel tracks to follow. The local Muslims came here to pray for fertility. Judging by the proliferation of children in Xinjiang Province, the traffic to the Tomb of Ulugh had been heavy.

We saw the remains of buildings abandoned 500 years before. Many foundations still remained, and the dry desert environment had preserved numerous wooden structures. There were hundreds of ancient home sites outlined by the reeds that once provided the support for the mud-plastered walls that covered it, just as rebars provide the binding strength for our modern concrete buildings. The sand and wind had worn away the mud walls leaving the dry reeds still standing. Each house had a fireplace for cooking and heating and many had survived. Potshards and ceramics could be found all over the desert floor of this area as the continually shifting sands exposed new levels of the life of this primordial place. Michael found a coin and gave it to Rajap Yusaf, the Administrator of Hotien Antiquities. He said it was from the Qin Dynasty (nineteenth century) and not very valuable. Auriel Stein's maps resemble treasure maps, identifying gold fields, jade sites, and places from which some of the treasures were taken and others left behind. I was carrying copies of the maps. All we needed was a shovel, a camel's hair brush, and permission to use them. Nothing, however, at these sites could be touched or even photographed without high level Chinese government permission. We could easily get the shovel, but being granted a permit would have taken years. Just visiting these places as the first foreigners since Stein was here about 1910 offered its own special excitement that is not easily explained, somewhat like walking on new-fallen snow. I walked down a street in ancient Pien and felt the aura of life and commerce that thrived here, half a millennia before.

Just north of Pien was an even older place from the Tang Dynasty (ninth century C.E.) that Auriel Stein identified as Uzum Tatli. We had to abandon that excursion when both tractors in tandem could not pull the trailer through the knee-deep powdery sand. It is ironic to see these large modern tractors with monstrous wheels bogged down in a desert that camels cross, unhindered at two and a half miles an hour. They say a camel is an animal designed by a committee. It has many neat features but to get all those capabilities built into one animal resulted in one ugly beast. After a lot of tractor maneuvering and cursing in many languages, we were once more on our way.

The town of Pien had changed since Marco Polo was here. Today it is an abandoned historic site partially buried under the Taklamakan. It was the unusual marriage arrangement that remained highest in Marco's recollection of Pien.

Unable to venture further to the north and deeper into the desert our guide took us to the East to another ancient site "Farhad Beg Deilaki." This was a real challenge. After taking hours to make our way to Pien, including the time to extract one tractor or another from the deep soft powdery sand we finally found it. I should really say our guide Dulkan found it. He was phenomenal. Without any GPS navigation system or compass (originally invented by the Chinese) he gave the tractor driver directions through the maze of sand dunes. Some of the dunes were molded by the wind alone while others have tall desert reeds and bushes that act as sand catchers and allow the dunes to grow to the height of a three story building. Dulkan walked ahead to direct the tractor drivers over the easiest route. As the day moved on and the temperature moved up, his white skull cap replaced the black karakul hat that he wore at the beginning of the day. Every now and then he scampered up a high dune to reorient himself. I climbed up one of the taller dunes to see the view but all I could see in every direction, to the horizon, were more dunes all about the same height. There was very little difference between them but apparently enough for Dulkan to find the way. Unfortunately, this journey also turned out to be a lost cause. The tractors just could not force their way through this part of the desert. Where were the camels when we really needed them? Our hosts of Domoko may have felt we would be more comfortable on posh couches instead of the undulating back of a camel in the hot sun. Still, it was not a wasted trip since we did reach our main goal; a visit to Pien.

After some strange maneuvering with one tractor pulling the other tractor out of one jam after another, we headed back to where we had left the jeeps, just three hours away.

A Dance in our honor started at 10 p.m. at the home of the director of the commune. He brought out a big portable stereo "ghetto box" with a selection of both Uighur and disco music cassettes. The local (Communist) party secretary, the head of the local medical clinic and teachers from the school also came to our impromptu dance party. In addition to the canned music, a live musical group including a drummer, a fiddler, and the local electrician fiddling on the two-string dotar added excitement to the festivities. I had met the electrician earlier when I asked to find a source of electricity to charge the battery for the video recorder. He spliced a wire connection into the lamp dangling from the ceiling of my room at the guesthouse.

After a lot of encouragement by the Director, Yusaf Khan, a couple of the women got up and soon everyone was dancing to the Uighur music. The party secretary (an appropriate title for a dance master) was trying to get everyone to dance to the disco music but most of the locals were more comfortable with the Uighur dancing. I joined in on the dance floor with what has become my traditional "chicken dancing" to the local music. Fruits, tea, rock sugar, and hard candy were served and everyone had a ball.

We found another Uighur wedding was taking place the morning we were to leave for Yutien. We went to the house of the bride and ate the obligatory mutton, nan, and salt milk-tea and took lots of pictures. This wedding had totally different rituals from the ones we had seen over the past few weeks. Here they carried the bride to the groom's house in a carpet held by a handful of the groom's friends. It was a big parade of well-wishers, men dancing and a troupe of musicians. At the head of the procession going down the road was the thirteen-year-old sister of the bride. She wore a red dress, dancing and clapping and being as much the center of attraction as was her sister. She was cute, vivacious, and a talented dancer. I felt this young girl was too talented for this little town in the middle of nowhere. I am certain she has left Domoko by now and living as a professional entertainer in some big Eastern city of China.

Michael liked a carpet that hung on the wall of the bride's house, so much that he bought it for 500 yuan (about $100).

Yutien was a sandy forty miles away and somehow our Toyotas were now ac-climated to the desert and had no trouble getting there in what seemed no time at all, or it could have been that the drivers were now more experienced. On arrival, a message was waiting. There was much conversation among the Chinese. They acted as if they did not want to tell me some bad news. I was a bit concerned. Fi-nally, I found out that it was a message from Justin, our young California friend, who said he would arrive in Yutien at noon on September 5 with some important "big" news. Michael and I guessed it was about a small group of Germans driving a couple of Audi sedans from Shanghai to Karachi. A couple of days ago we heard they had left Dun Huang in central China to cross the north side of the Taklamakan, on the New Silk Road. The whereabouts of the Audi Group had been a mystery for the last five days. To confirm this, we would have to find out the "big" news when Justin arrived. This was of special interest since we wanted to be certain that they were OK and also confirm that they did not reach the China-Pakistan border before us without our knowledge.

Thursday was September 5th and Michael's thirty-fourth birthday. I mentioned this to Luo Xiao Yun. She said they would try to make a birthday cake. I suggested eighteen small birthday candles for the cake, knowing that Michael would appreciate the significance of eighteen being the special number for life in Oriental and Judaic mysticism.

That morning we visited one of Xinjiang Province's largest rice fields with an area of 30,000-mu (5,000 acres). The problem was too much water—and this is the world's driest desert? The water comes from underground springs, and the land is so soggy, that tractors and other farm equipment got bogged down in the fields. As a solution they dug deeper canals around the fields to drain off the excess water. This water was fed into nearby rivers for use down stream.

Yutien had set up a very sophisticated irrigation system using radio controlled well pumps. They had about 120 pumps that were operated from one master control station that looked like a "B movie" version of a Pentagon War Room. There was a giant map on the wall with lighted numbers at each pump location. Digital displays using 1950s technology provided the control and flow rate of the water. It was a very impressive operation for this primitive part of China.

Even with all the water and water control, the day we arrived, the town's water was not flowing. And there was no running water at the guesthouse. Our only source of water, for the duration of our stay, was a well in a mud-brick house in the courtyard.

Sure enough, Justin Rudelson arrived about one o'clock in the afternoon. His cryptic cable telex (since there was no telephone service) could now be explained. Just after we left Hotien, the two Audis arrived with a group of Germans on their way to Karachi. We learned about this Audi project from a young German at the Shinar Hotel in Gilgit, Pakistan, a few weeks before. During a recent visit to Germany, the Chinese Premier Zhou had given permission for a German auto club to travel from Shanghai to Karachi over the Kunjerab Pass. The Marco Polo project did beat them to the pass.

While we were in Hotien we had invited Justin to a wedding but he had to be disinvited because only a limited number of visitors could attend. This was embarrassing but today we made it up by arranging for him to attend a Uighur wedding in a village at the edge of town. As we approached the bride's house I was struck by the dramatically different clothing of the married women. Unmarried women wore what we found to be typical Uighur womenfolk dress, skirts over slacks and brightly colored lace scarves over their hair. The skirts and scarves were sometimes decorated with fine ribbons of gold leaf. Many women also wore the Atlas silk as a one-piece sheath and some dresses had Atlas and synthetic silk

combination. The most common color was red. In contrast, the married women wore white shawls in the style of the chador of Iranian or Indian women, only at the very top of their head they wore a miniature black cap, the size and shape of an upside-down teacup, embellished with colorful embroidery. It was held in place with a long hatpin. The white shawl was worn over a long black dress. If they had children, a series of eight horizontal blue or aqua colored stripes were sewn across the bodice of the dress from the neck to about half way down their bosom. About fifty or sixty women stood outside the bride's house as part of the celebration. The bandstand was a large flatbed farm truck. A couple of drummers, a few stringed instruments and an ancient style single-reed clarinet played on the truck as the men danced in the streets. Inside the house the women were gossiping. In the rear courtyard giant woks over fire pits were cooking *palu* (rice, meat and vegetables) and boiling water for *cha* (tea).

The local imam officiated at the wedding, vows were recited, and there was a reading from the Koran. The couple was officially married after the race to eat bread dipped in the salt water. The groom won again.

After everyone was fed, the bride was carried out of the house on a carpet to a waiting jeep that served as the modern version of a horse and wagon. Three fully loaded large open farm trucks took the guests in a caravan from the bride's house to the home of the groom a mile away for more dancing and eating. Friends of the wedding party erected obstacles in the form of ropes tied across the road.

205 *The Deserted City of Pien*

Top left: Carrying the bride in a carpet to the wedding
Bottom Left: Displaying the dowry

Top middle: The sister and grandfather of the bride

Top right: At the wedding party the men and women are separated by a fence
Bottom right: The iman conducting the wedding service

In order for the trucks and guests to pass the barrier, one had to pay the keeper of the barrier with a dance before the keeper lifted the rope. There were many volunteers ready to dance. Partying, dancing, and eating continued for another day. We slipped back to the inn.

Preparations for Michael's surprise birthday cake were proceeding. The cook knew how to make a cake but had no round cake pans. The cakes of Yutien were always made in large rectangular baking pans. The local blacksmith came to the rescue and manufactured four round pans of welded steel within a couple of hours. Candles were also a problem. All the storehouses in the area were searched and finally four red, foot-long dinner candles were found. Red is the traditional good luck color throughout Central Asia and China. There were two for each cake. The cakes were made as two layer pound cakes with mandarin oranges between layers.

I once had an interesting experience in China regarding the color red. I was meeting with the director of a factory. As is the tradition before discussing business there is an hour of socializing; what some would call "smoozing." We were discussing birthdays and it turned out that we were both born during the year of the snake. The Chinese calendar has a sequence of twelve years, each called by the name of a different animal. The snake was the sixth to travel to Buddha to pay their respects on his deathbed. The director asked me a very bizarre question, "Are you wearing red underwear?" I was shocked and asked, "Why?" He said that he could not see any red on my external cloths so he thought I may be wearing red on something that he could not see. The director explained that during the animal year of your birth you should wear red every day for good luck. That evening I bought red underwear. I had a flight back to Seattle in a few days but for some unexplainable reason I went to the airport and immediately found a seat on a flight home. It was September 10, 2001. If I had waited one more day, 9/11, I would have been stuck in China for a month. The red underwear worked.

After dinner the lights of our dining room were turned out and to Michael's amazement Xiao Yun and Jin Bo Hong carried out the cakes, candles a blazing as we all sang "Happy Birthday" in Chinese, Uighur, and English.

The evening's entertainment at the local meeting house was a live performance of a Uighur dance troupe from the big city, Urumqi, Xinjiang's capital. After the show, everybody stayed to party, Chinese style…no booze. Dancing by most of the Marco Polo troupe and the Uighur Dance Troupe went on well past midnight back stage. A ten-piece Uighur band supplied music. I felt ill so I went back to the guesthouse early.

I decided to take the next day off and stay in my room most of the day. The rest of the group went to the power station (2,400 KW facility) and a large commune where they had lunch.

The bazaar at a small village outside Yutien almost turned into a riot. Michael was surrounded by hundreds of local people. They had never seen a red-haired

foreigner before and he was stuck on top of a truck snapping back at the hordes around him with the shutter of his camera. Justin left for Hong Kong by way of Urumqi. It was a warm but difficult parting. In what was a short period of time, Justin and I felt we had adopted each other as family. His father had died in a small plane accident at Santa Barbara Airport twelve years earlier and I was about his father's age. He had an objective to help world peace, to help bring Israel and China together. We both independently recognized the cultural similarities between these two nations and how much each needed the other both politically and economically.

Justin did a paper at Dartmouth in which he presented the similarities between Judaic and Confucius philosophy. Both countries were established in their present reincarnation at about the same time (Israel 1948 and China 1949). Both have histories and traditions that go back to the second millennium B.C.E. They both have been persecuted in their Diasporas and usually lived in Ghettos. They are both family-oriented societies and for thousands of years have admired intellect over brawn. Both have reputations for having innate business acumen…It may be also noted that both Chinese and Jewish families go to Chinese restaurants for Sunday dinner and on Christmas day.

By Friday evening, I was feeling better and we all went to the edge of town where civilization meets the desert. Here we found swells of sand rolling on towards the horizon as if it were a turbulent beige sea caught in an instant of time.

207 *The Deserted City of Pien*

Top: Preparing the wedding feast
Bottom row: Women guests of the wedding
who were married wore special clothes

The soft sand and the warm twilight gave the curving sand a very romantic, almost erotic, feeling. The sunset that evening turned the sand and sky into a wonderful work of art.

As we sat on top of a dune a shepherd with his sheep crawled amongst the dunes and continued into the night to some distant oasis.

All of the Chinese were worried about the desert between Ruoqiang and Dun Huang. The concern today was the weight in the jeeps. To solve the problem all excess baggage including the refrigerator for the film that I carried half way around the world was being packed up and shipped by the postal system to Beijing. FedEx had not made it to Yutien. Cooler weather was expected as we traveled further along the higher elevation Silk Road, so keeping our film cool was unnecessary. A local cabinet shop built the shipping container. The very expensive Luan Philippine Mahogany was the only wood available to make the box.

The trip from Yutien to Minfeng was an uneventful two-hour journey on a relatively good gravel road.

Minfeng was a town with a population of about 2,000 people. Its bazaar was small not only because it served a small community but because of its isolation. Minfeng was no longer on a road to anywhere. The distance to Urumqi was nearly 2,000 miles by road, or more appropriately it should be called a trail. Without

Above: Bringing home the Hami melons

an airport or train it was difficult to bring anything to Minfeng. Therefore, the bazaar was small.

Both in Domoko and here in Minfeng we saw most men wearing the tall curly black wool hats over the "dopa" (skull caps). As with the weddings that had individual and unique rituals at their ceremonies, local clothing styles for both men and women seemed to be regionalized and probably for the same reason…isolation.

On the way back from the bazaar I had a chance to visit the local TV station. They had a very low power (100 watt) transmitter, which provided TV coverage for just a dozen square miles— a sufficient range for this community and its suburban farms. The programming source was a couple of video cassette players and about fifty prerecorded tapes. There was also a consumer-type, Japanese made video camera on which local programs could be produced. We were told they received news programs every six weeks. These tapes were their only contact with the outside world.

Would you believe that there, in the middle of a desert, a fisherman brought in a catch of fresh fish for lunch? At Biwek Kol (Kol is Lake in Uighur), about twenty-four miles east of town, we found a small fishing industry. On one side of the road was a half dozen or so breeding ponds and on the other side there was a nine-mile long lake in which they stocked a good tasting fish. A couple of men went out in a rowboat and pulled in a nylon net that had ensnared a couple dozen

209 *The Deserted City of Pien*

Top and bottom left: Riding camels in the desert

Right: A family traveling along a desert road

fish. As we relaxed on cots, they cooked up a delicious fish stew. The soup must have had some magic ingredient since I felt especially great, maybe high, the rest of the day. Everyone in our group said the same thing. I have no idea what those fish may have been "smoking."

An explorer's work is never done. After lunch we headed south straight across the desert towards the Kun Lun Mountains. It was 42 miles from the road. We had to cross two riverbeds and bounced across some pretty rocky terrain. That is why they called our Toyotas off-road vehicles. Finally after a couple of hours we arrived at Yeyik —a commune surrounded by desert and mountains. There was nothing special about the place except its remoteness. Eight camels were waiting to help us follow Marco Polo in a manner that he no doubt used in this part of his travels. Those in our group who did not get a camel were entitled to a horse. We all saddled up and were soon crossing a wide river bed on our way to visit a family whose home was on the other side of this section of the desert. This time we had an appropriate transportation. As we started, the wind picked up and we found ourselves in a full-blown sand storm. It is not that you can't open your eyes to see where you're going, that is the job of the camels, nor is it the irritation of the blowing sand on your skin. No, the most annoying thing about the sandstorm is the total saturation of every crack and cranny of your body, clothing, and all else by minute particles of sand. The powdery granules manage to work their way into everything.

Only by riding a camel does one get to appreciate these beautiful lumbering beasts of the desert. Their feet have wide pads to distribute their weight over a wide area and are easily pulled from the enveloping sand. I rode two camels; one out and another one back from the farmhouse. The outbound trip was as if I were riding a well-padded rocking horse. It had a smooth gait as it easily climbed up and down the dunes. On the way up a steep dune you are sitting on the rear hump and the way down you are straddling the front hump. I felt safe and secure. The second camel was very different; its rocking motion required some effort to prevent the whiplash action from unseating me. At one point, I was the second from last in our caravan and the last camel broke rank. The leash that was tied to my camel broke. Suddenly, my camel leaped into the air almost throwing me to the ground. My video camera and tape deck flew out in different directions. Luckily they were well attached to my body with straps and cables, so I didn't loose anything. No one saw the actual sequence of events, but it was quite possible and very likely that the last camel bit my camel on the ass, which caused my camel to leap forward and into the air to get away. This is very typical camel behavior. Still, for all their orneriness and smelly breath, they are the best off-road means of desert transportation available.

We bid our farewells to Matnur and Yusaf since we were leaving their jurisdiction of the Hotien District. At 10:40 a.m. we left for the 200-mile journey to Qiemo (Charchan in Marco Polo's book). The dirt roads were no problem and we arrived at 4 p.m. Our arrival interrupted the Qiemo County weekly meeting and the group came over to offer us a "warm welcome." (Warm welcome is the translation of a Chinese expression that means just that.) Almost their entire government arrived including the following:

- County Director
- Party Secretary for the County
- Assistant Party Secretary for the County
- Head of County Construction
- Head of County Agriculture
- Head of Foreign Affairs
- A Uighur to Chinese Translator

I was surprised when they explained that even after all these years, some of the members of the government only spoke Uighur and others spoke only *Putong Hua* (Mandarin Chinese language) so a translator was often needed at government meetings.

Qiemo is a county in the Biangola Mongolian Autonomous Region. It has an area of 46,000 square miles—about the size of New York State—at an average elevation of 4,200 feet. The average annual rainfall is 19 mm or ¾ inch and the average temperature is 10 degrees C (50 degrees F). In this vast area the total population is only 33,000 people; about the same as a few square blocks of Manhattan. With so little rainfall they have to struggle to produce the wheat, corn, cotton, rice and garden vegetables needed for survival. Mining is the big source of income, and asbestos is the principal mineral, produced and processed right at the mine sites and exported by truck. The people are almost oblivious to its cancer-causing effect since the asbestos dust is everywhere. As I walked through town I saw asbestos accumulated in the corners where buildings or curbstones meet the ground. Only a few of the workers wore facemasks for protection. At least the government limited these young people to a maximum of two years of work in the mines.

In addition to the asbestos, they mine white jade and export about 20 tons per year. Qiemo is mostly known for its white jade. There are about 300,000 farm animals in addition to the produce grown on the eleven agricultural communes. Qiemo was moving into the modern world with a small TV station, and China Airlines (CAAC) was flying into the new airport on a once-a-week schedule.

The history of Qiemo, which Marco Polo referred to as Charchan, reaches back four to five thousand years. Some Stone Age sites can be found at locations along the Charchan River and back into the Kun Lun Mountains. Charchan has a written history dated to the Han Dynasty Period (100 B.C.E.).

Marco Polo tells of how the people of Charchan found safe haven in the desert:

harchan is a Province of Great Turkey, lying between south-east and east The people worship Mahommet. They are numerous towns and villages, and the chief city of the kingdom bears its name, Charchan. The Province contains rivers that bring down Jasper and Chalcedony, And these are carried for sale into Cathay, where they fetch great prices. The whole of the Province is sandy, and so is the road all the way from Pien, and much of the water you find is bitter and bad. However, at some places you do find fresh and sweet water. When an army passes through the land, the people escape with their wives, children and cattle a distance of two or three days journey into the sandy waste; and knowing the spots where water is to be had they are able to live there and keep their cattle alive, whilst it is impossible to discover them; for the wind immediately blows the sand over their track.

Quitting Charchan, you ride some five days through the sands, finding none but bad and bitter water and then you come to a place where the water is sweet. And now I will tell you of a Province called, Lop, which you come to at the end of those five days. It is at the entrance of the Great Desert, and it is here that travelers repose before entering the Desert.

MARCO POLO, 1298

It was more often the case that we were at the right place at the right time than the other way around. Today was another one of the serendipitous occasions. On arrival in Qiemo we found a group of the leading archeologists from the Xinjiang Museum, led by the Director of the Research Center, Dr. Kayum Hoja. They agreed to have a meeting with us that evening so we could pick their brains about Marco Polo. Our main question regarded the route that he followed. They confirmed that all of the sites and towns visited by Marco Polo along the Southern border of the Taklamakan are still in the same locations except for Pien, now known as Old Domoko, which we also visited. According to Dr. Kayum, Lop Nor (a lake mentioned by Marco Polo) is now completely dry. In 1949 it had one-meter depth but that too has evaporated. The people of that area were known as "Lop" and they were moved from the lake to the north in 1924.

Some recent discoveries of the Xinjiang Museum of Urumqi include:

- More than forty sites of the New Stone Age Period dating from 3000 B.C.E. to 1000 B.C.E. were found both North and South of the Tian Shan Mountains, which are located in Northern Xinjiang Province.
- In Tashkurgan they found an even older Stone City—that was dated to 6,000 B.C.E.—than the one we visited.
- Near Kashgar they discovered human fossils from 20,000 years ago.
- Some bronzes were unearthed in Northeast Xinjiang near Illi from 500 B.C.E.
- A tomb from 1500 B.C.E. was found near Hami, over 500 miles Northeast of Qiemo.

Also in attendance at this meeting was Ahmeh, a dirt archeologist who was the head of the fieldwork, and Dr. Dolkum, a research archeologist from the

Research Center.

Of special interest to Michael and me were their recent discoveries of rock carvings similar to what we had found in Northern Pakistan. These were found in the Kun Lun Mountains some 120 miles south of Qiemo. The drawings Dr. Kayum made for us looked the same as the rock drawings we found northeast of Gilgit, Pakistan.

Travel to Ruoqiang took over seven hours to go 200 miles, with a stop in Waxxan for a roadside lunch, plus a number of melon stops along the way. Melon stops were part of the ritual of our travels through Western China. After an hour or two of driving, our three vehicles would stop along the side of the road. Both Hami melons and watermelons were cut open with the dagger that Michael received as a gift from Jin Tulle in Kashgar. Mellon stops served many purposes. The break in driving gave us a brief rest from the stomach-churning road, a toilet break, and an opportunity to have conversations with those in the other cars. Melons are a good source of liquids, so badly needed when traveling across the dry, hot desert and the sugar gave us energy. They also tasted great. We made it to Ruoqiang without mishap.

In our room that morning we had a meeting with officials from Ruoqiang County of the Biangola Mongolian Autonomous Region. The county had grown from only 4000 people in 1949. Almost 60 percent are Uighur, 38 percent Han Chinese, and the balance Tarter (people from Mongolia), Kossak (from Russia), and Hui (Islamic) minorities. When we arrived in a new area the local officials went through the same ritual of welcoming us. This included offering us a long list of statistics about their jurisdiction and how it compared to 1949 when the Communist Government first had taken over all of China. There must be a little red book that is given to each of the local officials on how to greet new visitors, the various details on rainfall, average temperatures, and the number of tons of crops produced or minerals mined. The details on their small part of the world are interesting and did give us a sense of where we were and how this place was different from the rest of the world.

Just like each person on earth, each geographic place is unique. Every place we visited had its own personality, but more than that, its own natural geographic structure plus the modifications and structures that had been added by man. There was also the weather, the smells, and for me the immediate feeling that comes over me when I'm first introduced to a new place. This is difficult to describe but I always know if the experience was a good or bad. It becomes an intuitive response. Even small children will sense this when brought to someplace he or she has never seen. In watching my five children and their friends grow up I found they will either cling close to the adult who brought them or feel comfortable and want to investigate their new environment. It is the craving for these new experiences that has driven me to seek new places whenever I travel. To some it may just be boring numbers, but to me the statistics offered by these local officials added to the understanding and the special nature of their small part of China and the world.

We found that Ruoqiang, although located far from the more populated parts of China, is still very self-sufficient. There is about a half-inch (12 mm) of rain per year and an evaporation rate of 100 inches per year, making it one of the driest places in China. With the help of the river water from the Kun Lun Mountains and the 5,100 hours of sunshine per year (averaging over twelve hours a day), they produce for local consumption more than enough wheat, corn, rice, and beans, and keep 100,000 sheep and cattle. Their main source of income was the mining of minerals, which include 16,000 tons of asbestos taken from seven mines located both on the surface and below ground. They have surveyed a reserve of over 50 million tons of asbestos. Other minerals include gold, copper, and iron. They were concerned about their future since the market for asbestos does not look bright…thank goodness. A possible replacement for asbestos may be oil. We saw survey teams with big U.S.-made hydraulic earth pounders that were used to find oil. It worked like an ultrasound, examining the size and shape of the baby in the tummy of a pregnant lady. The machine pounds the ground and then detects the reflected noise to create a picture of what is below the surface.

Our room at the guest house was conveniently located 183 steps from the outside latrine. Sometimes the relative locations of the bedroom and the latrine can be really important, especially when you are in a part of the world with no refrigeration and other conditions that allow food to spoil quickly.

County Vice-Director Fang Zhong Gui, County Planning Director Yu Zhong Asar, and Cultural Director Tu Di Ashimul introduced us to Ruoqiang County. We were told that another American group would be coming on September 20. They had a joint project with the Xinjiang Mountaineering Association to climb Muztagh Mountain in the Kun Lun Range.

The group of sixty people from the U.S. would be surprised to find on their arrival a small sign on the latrine wall saying: MARCO POLO WAS HERE.

Milan is 48 miles northeast of Ruoqiang on a road that follows a beeline to the horizon. The land was flat with no vegetation to be seen in any direction. It was bleaker than a moonscape. Roads are easy to build straight on this type of terrain. We arrived in modern Milan and without stopping we continued on an ancient track to the Old City of Milan. In its heyday, the old city was huge for a city in the middle of a desert. It was once a vast metropolis, by desert standards, that was—3 miles east-to-west and 6 miles south-to-north. At its center we found the ruins of the citadel. Originally the structure was 210 feet by 170 feet constructed of reeds and mud. On the north side we found a series of storage rooms. We assumed they were storage rooms since they had no doors or windows and access must have been through a hole in the ceiling. In one of the rooms Michael found another coin that Cultural Director Mr. Tu Di said was from the West Han Dynasty (100 B.C.E.). The coin was destined for the local archives since, as usual; all things of antiquity belong to the state. We were able to identify two, dome-shaped mounds that were once Buddhist stupas (shrines). Someone searching for valuable artifacts had excavated the core of the structures.

The commune at Milan was established by a trainload of 300 students from Shanghai during the Cultural Revolution in 1966. It is a big achievement for a bunch of kids from the big city, who were taken out to a desert town with very little preparation and made it a productive and very profitable agricultural project. They grow wheat, and vegetables and have 15,000 fruit trees of apples, pears, and peaches. In addition they too have made a lot of money mining asbestos and shipping 10,000 tons each year.

In this world everything is relative. This is a very successful commune. Each worker is compensated in one of three ways: the first is by a fixed salary with a 25 percent bonus if they exceed their quota; the second is by direct sale to the free market for the products that have exceeded the quota; the third is by a negotiated contract to produce a specific amount for a specific price. Considering these conditions, which seem to be very fair, the average yearly income for each of the 3,700 employees of the commune was 700 RMB. Based on the exchange rate of 1985 it would be the equivalent of about $0.50 per day. This is again relative since a pound of rice sells for $0.04 and a watermelon sells for about $0.01 each. There are also special annual bonuses for asbestos miners of 500 RMB, but these young workers were most likely unaware of the health problems they would face later in life.

Farming in Milan is not as easy as it may be in Kansas. First, it is in a desert. Water must be brought in from the mountains and distributed by a system of irrigation. Second, the soil is contaminated with minerals and salt. Therefore, much of the water is used to wash the soil. The work is done by hand. There are no harvesters and "combines" or other mechanized farm machinery. They do have some tractors that are shared amongst the family farms and animals supplement these. It is not an easy way to make a living.

Justin Rudelson had told us, back in Hotien, that there was a ninety-five-year-old man in Milan who was the last person still alive who had lived in Lop Nor before it was abandoned. We walked down a row of mud-brick huts. Over the past month, we'd walked down the streets of villages all over Western China and, as I have said before, I felt that we'd walked into a time machine going back into antiquity. The people and their homes had not changed. The road we walked was dirt; primitive wooden farm implements leaned against the walls next to the door, left by the farmers who had just come in from the fields. The crops were the ones that Marco Polo recorded in his chronicles. What we saw today on our way to the old gentleman was another stroll back to the thirteenth century.

How fortunate am I to be able to witness an ancient world before it moves quickly into the twenty-first century.

The old man and his young seventy-nine-year-old friend were both born in Lop Nor. A third elderly man, who sat with us in the small dark room, told us his father worked for Auriel Stein eighty years ago. We talked about the problems of desert travel, especially the black storms. The old man said it could not have been that bad; after all, he was now ninety-five years old.

We left Milan early to follow the telephone lines forty-eight miles back across the Gobi to Ruoqiang. Gobi is a Mongolian word that means desert, but not necessarily sand desert. The Gobi is a wasteland, with no water and little or no vegetation; most of its surface of the Gobi over which we traveled was covered with brown, gray, black, and white pebbles or gravel.

That evening we went to the local cinema located just a few hundred yards from the guesthouse. This turned out to be a surprisingly different experience. They were presenting a comedy called *A Family Affair,* which was the best Jin Bo Hong could offer as a translation. We each paid the equivalent of five cents admission. When I was nine years old I paid five cents for admission to a movie house. The local policeman would give the kids in the neighborhood a pass for the Saturday matinee for a fifty-percent discount if they had not caused him any problem.

We walked through a narrow tunnel and found ourselves outside again. It reminded me of a 1950s drive-in movie theater with benches instead of parking spaces. The projection building and the white painted, plastered brick wall that served as a panorama-shaped screen looked new. I found out later it was just two years old. The benches were concrete slabs about eight inches wide. I would guess the capacity of the facility was more than 3,000, which exceeded the population of the city. This same architectural style was used in other cities in Western China. When there is very little chance of rain, a roof is not necessary and the cool evenings are better than air conditioning.

Jin Bo Hong sat between Michael and me and gave us a simultaneous translation of the dialog. The story, as the title from Jin's translation implied, was about a father, mother, twenty-six-year-old daughter, and a twenty-three-year-old son. The daughter is in love with the bright boy next door (actually, he lived across the courtyard in a high-rise apartment house). The son meets a saleslady at a bookshop and, as required by the formula, also falls in love. It is a comedy of errors, a little slapstick and some typical TV comedy situations. It all ends happily with everyone getting married.

CHAPTER 22

Aborted Adventure
Gobi, September 15 to 19, 1985

he length of this desert is so great that 'tis said it would take a year and more to ride from one end of it to the other. And here, where the breadth is least, it takes a month to cross it. But after riding for a day and a night you find fresh water, enough mayhap for some 50 or 100 persons with their beasts, but not for more. And all across the Desert you will find water in a like manner, that is to say, in some 28 places altogether you will find good water, but in no great quantity; and in four places you will find brackish water.
MARCO POLO, 1298

We left Ruoqiang for the 160-mile ride across the Gobi to Mongai. This remote outpost in the desert is another asbestos mining town. There was something depressing about every aspect of this place. As we approached, open trucks hauled full loads of the deadly fiber. Most of the people on the streets wore surgical facemasks that could be only partially effective against the fine particles of asbestos. In the U.S. if you must deal with asbestos, you wear the equivalent of an astronaut's space suit and a highly filtered breathing helmet. Everywhere we looked, we saw mounds of the gray-white fiber. Both the ground and the people were fiber dusted. Those coming out of the mine looked like bakers after kneading dough. Cracks in rocks and every hole and cranny were filled with asbestos in every part of town. China may have a Bureau of Mines or a comparable organization enforcing safety and minimizing health hazards but they must be occupied with other bureaucratic activities.

Even more depressing were the home styles. Apparently this high-altitude town got very cold in the winter. The houses were built below ground, and the roofs were at sidewalk level. The windows were more like skylights. Each one- or two-room cave-like dwelling had a metal stovepipe extending into the air eight or ten feet. The construction was similar to the dug-out dwellings used by the poor dirt farmers in the U.S. Prairies during the depression of the 1930s. The wealth of this community could be judged by the proliferation of outside TV antennas, like America before cable TV. Miners were paid a substantial bonus for their hazardous work, making home TVs affordable.

Lunch was prepared for us in a shed at the edge of a courtyard filled with the carcasses of abandoned truck and mining equipment. The noodles were not well cooked. The water at this altitude did not boil at a high enough temperature to allow the noodles to finish cooking. Marco Polo also described this phenomenon when he was on the roof of the world; he thought the fire did not burn as hot because of the cold, not the lack of oxygen as scientists have told us.

Marco Polo described in great detail the characteristics, application, mining, and processing methods of asbestos. His book explained to the Western world about this magic fabric that would not burn.

We departed Mongai as quickly as possible.

There was a town deep in the Gobi that was to be our next stop on our Marco Polo trail. According to the map we received from the local authorities, the place to turn off to Polo's Sarkole was forty two miles along the main, pardon the expression, road. We came to what seemed to be the obvious point, and we peeled off across the desert. The map showed only one road as a line of dots but in reality there were many forks in the trail and many truck tracks in the Gobi. We had no idea how long ago the tracks were made since this part of the Gobi is covered in grey/black pebbles. Once the weight of a truck or a heavy donkey cart makes its impression, it will remain until something other than weather obliterates it. The terrain was perfectly flat and apparently continued that way up to a parade of small mountains scooting across the skyline some 20 to 25 miles away. Each of our drivers and his passengers believed that the ruts in the gravel they chose to travel were the most likely route to Sarkole. After ten miles of meandering across this bleak desert plain, we were all hopelessly lost. We stopped at a place where the skeleton of a camel was set up in an eerie kneeling position. The camel driver Peng Qin Yuan who was to be our guide only knew the way after we got to Sarkole. Mr. Peng was forty-eight years old and had some experience in desert travel. He was a tall, lanky man from Dun Huang where he farmed watermelons. Peng was visiting his brother in Ruoqiang when he heard we were looking for a guide to take us along the old caravan route from Baskurgan to Sarkole and then across the Gobi to Dun Huang. Not only would he be paid as our guide but also he would save the price of the bus fare home. He explained it was not really his brother but someone who was like a brother to him.

The Uighur driver of the extra jeep that carried three drums of extra fuel plus 25 gallons of water felt we should keep on going. He was in the minority. It would be dark in two hours and the majority agreed we should go back to the "main" road. We possibly had a chance of getting directions from a passing truck…well, maybe. The other alternative was to go on to the next town that we thought might be some ten miles from where we turned off the main route. We turned around and sheepishly drove back to this point. A driver of a passing truck directed us to a house further down the road. He said these people were responsible for maintaining the local roads.

By the time all the details about the road to Sarkole were accumulated, the committee of ten (i.e. all the members of our entourage at that time) determined it was too late and we headed for the oil town of Hua Tou Gou. Lao Lu said he remembered staying at the town guesthouse. Lao Lu went in and came out a few minutes later waving a copy of a photo-journal of the oil industry for Xin Hai Province. He had edited the book many years earlier and a copy was sitting on the

desk at the inn. Lao Lu realized he knew a number of the local bigwigs. With their help we quickly acquired the best accommodations in town. Since we had now reached VIP status, they even built a fire in the boiler so we could take showers in the shower house. The place had a line of over 50 showerheads (not stalls) and a giant twelve-by-twenty-four-foot bathtub, either for King Kong or a bunch of friendly people.

Our three Toyota drivers did not want to go to Sarkole from the start. They felt their vehicles would be destroyed in this rugged, remote, and long forgotten region. Everyone we talked to said that we couldn't make it. Nobody knew the condition of the road except that it hadn't been used in many years. We had heard that a six-wheeled truck with a full road crew managed to get through a few years ago. Our camel-driver guide had made it with seventy-three camels in 1983. There was no current information on Sarkole at Ruoqiang but we still wanted to try. Marco Polo did not mention Sarkole but we knew that the Old Silk Road did go along the road through Sarkole. That had to be his path. We had enough fuel, food, and water. We were carrying enough camping equipment for everyone to be reasonably accommodated.

For some unknown reason, all three drivers were sick. Two had altitude sickness, headaches and vomiting and the third had a temperature of 103 degrees Fahrenheit. There were a number of choices. One, wait for the drivers to recover; two, abort this part of the program; or three, hire another truck or jeep to go along with our

219 *Aborted Adventure*

Above: Housing was built below ground in the asbestos mining town of Mongai

remaining fuel-carrying jeep. We chose the last. The drivers' reluctance to protect their Toyotas from the harsh terrain may have been an act and a contrived sickness but it is rather difficult to fake a 103-degree temperature.

The following morning Lao Lu contacted his influential friends in town and within an hour we had a Beijing Jeep and a young driver to handle it. By 10 a.m. everything was ready. Only three people from the six-member project would be able to go. It was to be Michael, an interpreter plus myself. Xiao Yun wanted to go and be the English interpreter. We insisted on Jin Bo Hong (with a better competency in English) or Zhang (the interpreter assigned to our project). This was too dangerous a project not to have someone along with a good command of English. Zhang preferred not to go since camping out was not really his cup of tea. Xiao Yun thought that we chose Jin Bo Hong because of friendship and she was a bit miffed. She did not want to miss this exciting photo opportunity. I told the rest of the group that if we did not come back in thirty-six hours to go on to Dun Huang and we would meet them there. This of course would depend on when the Toyota drivers recuperated.

Our Uighur driver handled the first jeep and the camel driver sat in the right seat as a navigator. The back seat was filled with the drums of fuel, a good supply of water and food, and the camping gear. In the second jeep our new young driver, eager for adventure, manned the wheel. I sat beside him while Michael sat in the rear with Jin Bo Hong. Off we went to the main highway, and this time we were certain of the place to turn off for the track to Sarkole. For hours, we drove over this bleak gravel ground. The road was so rough it was impossible to travel at more than 20 miles an hour. Out in the middle of nowhere a big six-wheel truck lumbered towards us. We all got out, checking with the driver and confirming that we were on the right road to Sarkole. "Yes," he said, "you have only three more hours of driving." On three occasions my heart sank as we got lost following truck tracks that led us to unknown places. I began to feel that we would be forced to go back again before we found Sarkole. Michael climbed up on a ridge and thought he saw the right trail. It is important to understand that we were not following a marked road. In the Gobi we saw marks and ruts that could have been from animals, trucks, or jeeps as well as ridges that looked like tracks. Since it is the Gobi and not sand, some of the tracks could have been many years old; if it were sand, the wind would have allowed us to see only the most recent tracks or nothing at all. We continued to bounce down the trail. We made our way over a 12,000-foot pass then down to a flat plain at 10,000 feet altitude. I carried an altimeter with me to hopefully keep track of our location on our aeronautical maps that recorded elevation. It was a good idea but didn't work. We still did not have any notion of where we were

At the end of a vast plain we were confronted by another row of mountains that stood as sentries trying to hold us back. Just as we expected, the backside of these mountains emerged another dusty plain. The bottom of my backbone was beginning to bruise from my belt rubbing every time the jeep bounced. After our fourth or fifth range of mountains, we were following the switchback trail down the far side when we saw some sort of structure off in the distance on the far side of another flat valley. The trail headed straight across the valley floor towards this object. As we drew nearer the structure turned out to be the ruins of a single building. The valley was about six miles wide and we could not see its beginning or end…no vegetation, no hills, no boulders, and no water, nothing except this one ruin. To our shocked amazement, a small barely discernable sign in Uighur said this was Sarkole. The people who lived in this oasis had departed, not even leaving a single building with a roof. It was a dead, desolate nothingness.

As we investigated the area looking for some remnant of the past, we saw the plume of dust made by a vehicle heading straight for us. We watched it cross the valley. It was a police truck from Mongai, which joined us at the ruins of Sarkole. They were sent here because three prisoners had escaped from the jail at Milan. The theory was that since the prisoners were from Eastern China, they might try to cross the desert along this abandoned route. These police would be ready to nab them. We left the police to their duties and put our expedition on the road again. We were on the Marco Polo trail heading across the Gobi east towards Dun Huang or so we thought.

Even though we had one camel driver as a guide at this point anyone could have led the way on this obvious trail. After traveling for another hour, our convoy decided to stop to review our situation. The distance marker along the track indicated 340 miles to Dun Huang. Our maps indicated less than 240 miles. The fuel in the jeeps plus the extra fuel might not be enough to get us all the way, especially if we had extra-difficult terrain to cover. Our camel driver said there was a section of 48 miles, which would require us to make our own road. Everyone we asked said the route we were attempting was impossible. In Ruoqiang the only knowledge they had of travel along the abandoned road was the survey truck with a road building crew. It was the only vehicle to have traveled the 450-mile corridor since the late 1970s. No one in nearby Mongai or Hua Tou Gou knew how to make the journey but we were determined to give it the old college try.

Michael and I had had a great deal of experience in open desert travel. With two four-wheel drive jeeps and plenty of fuel, we were certain we could do it. After hearing horror stories about traveling across this desert from our camel driver (wolves, thieves and the like), the other two drivers became apprehensive. To our horror, the drivers then told us that our reserve fuel tank was used to fill the Toyotas and had not been replenished. Michael and I were furious. Were the jeep drivers telling us this so that we would abandon moving ahead to Dun Huang or were we really going to run out of fuel? With a marginal fuel supply, unconfident drivers, and a questionable road, to continue would have been foolhardy. We were told that it was Luo Xiao Yun who authorized the removal of the fuel. I could not imagine her reason for doing this.

The area between Sarkole and Anabar (the next abandoned town on the map) was over 150 miles with many ravines. These are ditches carved into the earth by run-off water from the mountains in the spring. The camel driver said they were as deep as a man's height and twice his height across. This we realized would have been almost impossible for our jeeps to maneuver. The decision to abort that route to Dun Huang was the right one.

The place where we had stopped was a desolate spot near the edge of the valley next to the mountain wall. Michael suggested we camp there. Wolves were also inhabitants of this area and there was concern about the escaped desperados. One of the jeep drivers worked for a petroleum company and knew of an oil-drilling camp only two hours away. It was too late to go back to Hua Tou Gou, so we headed for the oil camp. As we passed the Sarkole ruins the police were still there. We drove along a road in a southerly direction for more than an hour. Far off to the east we saw a single object on the horizon, an oilrig. We turned left and headed towards it but no matter how far we drove it seemed the same distance away. Illusions of this type are typical in the desert. After another forty minutes it started to look closer but now the road was so rough that the jeeps could not travel more than three or four miles-per-hour. We could have walked faster. We were being bounced out of our seats every few feet. There were no seat-belt requirements in China in 1985. Our Marco Polo project had taken us across rough roads but this was ridiculous. It was like driving up thousands of irregular stone steps. The surface of the earth was salt encrusted, which had turned to irregular waves of a concrete-like material that even the weekly pounding of oilrig supply trucks could not wear down. We reached the camp in another twenty minutes but it seemed like hours on this bronco ride. After we told our story, they found some space for us to sleep on the floor of one of the storage trailers.

There were about ninety workers and eleven were women. The site was called Crescent Moon Mountain. We met the twenty-six year-old vice manager Shi Wei Hua from Guangzhou (Canton). He had six years experience in this business and from all indications he was one of the oldest people in the camp. Thirty of the men were married but only one was with his wife. Compensation was pretty good by Chinese standards. Starting salary was 70 RMB per month (about $20) and with three to four years experience it increased to 300 RMB. If the oilrig made a hit, there was a bonus of 40 to 50 RMB per month. Jin Bo Hong mentioned that with many years experience as a photographer he had less income per month. We pointed out to him that he had some travel benefits, like staying at an oil camp on the floor of a cold trailer.

Because the ground was so hard they could not dig holes in it for the outhouses. It would take dynamite to penetrate the surface. Instead of a ground-level floor over a hole in the ground, they built an outhouse with a floor inside that was about three or four feet above ground. A few steps were built up to this height and the door. Inside was the traditional hole over which one would squat. When "the pile" reached the level of the hole, the entire wooden structure, which was no more than four-foot square, would be lifted and carried another fifty feet away. The old pile would remain to decay since there was no place to bury it. Such is life on the desert.

Dinner consisted of the freeze-dried foods that we brought from the REI outdoor sports store in Seattle. Jin Bo Hong went to the kitchen trailer to cook it in boiling water, but could not get the water hot enough because of the altitude. Jin solved the problem by stir-frying our meal, Chinese style. We had chicken curry with walnuts and a vegetable stew. The kitchen staff gave us some nan with warm tea. It was a very satisfying meal.

About thirty young men from the camp crowded into our trailer. We sat and drank tea and threw questions back and forth. "How far do they drill into the earth in a day?" *"About 650 feet."* "What is it that young people do in America in their spare time?' *"Music, cars, movies and girls."* We did not want to corrupt them with the addition of booze and sex. "How far will you drill this hole into the earth, and by when?" *"13,000 feet by October 1."* "Is there crime in America?" *"Yes." (With details)* "What do they do for recreation at the camp?" *"We study, play ping pong and chess, and read, but sexual fraternization between unmarried couples is forbidden."* It sounded boring to me but they may have been as discreet as we were.

The highlights of the evening were the stories told by our camel-driver guide, Peng. Mr. Peng's story started in 1972 when he wanted to visit this brother. He had little money at that time and was looking for a cheap way to go from Dun Huang to Ruoqiang. Someone told him that if he took the shortcut across the desert by donkey, it would only take him seven days to Baskurgan where he could get food and water and only a couple of more days to Milan and Ruoqiang. With only eight liters of water (about two gallons) and a small supply of food, he left with his donkey. It was July in the hottest part of the summer and he traveled by night and slept by day. The journey, much to his chagrin, was considerably longer than he was told and for which he was not prepared. As he began to realize his predicament he rationed his water to a cup a day. Two things saved his life. There was still some water in a couple of rivers he passed and between Anabar and Sarkole it rained. After twenty days he was near death and just one day from Baskurgan when a pack of seven wolves surrounded him and his donkey. He had taken an old army sword with him as a weapon and in his weakened condition he managed to hold off the wolves for half an hour. Finally, they quit and he continued. On the twenty-first day he arrived in Baskurgan and the few families who lived there gave him food and water. He again moved on to visit his brother in Ruoqiang.

Peng became famous as the crazy one who had crossed the desert alone by donkey. The donkey did not have any problem because it ate from the wild bushes that grew here and there in the desert.

Ten years later when someone wanted to take a caravan of camels across this same route from Dun Huang to Ruoqiang, everyone remembered the crazy melon farmer who had gone this way by donkey. He was hired to be the guide. This time he went in November, which was the best time of the year for camels. Even in October there is still a high level of evaporation, and the camels need more water. In November, they can go for ten days without water. The caravan Peng took included seventy-three camels that were not tied together but they were herded like sheep. They all made it to the market in Ruoqiang. It took them eighteen days, traveling at about twenty-five miles per day.

The director of the oil rig camp called Hua Tou Gou Guest House by radio telex that evening. "The Marco Polo Expedition has arrived safely at Well Number 799 and will return to Hua Tou Gou in the morning."

It was fifty miles to Hua Tou Gou, and the road was very slow. It took over three and half hours including a short break for breakfast. When we arrived, we found Lao Lu standing in the middle of the road. He stopped the jeep before we got to the guest house to talk to Jin Bo Hong; Lao Lu did not speak English. He was in tears. Apparently, because we chose Jin Bo Hong to be our interpreter instead of Luo Xiao Yun, she was upset. Xiao Yun had called the director of the CNS and complained that Michael and I were not following the direction of the CNS as per the contract. She came out to meet us also and tried to intimidate Jin Bo Hong but he would have no part of it. I can understand her concern; it could have provided a number of good photo opportunities, which she missed. She was also right regarding the contractual requirements, since she was part of the CNS and Jin Bo Hong was an independent photographer. CNS was our Chinese sponsor but I felt it was a matter of safety for the two English-speaking participants to have the best interpreter to handle any unforeseen circumstances. I tried not to get involved in a debate with Luo Xiao Yun but Lao Lu was the senior person for the CNS group and he and I were in complete agreement. When there were problems, both Lao Lu and I were flexible and solutions were always found without difficulty. I decided it was prudent not to mention the problem we had the previous day with the fuel.

We were packed, the Toyotas were loaded and the drivers had recovered. Our caravan was ready to take off for the 240-mile trip to Leng Hu (Cold Lake). Here, too, Lao Lu knew the Director of the Xin Hai Provincial Petroleum Company. On our arrival Mr. Xin warmly welcomed us with a classical Chinese banquet including many very expensive dishes. I was impressed with his hospitality since we were still on the edge of a vast desert almost a thousand miles from a major city. There was fresh fish, prawns, white tree fungus soup and more than a dozen other dishes. The drinks included Mao Tai (a 120 proof Chinese firewater), a sweet wine and the best of Chinese beers, Qing Tao. (Qing Tao was started in China by a German

Company in the 1920s and now a world wide favorite.) There were many toasts and it was a joyous celebration since we had much for which to be thankful.

After dinner, we were treated to hot showers in the Leng Hu bathhouse. A videotape deck was brought into our guesthouse and we watched a Kung Fu movie. No subtitles were needed.

As gifts, we were given copies of the photo journals that Lao Lu had consulted and edited. The book designer lived in Leng Hu and was the resident artist. Two very attractive murals that he created were in the reception room and in the court-yard of the guest house. He and his very charming, petite and beautiful wife were there when we arrived and they joined us at the banquet.

Early in the morning everyone was there to wish us farewell. On the way to Dun Huang we were allowed to travel through Aksay, which required special permission. The government did not want Americans traveling through this area. There must have been some secret missile and atomic testing-ground nearby—why else were they so concerned? Originally, we were denied access to this route, but, when it was determined that to take a back road was impossible, permission was reluctantly granted. Our driver either on his own or by someone's direction, started down a hill from a 12,500-foot pass at over 85 MPH. We were on a road outside the city so very little could be seen. All governments are afraid of the wandering eyes of foreigners around secret places. It would have been the same in the U.S. if we were taking Soviet citizens at the height of the Cold War past Los Alamos. This was a very military-sensitive part of China and without the help of the CNS and Luo Xiao Yun's father the Marco Polo Expedition would not have taken place.

Dun Huang was a very new town. The ancient Dun Huang was just on the outskirts. It had a population of 30,000 people during the Han Dynasty (110 B.C.E.) and about 60,000 residents during the Tang Dynasty (800 C.E.). After two thousand years it had over 100,000 people. That shows that the population doubled every thousand years. This type of slow growth shows stability and makes life easy for the urban planner. The ancient city was inhabited for three or four thousand years up to 1720 C.E. A tower was all that was left of the old city wall.

Tourism was becoming a major industry. Mr. Li, head of Dun Huang tour-ist office, told us that they had 130,000 in 1984; over 10,000 were foreign, mostly from Japan. They were planning five new hotels with capital from Hong Kong and Japan.

Raoqiang

Dunhuang

Zhengye

City of Pien

Lanzhou

CHINA

Hohot

Shangtu

Beijing

Huang He

Yellow
Sea

ET

CHAPTER 23

A Junction of the Silk Roads
Dun Huang, September 19 to 24, 1985

After you have traveled thirty days through the Desert, as I have described, *you come to a city called Sachiu, lying between north-east and east; it belongs to the Great Khan, and is the province called Tangut. The people are for the most part Idolaters, but there are also some Nestorian Christians and some Saracens. The Idolaters have a peculiar language, and are no traders, but live by their agriculture. They have a great many abbeys and ministers full of idols of sundry fashions, to which they pay great honor and reverence, worshipping them and sacrificing to them with much ado. For example, such as have children will feed up a sheep in honor of the idol, and at the New Year, or on the day of the Idol's Feast, they will take their children and the sheep along with them into the presence of the idol with great ceremony. They will have the sheep slaughtered and cooked, and again present it before the idol with like reverence, and leave it there before him, whilst they are reciting the offices of their worship and their prayers for the idol's blessing on their children.*
MARCO POLO, 1298

Our first day in Dun Huang was devoted to the main attraction of the area, the Mo Gao Ku also known as "Qianfor," or Grottos of a Thousand Buddhas as Marco Polo referenced in the above passage from his book. These were the best-preserved Buddhist Grottos in China and because they represented a national historic site they were not obliterated during the Cultural Revolution. So many historic sites described by Marco Polo, as well as other places important to the cultural and artistic heritage of China, were either totally destroyed or disfigured by the vicious vandals instigated by the Gang-of-Four. (The Gang-of-Four were leaders in the Communist Party who were responsible for inciting many of the atrocities and horrors of the Cultural Revolution). Mo Gao Ku has 492 caves left of the original 1,000. Many were lost from earthquakes and other natural disasters such as erosion. It is essentially China's largest museum, with some 400,000 square feet of frescoes, dating back to the fourth century, on its walls offering a detailed history of China. They were built on several levels on the face of a stone cliff displaying Chinese art and culture up to the fourteenth century. It describes daily life, cultural exchanges with foreigners, and many Buddhist stories. Within this complex there is a statue of Buddha that stands 100 feet tall and is the largest of the 2,000 Buddha statues remaining in the caves. "Cave 17" is the repository for 60,000 pieces of written scripture, documents of many types, manuscripts, and copies of block printings and rubbings. These were produced by calligraphers of the highest stature recording all manner of subjects. It includes detailed information for the study and the understanding of linguistics, politics, geography, history, music, science, religion

and everyday life that took place in these ancient times. There is now a new science known as Dunhuangology being studied here in the Dun Huang Cultural Research Institute as well as at many other facilities of higher learning throughout the world. Mo Gao Ku is truly a treasure trove of knowledge on China and the world. Its immense collection of the written word that was originally archived in Dun Huang would be the comparable to the U.S. Library of Congress or the Library of Alexandria of Ancient Egypt. The Mo Gao Ku must be considered one of China's greatest treasures.

The caves were carved out of a mountain about twelve miles from town. It all started at the time of the Six Kingdom Dynasty in 366 AD and continued up to the Yuan Dynasty, 1271 to 1368, when most of Asia was under Mongolian rule.

Remarkably, Marco Polo's book, which had an impact on the economy of all of Asia and Europe, could be blamed in part for the fact that work on the Mo Gao Ku had stopped. His book *A Description of the World* described an easier sea route to the East from Europe and as a result the traffic along the Silk Road decreased dramatically. Fewer and fewer people came this way to support the work of these Buddhist monks…so it was abandoned.

In addition to the caves that housed the many works of art, there were many caves in which the monks and others had lived and worked. We asked how many Buddhist clergy had worked at one time documenting the history and culture of China in words and art. There is no exact record but Mr. Li, our guide, said that in one day they would consume 300-jin (pounds) of rice.

Above: The Mo Gao Ku caves of Buddhas Dun Huang

In the later part of the nineteenth century, a Buddhist monk by the name of Wang Yuan accidentally discovered the long-abandoned caves and became the self-proclaimed guardian and curator of the Mo Gao Ku Grottos. He spent his life cleaning and maintaining the contents of the caves. In 1907, Auriel Stein, the explorer/archeologist, came to Dun Huang and became friends with Mr. Wang. As a result, Stein removed some 13,000 scrolls and artifacts including a gold Buddha that was sent to the British Museum. He visited Dun Huang five times between 1907 and 1930 and paid very little money for these priceless treasures. Amongst the many other "foreign devils on the Silk Road" (as identified by Peter Hopkirk of the London Times in his book with the same name) was a Dr. Langford of the Fogg Museum of Harvard who used a glue solvent that could remove the frescoes without damaging the walls. The scrolls, taken by these and other cultural desperados, were written in Chinese, Hebrew, Sanskrit, Tibetan, Ancient Uighur, Persian, and many other languages. It represented a goldmine of knowledge created over a millennium.

Marco Polo came to Dun Huang by entering the Southern Silk Road Gate to China through what is called Yang Guan Pass. All that is left of what was a massive wall and gate is a beacon tower perched on a hilltop. The Old (Southern) Silk Road threaded its way through this valley. It was here that Auriel Stein also found 800 Chinese writing sticks. These bamboo strips were from the Western Han Dynasty (112 to 111 B.C.E.) when an immigration and customs control station was in operation. The sticks were letters of introduction for business purposes and were the visas needed to allow passage along the Silk Road. Long straight sticks were used because the old Chinese calligraphy was written vertically (or Chinese calligraphy is written vertically because bamboo sticks were readily available). Apparently bureaucracies as we know them today haven't changed in over two thousand years

To the northwest of Dun Huang was the Yumen Guan, the famous Jade Gate to China and terminus of the New Silk Road (the northern route around the Taklamakan) before entering China. To reach it from Dun Huang we traveled west for 20 miles and then made a sharp right turn straight across the Gobi. The tough terrain was covered with ageless tracks of donkey carts, trucks and camels. There was no road and we traveled in a northerly direction for 50 miles before arriving at the Gate in the middle of a vast plain. There were no points of reference, no mountains in the distance, no vegetation or perturbations in the earth to use as a guide. It was another one of those flat bearingless wastelands. After hours of slowly moving across the ruts of the Gobi and certain of being lost there, you see on the horizon, a giant mud cube known as the Jade Gate for over 2,000 years. There are two stories that explain the origin of the name, Jade Gate. One was that this was the gate through which the jade came on its journey to the east from Khotan (Hotien). Instead of going along the Old Silk Road by which our expedition came, in the earlier years before Marco Polo there was the Phoenix

River that crossed the Taklamakan for a shortcut to Dun Huang by way of the site we now call the Jade Gate.

The other story was based on the legend that when camels came to this gate, they became ill. It was believed that the jade the camels carried objected to being removed from Xinjiang Province into the Gansu province of China. This made the camels sick.

Marco Polo told a story that tied in with this legend. He said that when animals that were not indigenous to this area were brought to this country that he called Tangut (an old name for the Gansu Province) they ate an herb that was poisonous. Local animals knew this plant and avoided it. If Marco Polo's story is true then it could indeed be the cause of the sickness of the camels coming from Khotan, and also explains the legend.

The evening of September 20 was a clear moonlit night and ideal for camping. We had traveled to a spot where an ancient legend took place. The sands around Ming Shan Mountains outside Dun Huang were still warm as we set up our tents. We were at the base of a massive sand dune that took Michael almost 15 minutes to climb. Darkness came and our world became quiet; as I gazed up I saw the soft flow of the Milky Way cross a sea of diamond-bright stars that lit the sky; just one of those perfect nights to sleep out of doors. The quiet was broken by strange voices. It was eerie. Everyone in our group was asleep and no one else could be seen. Remembering Marco Polo's story about how the Taklamakan would lure the unsuspecting desert traveler deeper into its unknown parts seeking the source of these alien voices, I too had no idea of what was happening. It may have been the shifting sands that made these strange sounds but for me, it still remains a mystery.

The legend of the Ming Sha Shan was about a Chinese General who came with his soldiers to camp at this same spot but at that time it was a large oasis. His soldiers were so taken with the site, they started to hoot and holler in celebration of the perfect campsite. Unbeknownst to the Chinese army, their enemy was quietly camped a few miles away and their sentries heard the noise. That night while the Chinese Army slept, the enemy invaded their camp and a great battle ensued. There was a great noise from the clatter of the swords, drums, trumpets and the shouts of the fighting soldiers. At the height of the battle a great black sand storm came

This page: Camping in the desert

and quickly covered the battle site and continued to rain sand until mountains of sand covered the place. One can still hear the sounds of the battle cries in the sand. This may have been the answer to my mystery.

On September 22, the Marco Polo Expedition went through the Jade Gate and our project experienced a metamorphosis. No longer were we to be subject to the sometimes-primitive conditions and rigors of desert travel. The Jade Gate is near the western end of the Great Wall and has been historically known as the door to Old China. Here the dominant religion changes from Islam to Buddhism. In the far western province of Xinjiang we found mosques in nearly every village. I define China as the area of the People's Republic of China where the ethnic Chinese, known as Han, are the dominant population. After entering Eastern China, we discovered the mosques were gone, replaced by some of the old and many restored Buddhist temples. During the Cultural Revolution (1966 to 1976) most of the temples were partially ravaged or totally destroyed. The great bronze Buddha statues were melted down for scrap, wooden Buddhas burned, and those of stone pulverized. Much of the art and beauty of ancient China was gone. On one hillside, a hundred life-size stone Buddha statues were decapitated. Because of this devastation we can no longer see many of the places that Marco Polo described. A few of these places identified by the central government as of historical importance had been saved. The 110-foot reclining Buddha that Marco Polo saw in Zheng Ye survived. The Buddhist monk who was now the caretaker of this ancient temple had spent twenty-two years in labor camps because he had refused to renounce his religion. All this changed under Deng Xiao Ping.

In 1979, freedom of religion had been given back to the Chinese. Many temples and religious shrines were now being restored. As one Chinese gentleman told me "God is now looking favorably on China because since 1979 (and freedom of religion) the total Chinese economy has increased 10 percent to 15 percent per year with a minimum inflation."

We found the farmers were also doing especially well. Privately owned enterprises were flourishing throughout the country and executives of profitable companies received big bonuses. This was part of the new free enterprise system established by Deng Xiao Ping.

Above: Camels, the ideal desert transport system

In a few days we would be traveling down the Silk Road through the Gansu Corridor surrounded by mountain ranges with the Great Wall meandering back and forth across our trail. In Gansu Province, we would no longer have to breathe the dust of the desert. We would be in valleys painted green by the water of ancient irrigation systems with an overwhelming proliferation of fruits, grains and vegetables of every description and some that were indescribable.

It was along this stretch of road that Marco, his father, and his uncle met a welcoming committee of the Kublai Khan who escorted them to Shangtu, Kublai Khan's summer palace. They had been traveling for over three and a half years since leaving Venice. We too were being given royal privileges by the Chinese government allowing us to visit ancient sites not seen by foreigners since the establishment of the Peoples Republic of China. We felt like pioneers opening a road through a vast new and exotic world. It had been three thousand miles of traveling along the Silk Road since we crossed the Kunjerab Pass between Pakistan and China. In the city of Lanzhou at the far end of Gansu Province, our Marco Polo trail left the Silk Road and headed north along the Yellow River to Xanadu, as Samuel Coleridge branded the Great Khans' "stately pleasure-dome" and summer home.

After a few days of traveling west to visit the Jade Gate and other sites in the desert, we returned to the Dun Huang Hotel. A group of English-speaking tourists from Europe and America were now visiting the hotel. After a few conversations, they asked if we would present an impromptu talk about Marco Polo and our project. A meeting room was arranged and that evening about fifty people attended. Michael gave some introductory remarks and details about our project and the Marco Polo Foundation. He explained how our educational foundation was set up to carry on the work of Marco Polo to introduce the East to the West with books, magazine articles, film/videos and lectures like the one we were giving that night. I then presented the story of Marco Polo and our expedition. During the question-and-answer period, Michael told how disaster after disaster followed wherever we traveled. Michael explained, "There was a major earthquake in Agri, Turkey, killing almost 4,000 people. Tabas, Iran, was destroyed as 12,000 died of the 14,000 people who lived in this oasis in the middle of the desert. Everyone knew what happened to the Shah of Iran and how Afghanistan fell victim to the Russians just after the Marco Polo Expedition left these countries. As we crossed a mountain pass in Pakistan, an earthquake of a level of 6.1 on the Richter scale killed hundreds and left thousands wounded and homeless. Just a few weeks ago there was an earthquake in Eastern China that was so shocking that Harry and I jumped out the window of the building in which we were having dinner. There was no question that wherever the Marco Polo Expedition traveled a catastrophe was sure to follow." A gentleman from the British touring group asked when we were leaving. We said in about five days. He said, "Good, we're leaving tomorrow. We don't want to be leaving after you."

The next day, the person who inquired about our departure date, a surgeon, was riding in a car leading the bus carrying the other British tourists. A Beijing 212 jeep was traveling in the opposite direction. The two vehicles crashed head-on, as they rounded a sharp curve on a mountain road. The surgeon was killed. Three others of his party were in hospitals. The driver for the British tour group lost his legs and eyes. The driver of the other car was killed and his five passengers were injured.

A few days later, we drove from Dun Huang to Jiuquan. There, along the mountain roadside, were the two wrecked carcasses of these vehicles, left at the scene as a warning to other drivers. The surgeon was traveling in a black Shanghai Car, a large sedan made in Shanghai. It was folded in on its driver's side as if a giant sledgehammer had hit it. The Beijing Jeep had been totally devoured by fire, leaving nothing but bent metal. All that remained of its tires were a few steel wires. It was not until that moment of seeing this scene of death that the full impact of my involvement with this tragedy hit me. These were the people with whom I had shared my Marco Polo story, recounting to them as an aside the disasters that had followed our path. I was profoundly moved. No, I was shocked and I hurt inside, as if in some way I was responsible. There was nothing I could do. Later, I tried to visit the survivors and was told I could not because it was a military hospital. Army helicopters took the British accident victims to the hospital. I was told everything possible had been done to save the doctor's life and to help the others.

As I walked out of the meeting room at which the Marco Polo lecture was given, the French tour leader of the Jules Vern Travel Group said he wanted to introduce me to someone special. It was Liu Yu Tien, probably the most famous modern-day traveler in China. He had walked the entire length of all the Great Walls of China during the previous year, a distance of over 10,000 Li (about 3,400 miles). He did this with no support team, no animals to carry food and water, no rendezvous points where the comfort of a tent and refreshments could be provided, nothing but his two legs and an extremely strong and durable body, and he was the first person known to have accomplished this feat. Part of his conditioning for the long march along "the wall" was to walk on broken glass to toughen the soles of his feet. Just looking at this medium build man of forty-two years told me immediately, that this was a special person. A thick dark skin that had survived endless days in the hot sun belied his modesty and humility, as do the many hundreds of nights sleeping on the frozen, snow covered ground. He maintained himself with a 20-pound backpack that contained all the food, water and clothing he felt he needed, plus a camera to document his journey. Two years earlier he had retired from the Railroad Bureau in Urumqi, and was now supported by the Old Soldiers Society.

His wife and daughters, nine and thirteen year old, waited for him in Urumqi. He started walking the Great Walls from the Po Hai (a sea on the Eastern Coast) on May 13, 1984, and arrived at the western end in the Taklamakan in February 1985. In March 1985, he started to follow the Old Silk Road from Xian, the ancient capital of China. His goal was to walk to Islamabad. He would be following part of our route in reverse. That night we stayed up late to talk with this warm, beautiful person. He told us how his children clung to his legs pleading that he should not go. My children had said the same thing to me. He and I truly understood one another, yet we had no common language. It was the desire to pursue the unknown and to be pioneers by following the rarely traveled roads of history, to meet and win the challenges not reached by others.

When we suggested that he take a donkey with him across the desert, his face wrinkled and his hands gestured total rejection to the idea. The same response I would give someone suggesting I take an easier route for my Marco Polo project. There is an expression in Chinese "*Xin Shi Zou Kou*" which means "Walking Body Dead Spirit." It is the path so many people take. When they are young they have special dreams and aspirations. They then choose a life that is easier to follow and their spirit or soul dies while their body lives on to an old age.

We agreed to meet with Lui on Monday morning when we would all go out to visit the White Horse Pagoda (*Bei Ma Ta*). It was just a couple of miles from the center of town and a few hundred yards from the only section left standing of the old city wall.

The name "White Horse" was also based on another legend. A Buddhist monk was making his way from India to China and traveling on a white horse. When they arrived in Dun Huang after passing through the Jade Gate the horse became ill. That night the monk had a dream. In the dream the horse spoke to him and told him that he was a dragon horse (or heavenly horse). The Gods had sent him to carry the monk to China. By going through the Jade Gate they had reached China, and his mission was complete. The horse said he must now return to heaven. In his dream the monk grabbed the horse by its mane and said he had a great distance to go. The horse replied that there was another dragon horse nearby who would serve the monk. The next morning, the monk woke up and found the white horse died during the night. To honor the horse and the legend, a pagoda was built in memory of the heavenly white horse.

I said goodbye to and wished Liu Yu Tien well on his journey to Islamabad. From his backpack he took out a white silk scarf. It was a Kata, the sacred Buddhist scarf that is an auspicious symbol and sometimes blessed by a Lama. It offers a positive note to the beginning of a relationship or enterprise to show the good intentions of the person offering it. The Kata is usually given when meeting a Lama or the Dalai Lama. Liu placed the Kata around my neck in front of the White Horse Pagoda and we quietly bowed to one another.

Liu and I had both arrived at Dun Huang on the same day. This was the halfway point for both of us on our travels across China in opposite directions; and

we met at Dun Huang, one of the most sacred Buddhist sites in China. Here we were, two travelers pursuing challenges that others have not conquered, meeting at this obscure junction of the old and new Silk Roads. This was another one of those unfathomable coincidences that made my journey really special.

235 *A Junction of the Silk Roads*

Above: The White Horse Pagoda

CHAPTER 24

Beyond the Jade Gate
Gansu Province, September 24 to 29, 1985

heng Ye is also a city in Tangut (Gansu) and a very great and noble one. Indeed it is the capital and place of government of the whole province of Tangut. The people are Idolaters, Saracens, and Christians, and the latter have three very fine churches in the city, whilst the Idolaters have many ministers and abbeys after their fashion. In these they have an enormous number of idols, both small and great, certain of the later being a good ten paces in stature; some of them being of wood, others of clay, and others being of stone. They are all highly polished and then covered with gold. The great idols of which I speak lie at length. And round about them there are other figures of considerable size, as if adoring and paying homage before them.

Now, as I have not yet given you particulars about the customs of these Idolaters, I will proceed to tell you about them.

You must know that there are among them certain religious recluses who lead a more virtuous life then the rest. These abstain from all lechery, though they do not indeed regard it as a deadly sin; howbeit if any one sin against nature they condemn him to death. They have an Ecclesiastical Calendar as we have; and there are five days in the month that they observe particularly; and on these five days they would on no account either slaughter any animal or eat flesh meat. On those days, moreover, they observe much greater abstinence altogether than on other days.

Among these people a man may take thirty wives, more or less, if he can but afford to do so, each having wives in proportion to his wealth and means; but the first wife is held in highest consideration. The men endow their wives with cattle, slaves, and money, according to their ability. And if a man dislikes any one of his wives, he just turns her off and takes another. They take to wife their own cousins and their fathers' widows (always excepting the man's own mother), holding to be no sin many things that we think to be grievous sins, and, in short they live like beasts.

MARCO POLO, 1298

It was a long 264-mile ride from Dun Huang to the city of Jiuquan. Our small convoy of Toyotas stopped in the town of Ansi for the Hami melons.

During the Ming Dynasty (after 1368 C.E.), a giant fortress was built at this western end of the Great Wall known as Jiuquan Pass. The earlier Great Wall built by the Han Dynasty (100 B.C.E.) was still there. As we approached we found Imperial Yurts, of the type used 1,000 years ago, set up within the walls of the Jiuquan Fortress. To our surprise we had just stumbled on to the set for a major movie. The yet unnamed film was based on the romantic true tale of an envoy from Tibet by the name of Lu Dong Zan who was sent by his king to win the hand of Princess

Wen Cheng, the beautiful and talented daughter of the Tang Dynasty emperor, Tang Tai Zong. Five envoys represented the applicants for marriage to this desirable Princess. The Emperor devised five tasks to help him make this critical decision. The Princess would marry the master of the cleverest envoy.

The first task was to thread a silk thread through a giant pearl whose narrow hole twisted and turned in nine directions before exiting. Four of the envoys failed. Lu Dong Zan tied the thread to the body of an ant and blew upon the ant until it exited from the other end with the thread. For the second test, they were all shown a hundred mares and the same number of colts. The five contestants were asked which colt belonged to which mare. The others were again at a loss, but the Tibetan envoy told the grooms not to give any of the colts any water in the evening. In the morning, their thirst drove them straight to their mothers to be nursed. Lu Dong Zan won again. The third and fourth tasks were passed without difficulty. The fifth was to pick the princess out of 2,500 maidens. He learned of a concealed birthmark from her former attendant who ran the Inn where he stayed. It was a clean sweep, and he won the grand prize, the hand of the princess for his master.

It was the year 641 C.E. and Tibet was then known as the Kingdom of Tufan and still quite backward. The road from Xian to Lhasa took two years to travel through icy passes, turbulent rivers, and the world's highest mountains. Princess Wen Cheng's huge dowry of gold, silver, silks, and jewels were hauled by hundreds of camels, yaks and packhorses. She also brought much of her sophisticated Chinese culture and lifestyle including Buddhist and Confucian classics. There were books on horticulture, medicine, and engineering technology, plus seeds known to grow in dry, cold climates. In her entourage were a number of artisans and medical practitioners.

Above: Jiuquan Fortress at the western end of the Great Wall

On arrival she was married to the King of Tufan. The Potala Palace, which was built as her residence, was the grandest and most luxurious for its time. It stands today as a great work of engineering excellence. The new queen was a devout Buddhist and she introduced this religion to Tibet.

The memory of this majestic lady is still revered today. She is credited with the design of two monasteries and some four hundred temples. Tibetans believe that the princess introduced and taught the techniques of weaving, spinning, and embroidery. Princess Wen Cheng lived for forty years in Tibet and died in the year 680 C.E. There is a statue of her in the Potala and two festivals are celebrated each year in her honor.

Hanging around the fortress during the filming of this story was very exciting. It offered many opportunities for photographs of handsome camels and beautiful actors in seventh century costumes against the background of this ancient monument in a totally isolated part of the world. One of the biggest advantages of taking a photographic expedition across a desert is that the weather is always excellent for taking pictures. This encounter with the film production was another one of those lucky happenstances that continually occurred.

Jiuquan is a city whose name means "Wine Spring." During the Han Dynasty, as the story goes, a general came to this city to celebrate his army's victory and share wine with his men. Since he did not have enough wine to go around, he poured the wine he had into the town well, a well that had always produced pure water. After the general's contribution, nothing but bubbling wine was drawn from this well for hundreds of years. Even today we found the smell of wine permeates the air around the well, now located at the center of the city park. No one seemed to have an explanation.

Above: The wine spring in Jiuquan City

Jiuquan is also famous for the jade it brings to market taken from the Qilian Mountains nearby. The jade is smooth and transparent and has beautiful veins of different colors running through it. We visited a factory where the special jade cups called "Moonlight cups" were made with walls as thin as an eggshell. This jade came in the unusual colors of blackish green and yellow in various shades up to a cheese white. Cheese white was unique for jade but it was the name of the color the workers gave us as we toured their factory. We attended many banquets in this area where these cups were never used for the wines. They were considered decorative; I bought two of them to display in my living room at home.

Not far from Jiuquan and within sight of the smoke stacks of its steel mill, Chinese archeologists discovered fourteen Han Dynasty tombs. The one we climbed down to visit was about thirty-five feet underground and fairly well preserved. The walls and the vaulted ceiling were all constructed of fired brick and something of which a modern day structural engineer would be proud to have built. The most interesting feature of the tomb was the individually painted bricks. The face of each brick was about five by eleven inches and each had a different pictorial story. On one wall, bricks were displayed with two-thousand-year-old stories of the daily life of the master buried in that tomb. He must have been a fairly rich person as depicted on the scenes we saw. To afford such an elaborate tomb also indicated his great wealth. The paintings also showed his dealings with other high-ranking officials. I would also say he was a bit pretentious. There was a picture showing him using a large jewel encrusted three-pronged fork. He was not using it to pick up food but as a skewer for cubes of meat to make shashlik (shish-kabob). It was a very expensive triple skewer.

I once heard the story of a woman who was having her portrait painted. She asked the artist if she would paint her wearing a necklace of large diamonds supporting a huge ruby in a pendant. The artist said, "Of course." The woman said, "I would also like you to paint a bracelet of large diamonds and giant diamond earrings." The artist agreed but asked, "Why?" The woman answered, "If I die before my husband, I want his second wife to go crazy looking for the jewels."

On the opposite wall were thirty bricks showing the daily life of the master's wife. It was like seeing home movies of a family who lived 2,000 years ago.

On a back street in downtown Jiuquan was an old mosque. As we walked down the narrow dark alleyway to its entrance, we saw workers repainting the outside columns. It was being totally rebuilt since the Red Guard left it in ruins during the Cultural Revolution. The term Cultural Revolution revolts me since it implies a peaceful change in the culture of the people. After traveling to many parts of China and seeing the devastation of this revolution, I would consider calling it a "Cultural Holocaust." It was a mass destruction of artistic, spiritual, and intellectual institutions and everything they represented, at every level, plus all the people with whom they were connected. They destroyed all that was beautiful and related to the essence of what we think of as being Chinese. Many of the people who held Chinese and other endemic cultures dear to their hearts and soul were also lost. All the people of China were touched in some painful way during these ten years of insanity. I found very few people in China who wished to speak about this period.

The mosque was a typical example of the thousands upon thousand of heinous acts that occurred between 1966 and 1976. The prayer books (the Koran) and religious reference books were burned. The new imam, Ma Sha Li, showed us a few they had saved by burying them. Since 1976 the government had published many new books to replace those that were lost. The Cultural Revolution forced all of the one thousand Islamic families of this area to leave their homes in Gansu Province and flee to the Muslim-dominated province of Xinjiang. Since 1979 over two hundred families had returned and were supporting the mosque and the imam. Every Friday about one hundred people came to pray.

The Imam Ma was forty-six years old and has been married since he was 19. They had two children. They too left Jiuquan in the late 1960s. He was jailed and forced to work in the countryside. After 1976, he studied Islam in Urumqi and became an imam. His first mosque was in Hami. Typical of bureaucratic screw-ups, he was a Sunni Muslim assigned to a Shiite mosque. He of course had no support from his congregants. The Muslims who returned to Jiuquan were Sunni and wanted to reestablish their mosque. They applied for a permit and went to Hami to invite Ma back to Jiuquan. The local Muslim families and businesses gave 2.5 percent of their income to support the mosque. The farmers gave 1% of their grain. This was called *zekat*.

In the reception room of the mosque there were two clocks in case one failed. The time for prayer is very critical. A tapestry of the Great Wall hung on the wall with three calendars in Arabic. A bed, a bookcase, a standing closet, a desk and chair, a fluorescent ceiling fixture, a couch and four soft chairs made up his entire home. The floor was brick.

According to the good imam there were numerous differences between the Sunni and the Shiite. The Chinese Culture has had substantial influence over the Shiites. He said, for example, the Shiite burn incense during a funeral. They have learned to greet each other with clasped hands in the Chinese fashion where the Sunni greet their comrades in the traditional Islamic manner of holding the right hand over the heart and saying *Salam Aleikum* (Peace be on to you). However, the fundamental difference between Sunni and Shiite is that Shiite believe Ali, son-in-law and cousin of Mohammad, was his successor and Sunnis do not. A hundred years ago the city of Jiuquan had over 100,000 Muslims. The conflict between Sunni and Shiite is an issue all over the world as it has been for centuries. I believed that the strong Chinese government and their policy of integrating a large Han Chinese population into Western China has kept the problem quiet. The Uighur population of Xinjiang Province has always wanted their own Muslim state.

Since 1979 and the implementation of what Deng Xiao Ping called the Responsibility System, the organization that was once called a commune was now known as a township. A production brigade became an administrative village and a production team was now a natural village. The natural village of Sui Me Gou which was part of the township of Quan Hu (Spring Lake) was our destination. The director of Quan Hu was a twenty-eight-year-old middle school graduate by the name of Ma Guo Jian. He was the leader of 8,440 people for which he received a salary of 100 RMB per month (less than a dollar a day). There were ten villages and ninety natural villages with a total of 4,440 workers. The total farmland covers 40,000 Mu (6,100 acres), growing mostly corn and wheat. There were of course many other vegetables and a type of hemp called "wu mu" that provides a seed used for making a cooking oil.

This would be called a "model township," which is probably why they showed it to us. The average income per family had doubled in the past five years. The extra money these peasants received was used to buy new houses, TVs, house appliances or farm machinery. The new Responsibility System now allows the establishment of private enterprises. As a result the Township has 122 different private businesses in building construction, blacksmiths, transportation, and retail operations. The township was also investing in enterprises such as asbestos mining in the nearby Qilian (pronounced Chilean) Mountains. The local government, as in Marco Polo's time, considered asbestos an important source of revenue.

Mr. Ma said that the success of their township was due, in a large part, to what we would call the "private sector" that now represented 50 percent of the economy. Their annual income to spend on the community was about 500,000 RMB. This would be used to improve schools and hospitals. Roads were partly funded by the Township and the balance by those who will benefit from it.

Interesting stories can pop up in unusual places. We had asked about the various minorities and in particular the Yu Gou minority who were from the Qilian Mountains. It turned out there were a few Yu Gou families in the township and arrangements were made for us to meet one. This particular family was given a special permit to engage in a transportation enterprise that would compete with a government operation. We met Ba Ji Ren, a thirty-six-year-old Yu Gou man and his wife, who told us about their lives and enlightened us about the Yu Gou culture. The Yu Gou minority believes in the yellow branch of Lamaist Buddhism (the Tibetans worship in the black branch). Their garments, however, were similar to the Tibetans.

Marco Polo mentions many unusual sexual mores as he traveled through China. This interview with the Ba family introduced us to a custom that would be considered not only unusual but immoral by either Western or Chinese standards of propriety. The age for a Yu Gou girl to marry is not important. Some marry as young as thirteen years. Mr. Ba's eyes flashed with pride and excitement as he proceeded to describe the lifestyle of his people. He said that a father would build a separate room or a small house for his daughter after she reaches a marriageable age. She then becomes sexually independent and may invite whomever she pleases to sleep with her in her new home. This, we were told, was not considered to be promiscuous behavior by their cultural standards. Her guest would be someone she might consider a good prospect for marriage. If she became pregnant, the new parents generally wed after the baby was born.

Regarding food, the Yu Gou people were forbidden to eat horse or donkey meat, fish, or the heads of chickens. (A delicacy at many Chinese banquets that I have attended was sparrow soup in which the head of the sparrow is floating.) They did not have a written language, but they had their own spoken language. It was believed that they came to the Qilian Mountains 2,000 years ago during the Han Dynasty from Mongolia. Today they were a relatively small minority with over 2,500 people living in Jiuquan County and an additional nine thousand Yu Gou people still lived in the nearby Qilian Mountains. There were only six family groups with the following surnames: Ba, Tau, Cha, Leng, You, and Gong.

They had three funeral ceremonies. The choice was Earth, Fire or Sky. The Earth was the standard method of burying the body in the ground. For Fire, the procedure was to cremate the body. Placing the corpse on the back of a yak and sending it off into the mountains carried out the last choice for a funeral ceremony. This was called the funeral of the Sky. Wherever the corpse fell off, would be where vultures, eagles, and hawks ate the flesh. This place was then considered the paradise for the deceased.

To our surprise the Ba family was extremely rich by Chinese standards and relatively rich by any standards. They lived in a modest three-room house of mud and fired brick with a courtyard around the main building. In the back was a shed that held what looked like a ton of green peppers. Farming green peppers was a sideline business. Mr. Ba's prime source of income was a transportation project that he had started about a year earlier. He now owned two buses for which he paid a total of 110,000 RMB. Even with the taxes, his net income was between 60,000 and 70,000 RMB per year. He could retire within a few years and live comfortably off the interest his nest egg could generate.

In 1984 the Central Committee of the Communist Party suggested families get into specialized businesses. Ba Ji Ren studied various possibilities and determined that transportation could be the most profitable. He chose the Jiuquan to Dun Huang bus route because it always seemed crowded with tourists and workers who lived in Jiuquan and worked in the asbestos mines. It was also the ideal distance to make a round trip each day (240 miles each way). His competition was the state-owned bus line. He charged exactly the same fare but he offered cool drinks in the summer and tea and bread in the winter. We received a sample of the cool drinks at his house. Because of the better service, he had taken a lot of business away from his competition, the Chinese government.

He was not certain about the future. There was a great deal of pressure and responsibility in running a business, and he was concerned the state might take over his bus enterprise. If things looked more promising over the next year, he planned to run it for a few more years and then return to his first love, raising green peppers.

As we traveled easterly down the Gansu Corridor we were always in sight of the snow-covered Qilian mountains to the south. Before liberation (1949) they were identified as the Rickover Mountain Range, in honor of the German geographer (Von Rickover) who traveled and documented China starting in 1868. Another term for the Gansu Corridor between the Qilian Mountains and the various ranges that parallel them to the north is He Xi. This refers to the Huang He (Yellow River) and Xi meaning west and Marco Polo called it Tangut.

From Jiuquan it was 150 miles to Zheng Ye along a good two-lane paved road bisecting the wheat and cornfields of the Prefecture. Our Toyota Land Cruisers had to jog and maneuver wide to avoid camel carts, donkey carts, man-pulled carts, bicyclists, hand trucks, and both men and women farmers with heavily loaded bamboo shoulder sticks across their backs. Tens of thousands of farm trucks and buses rumble down the roads of China. Now and then we saw the occasional passenger car or jeep, most likely owned by a state organization or industrial enterprise. The equivalent of a privately owned Mercedes in China was the Suzuki 100. In our travels, the Chinese-made motorcycles and mopeds that were starting to proliferate throughout the country were becoming the main people mover. In our travels through Iran in 1975, the motorcycle was beginning to replace the donkey for carrying hay and other farm produce.

One of the most important sites to visit for a modern day explorer in Zheng Ye was the Temple of the Giant Sleeping Buddha that our Thirteenth Century explorer described. He referred to Buddhists as Idolaters.

He said this reclining Buddha was 10 paces long, which was very close to the true measurement of thirty-five feet. The distance between steps for an average height man is about three feet, which at ten paces would be thirty feet and close enough to Marco Polo's estimate of the "statue" of the Buddha.

When Marco Polo was dictating the story of his travels to Rusticiano in the jail in Genoa, he had asked that his diaries and references of his travels be sent to him from Venice to help him remember the trip that he took twenty years earlier. The accuracy of such a minute detail, such as the length of a sleeping Buddha in remote Western China, gives further credence of the authenticity of the Marco Polo book.

CHAPTER 25

Fortune Cookies and Bound Feet
Inner Mongolia, September 29 to October 9, 1985

N ow it came to pass in the year of Christ's Incarnation 1187 that the Tartars made them a King whose name was Genghis Khan. He was a man of great worth, and of great ability and valour. And as soon as the news that he had been chosen King was spread abroad through those countries, all the Tartars in the world came to him and owned him for their Lord. And right well did he remain the Sovereignty they had given him. What shall I say? The Tartars gathered to him in astonishing multitude, and when he saw such numbers he made a great furniture of spears and arrows and such other arms as they used, and set about the conquest of all those regions till he had conquered eight provinces. When he conquered a province he did no harm to the people or their property, but merely established some of his own men in the country along with a proportion of theirs, whilst he led the remainder to the conquest of other provinces. And when those whom he had conquered became aware how well and safely he protected them against all others, and how they suffered no ill in his hands, and saw what a noble prince he was, then they joined him heart and soul and became his devoted followers. And when he had gathered such a multitude that they seemed to cover the earth, he began to think of conquering a great part of the world.

MARCO POLO, 1298

Each town we visited had its own identifying character; sometimes the people and their culture, sometimes the place and its environment; it could be an unusual community tradition, but always something special. This is what makes traveling so exciting, today or as it was 700 years ago when Mr. Polo went this way. Black Water Town could be just another backwater town along the Silk Road but the night we spent there was party time with a full moon, to boot. In America we call this the harvest moon but in China they celebrate the Mid Autumn Moon Festival or Zhong Qiu. There were lantern processions, candy for the children, and moon cakes for everyone. It was very much like an Oriental Thanksgiving combined with the Fourth of July. Red foods such as tomatoes, peppers, cherries, berries, apples, and red potatoes were favored for good luck. The moon cakes were shaped like a moon (surprise!) and filled with sesame seeds, ground lotus seeds and duck eggs. Eating the moon cake was a tradition that can be traced back to the early fourteenth century. A fascinating ancient tale about this tradition occurs at the time the Chinese started their revolt against the Mongolians. The Chinese formed an army under the command of General Chu Yuen-Chang and his deputy, Liu Po-wen. They conceived a secret moon cake strategy as a way to launch an assault against the heavily fortified Black Water Town. Liu, disguised as a Taoist priest, entered the city to distribute moon cakes. When it was time for the Zhong-Qui moon festival, the people opened the moon cakes and found a hidden message inside advising them to coordinate their uprising with the troops who were to attack the citadel from the outside. Chu Yuen-chang took the city and became the king. The tale was somewhat like the "Trojan Horse" story, with fortune cookies.

That evening we attended a banquet of the Autumn Moon Festival (the 15th of the eighth month on the Moon Calendar) and for desert we enjoyed, what else, moon cakes with entertainment by beautifully dressed ladies dancing and singing. It was party time.

The trip to Wu Wei is 138 miles from Black Water Town. It was a small town by Chinese standards (population about 25,000) but very old. It dates back to before the Han Dynasty (206 B.C.E.). This traditionally strategic site was located where roads (and now railroads) from Lanzhou to the south and Ningxia Province to the east were joined to form the main Silk Road heading west. In ancient times it was called "Silver Wu Wei" because of the prosperity and wealth created by Silk Road commerce. Wu Wei had seen its day and now was just a shadow of what it had been in ancient times.

It was here in Wu Wei, after excavating the two-thousand-year-old Han Tomb of Leitai, archeologists found hundreds of gold, silver, bronze, iron, jade, bone and pottery artifacts. The ninety-nine bronze warriors and their horses were the prize pieces of this treasure. It was the bronze flying horse, more often called the "Heavenly Horse," that became most notable. These Heavenly Horses have become the internationally recognized logo for Chinese tourism and now a symbol of China. It is seen and used everywhere in China and as promotional material around the world.

To get to the tomb, we had to go through a narrow underground tunnel, some seventy feet long. We entered a series of three coffin chambers, each with a side chamber where some ancient potentate and his family were buried with much of their most treasured worldly possessions. We had visited many underground tombs, and they all had that same eerie feeling, as if the spirits of the deceased were still hanging around. I may have been reflecting the reaction I had to the scary ghost movies of my youth but cramped underground tombs were still spooky.

In the afternoon we had an opportunity for another "exciting" visit to a Bell Tower. (Was I getting burned out on the repetitious tourism visits?) We'd walked through, up, and down dozens of Bell and Drum towers since entering China through the Jade Gate. These monstrous percussion devices were used to announce the opening and closing of the city gates, sunrise, sunset, time of day, or possibly a call to arms. These bell towers were an exaggerated version of the rural American town clocks.

One of the most interesting and visually rewarding places we visited in this area was the Hai Zang Temple, located about a couple of miles northwest of Wu Wei, with a large complex of ancient buildings. Wu Wei had an overabundance of ancient buildings for a town its size. The Hai Zang Temple was found within a

labyrinth of well-preserved gateways, archways, walkways, pavilions, and temples from both the Ming and Qing Dynasties (1368 to 1911). A river, a lake, and age-old trees made the park a quiet, peaceful place to stop, meditate, and absorb the spectacular scenery surrounding the complex.

As we left the temple grounds we saw four very old women struggling down the path. They could barely walk, not because of their age or lack of strength, but because they had been subjected to the ancient Chinese tradition of having their feet bound as children. We asked to talk with them. They were all over sixty and one was over eighty years old. They were dressed in identical clothes, all black from head literally to toes, which they may or may not have had. Children with bound feet usually lost their toes to gangrene. Each old woman wore a black skull cap with a black, loose fitting shirt. It looked as if the shirts were made from two pieces of a heavy black cotton cloth shaped in the form of a "T" and sewn together with openings for the head, body, and arms. The black pants were probably made in a similar fashion but shaped like an inverted "V." On their tiny feet they wore homemade, heavy, black cloth slippers. In the countryside and in the smaller cities and towns, most of the older women were similarly dressed, totally in black.

The feet were bound in order to make the foot smaller, daintier, and more beautiful in the eyes of Chinese men. It was called "San Cun Jin Lian" meaning three golden lotuses. The goal was for the foot to be no more than three or four inches

Top row of left and right page: Various sections of the 2300 year old Great Wall that was crossed by the Marco Polo Expedition

Middle: The Great Wall built after 1368
Bottom: Modern renovated Great Wall near
Beijing

in length. The girls with bound feet could barely stand and would walk hobbled. Men viewed this teeter-totter sway as erotic. When not assisted by someone else, it was usually easier for these women to get around by crawling.

They told us the harrowing story about themselves as children subjected to this trauma. When a girl turned three or four years old in China, before Liberation, her mom, who may also have had bound feet, would rip up strips of cloth and start binding her feet. The wrappings would be taken off each night then rewound the next day tighter. Sometimes the toes would be broken so they could be folded under the foot. The bones on the top of the foot would also be broken and the ball of the foot buckled in then wrapped to the heel. All this pain and suffering was considered insignificant in the quest for tiny feet and the prospect of a more prosperous marriage. Thank God the practice of binding feet is now illegal.

We said our "thank-yous" and goodbyes as the four women hobbled off down the path, supporting one another.

Marco Polo's book did not make reference to the practice of foot-binding, Chinese calligraphy or even the regular drinking of tea. Historians are not certain if he did or did not mention these three aspects of Chinese culture. The original two books dictated by Polo and written by Rusticiano were lost over 500 years ago and only 136 copies of the original survived. They were written in many different languages by copyists who made their own translations and interpretations of what they read. In addition, we do not know what may have been edited in or out of the manuscript by Rusticiano. Bound feet may have been such a ludicrous custom in the mind of Rusticiano that he told Marco no one would believe it, so it may have been taken out of the text. We just don't know. The Polo book rarely mentions his daily life, his clothes, his method of travel or what he ate each day. In addition, Marco Polo, his father and uncle were the guests of the Mongolians not the Chinese, which would explain why many things related to Chinese life were not referenced. Most of the descriptions and name places were written in the Mongolian language not Chinese. *The Description of the World* was the story of a man and what he saw and heard on a journey that occurred four to twenty-seven years before he dictated the book. The travels covered almost 50,000 miles and 23 years; all crammed into a single volume that was hand written. It was very obvious that he had to leave some things out of his story.

The true story may never be known, but as we traveled further along the trail that Marco Polo described we were able to verify the accuracy of more and more of the minutiae in his book.

There are those who dispute that Marco Polo went to China because of omissions. He does not mention the Great Wall yet he had to have crossed it many times as we did. This oversight could be justified since, at the time he traveled, the Great Wall was not great. It was no more than a large mound of earth. The wall that the world now recognizes was built during the Ming Dynasty, almost a hundred years after Marco Polo came to China. In the thirteenth century walls were everywhere. Every village, town and city had one. In addition, the Great Wall was originally built to keep the Mongolians out of China and mentioning these walls may have been an affront to his hosts. To have included all that he saw, heard and experienced would have filled many volumes and as Marco Polo said on his deathbed, "I have not told half of what I saw."

Travel to Lanzhou, the largest city in Gansu Province, was 155 miles.

I woke up early on our first day in Lanzhou to go jogging for a few miles, a ritual that I started in 1970 when I realized that being in good physical condition would be a prerequisite for my Marco Polo trek. The sun was up, and there were many bicyclists on the streets heading for work. On leaving the inn I noticed the air smelled really bad and I made all sorts of rationalizations as to its source, maybe an overflowing sewage line, perhaps a fertilizer or chemical plant nearby, stockyards—whatever, something was rotten in Lanzhou. As I ran, it seemed the whole town stunk. I have visited places all over China, and other poor countries around the world, but this was the worst. As I contemplated these various explanations, I looked down the road. To my surprise I was running about twenty yards behind a man peddling a three-wheeled "night-soil" barrow. I sprinted for a few minutes to get ahead of the source of my discomfort. The peddler of the cart had been collecting night soil in town to carry back to the farms in the suburbs. This was a very simple solution to what would have been a very difficult municipal environmental problem for a city without a sewage system.

I found Lanzhou to be a very clean city, normally without obnoxious odors, and the handling of waste products seems to be under control. They did not flush their sewage into the Yellow River. Chinese agriculture is based on the use of human waste to nourish their crops and is carefully collected and composted into fertilizer. Sewage is not despised in China but considered a national asset and treasure.

During the Cultural Revolution, Chairman Mao Tse Tung preached against the idea that human excrement was dirty. He proclaimed, "Workers such as the shit hauler or others with shitty jobs were pitied only through the insurgent view of highbred intellectuals who can never be true Communists."

Swallow Island was two miles from Lanzhou on the Yellow River (Huang Ho) and had a giant apple orchard. The manager, Mr. Ma Shi Lu, told us they are breeding 130 varieties of apple and shipping eight thousand tons of this fruit each year. The Lanzhou area is a major producer of many kinds of fruits, including a wide variety of melons. We were told the former U.S. Vice President Henry Wallace, under President Franklin Roosevelt, introduced the greenish cream-yellow honeydew melon to this area. Wallace was also the former secretary of agriculture and an agricultural scientist. He had visited Lanzhou in 1948 and subsequently sent the officials of Lanzhou the seeds of this sweet fruit to grow in Gansu Province.

Our Sunday excursion around Lanzhou was by way of a small riverboat. The Thousand Buddha Caves of Bing Ling Temple was only accessible by boat since there were no roads to the Jishi Hill from which the caves were excavated. Traveling down the river from the Liujiaxia Dam was like floating into a classical Chinese painting…giant fingers of stone reaching hundreds of feet tall, probing the heavens and repeating themselves as far as we could see…small peaks were scattered amongst the forest of vertical megaliths and at times we could see a wisp of cloud floating high and hugging their peaks. Everyone has seen this scene illustrated by Chinese landscape painters, who I had believed drew these perceptions from their imagination, but these were real! Hundreds of Japanese and Western tourists at the caves were recording these images with their cameras.

Clinging to the side of Jishi Hill were wooden stairs and walkways whose tenuous attachment to the wall was questionable. However, they provided the only access to the many caves and carvings on the face of the hill that dates back to 420 C.E. These walkways led to some 183 niches filled with 694 stone statues of the Idols of Buddhism. Nine thousand square feet of murals covered the walls of the caves. The imposing statue of a sitting Maitreya (the Buddha of the Future), which stood over eighty feet high, dominates the valley as you approach by the river. This vast complex of ancient art was over six hundred feet long.

I'm certain that Marco Polo did not visit the Lanzhou zoo with its small exhibit of pandas. But what is now known as "The Five Springs Park," which lies at the foot of Gaolan Hill, was known to be there in 1274, during Polo's time. The park got its name from the park's five crystal springs. The legend about the spring's origin came from when General Huo Qubing ran out of water for his army during an attack by the Huns in 126 B.C.E. The general, in a rage, beat on a rock with his sword and out gushed five clear-water springs. Those springs are still flowing.

We had lunch at the park.

Our entire group met with historians from the Lanzhou Museum and the Lanzhou University. We discussed Marco Polo's book and the authenticity of his descriptions of China during the time of Kublai Khan and the seemingly fantastic stories of his travels. The professors confirmed, as has every other historian and authority of the Yuan Dynasty in China, that the stories and details of China by Marco Polo were somewhat exaggerated but essentially true in that they could have only been told by someone who had been in China at that time.

CHAPTER 26

Wrestlers and Horses
Inner Mongolia, October 9 to 20, 1985

ow you must know that Kaidu Khan, nephew of the Great Khan, had a daughter whose name was Aijaruc which in Tartar is as much to say "The Bright Moon." This damsel was very beautiful, but also so strong and brave that in all her father's realm there is no man who could outdo her in feats of strength. In all trials she showed greater strength than any man of them.

Her father often desired to give her in marriage, but she would not have none of it. She vowed she would never marry till she found a man who could vanquish her in every trial; him she would marry and none else. And when her father found how resolute she was, he gave a formal consent in their fashion, that she should marry whom she list and when she list. The lady was so tall and muscular, so stout and shapely withal, that she was almost like a giantess. She had distributed her challenges over all the kingdoms, declaring that whosoever should come to try a fall with her, it should be on these conditions, viz., that if she vanquished him she should win from him 100 horses, and if he vanquished her he should win her to wife. Hence many a noble youth had come to try his strength against her, but she beat them all, and in this way she had won 10,000 horses.

Now it came to pass in the year of Christ 1280 that there presented himself a noble young gallant, the son of a rich and puissant king, a man of prowess and valiance and great strength of body, who had heard word of the damsel's challenge, and came to match himself against her in the hope of vanquishing her and winning her to wife. That he greatly desired, for the young lady was passing fair. He, too, was young and handsome, fearless and strong in every way, insomuch that not a man in all his father's realm could vie with him. So he came full confidently, and brought with him 1,000 horses to be forfeited if she should vanish him. Thus might she gain 1,000 in a single stroke! But the young gallant had so much confidence in his own strength that he counted surely to win her.

So a day was named for a great gathering at the Palace of Kaidu Khan, and the Khan and Queen were there. And when all the company were assembled, for great numbers flocked to see such a match, the damsel first came forth in a strait jerkin of sammet; and then came forth the young bachelor in a jerkin of sandal; and a winsome sight they were to see. When both had taken post in the middle of the hall they grappled each other by the arms and wrestled this way and that, but for a long time neither could get the better of the other. And last, however, it so befell that the damsel threw him right valiantly on the palace pavement. And when he found himself thus thrown, and her standing over him, great indeed was his shame and dis-comfiture. He got him up straightway, and without more ado departed with all his company, and returned to his father, full of shame and vexation, that he who had not found a man that could stand before him should have been thus worsted by a girl! And the 1,000 horses he left behind him...

Now I will leave this story and tell you of a great battle that Kaidu fought with Argon the son of Abaga Lord of the Tartars of the Levant.
MARCO POLO, 1298

Our group, the four photographers from China plus Michael and me, had become like a family. We had been traveling together for almost two months and, as in any family, there were a few spats but primarily we supported each other with the common goal of making this a successful journey: seeking to gather and document the morsels of data we found about Marco Polo along our way. This would have not been possible without the help of the local government officials that paved the way for us. We were truly indebted to them.

The entire group left Lanzhou at 6 a.m. for the five-hour drive into Ningxia Hui Autonomous Region, traveling along its border with Inner Mongolia on our way to the Zhong Wei Hotel in downtown Zhong Wei. This town was also the site of a major research facility, the Sha Huang (Desert) Research Institute. The goal of the Institute was to reclaim the desert. With the help of consultants from Israel, they came up with a technique that may work. Zhong Wei was at the edge of a vast desert known as "The Tengger," and this desert has always challenged the survival of the areas' inhabitants. In 1958 the local people and scientists from the Institute started battling the desert.

The scientists at the Institute showed us a desert being laced over in a cross-hatched pattern with rope made of loosely rolled hay and straw. The rope, about eight inches in diameter, was laid out into giant squares, about six feet on each side. Grass seeds were placed in the rope from which they received their nourishment to sprout and grow. Regular watering was a necessity. The rope also kept the sand in place to prevent wind erosion from covering the new grass seedlings. During the non-growing season the dead grass decayed and this cycle would be repeated over a period of years, eventually allowing the new seeds to grow in what should eventually become a healthy soil. We only saw the beginning of this process with the squares of straw rope spread over many acres of desert.

Since ancient times man has depleted the soil of its nutrients, destroying plant life while simultaneously cutting down the trees that held the earth together and stored the moisture. The result has been deserts. These deserts would expand into this barren campestral land, never to be regained for vegetation. Perhaps modern China has found an answer for this age-old problem with the help of Israel, a country that has already converted its deserts to flowering oases.

The waterwheel on the other side of the Yellow River was to be our destination. The easiest but most hazardous means of reaching the left bank was by goatskin river rafts like the ones which Michael and I had made our way down a river in Pakistan. The design was the same. The skins of a half dozen sheep were tied to a frame of bamboo poles (tree branches were used in Pakistan). They were blown up by the owner using an opening left at the end of one of the sheep's legs. As experienced goatskin "rafts men," our whole crew took the plunge and went by raft. I don't know why I do such crazy things, since I never learned how to swim and I don't think they'd ever seen a life jacket on the Yellow River. Besides, the last goatskin raft on which I traveled in Pakistan blew a skin in the middle of the river. The river flows slowly at this point so it was an uneventful trip. Although if this raft were to have capsized, I would have grabbed one of the bloated goatskins and between here and the Yellow Sea 1,500 miles away, I'm certain I would have reached the shore.

As we traveled east, getting closer and closer to Beijing, I felt less the explorer and more the tourist. The adventurous experiences and the threat of the unknown made the earlier segments of this voyage very exciting. This part of our journey was more of a learning experience, with the possibility of surprises.

The trip to the capital of the Ningxia Hui Autonomous Region, Yin Chuan, was uneventful. The Yellow River skirts the city and feeds water to irrigate the land around it. The irrigation system here had a two-thousand year history. The Great Wall, just west of Yin Chuan was built at the same time. Over the centuries Yin Chuan found itself between two Great Walls. In fact, along the thousand miles between Gansu Province and Beijing there are two walls in many places, wandering across the mountains and valleys along the path of Marco Polo. This area is known as one of China's leading farming districts due to these age-old irrigation canals. We saw vast areas of rice paddies, pools of reeds, and weeping willows bowing at the water's edge. These farmlands are so fertile and beautiful they can well be compared to slabs of jade, inlaid between the mountains and the Yellow River. You get the feeling that you are in the succulent subtropical land south of the Yangtze River, a thousand miles to the South.

The city of Yin Chuan has long been an important stopping point along the Great Wall. Marco Polo in one of his sojourns for the Great Khan stayed nearby. His book tells of the camelhair cloth produced here, describing it as the finest weave and the most beautiful sort of fabric known to the world.

Karakul sheep are found all over Central Asia. The sandwich of two slices of liver and a slice of fat that I was served in Tashkurgan, our first stop in China, was from a karakul lamb. The lambs were mainly raised for their wool, which were known worldwide as the Persian lamb, but they had a very fatty tail...delicious. In this area they were not raised for their meat (or fat) but for their wool. Archeological research had found the existence of Persian lambskin in the 14th century B.C.E. and drawings of these fat-tailed sheep were found on the walls of Babylonian Temples. Even the Bible describes the karakul lamb as the sacrificial lamb used by Moses.

The oldest and most important industry of Central Asia was raising karakul sheep. At a karakul coat factory, in Yin Chuan, we saw the process of making coats

of this very long curly wool. They claimed they only use wool with a minimum of eight curls, which is the highest quality.

On the roof of the factory we found half dozen tall beautiful Chinese women, wearing very high heels, and sleek black, body-hugging dresses, who in no way resembled the women we had seen anywhere in Ningxia Province or anyplace in Western China. They were producing a TV commercial promoting these very beautiful coats. I was so taken with this very luxurious material that I bought a white, waist-length karakul coat to take home.

In the afternoon we visited a Hui (Muslim) family. The lady of the house showed us her prize possession, an ancient photograph of her grandfather. We sat in the living room of her mud-brick home. The "living room" was a very descriptive phrase since this is truly the room in which they lived, ate, cooked, prayed, and listened to the boom-box-like radio. The one bedroom for the family of eight was in back.

A few miles south of Yincheng's city center were the remains of one of the deteriorating Great Walls, which was no more than a mound of brown dirt that stretched to the horizon in both directions. It was only significant as the historical site of an architectural wonder of 2,000 years ago but of no importance today or in Marco Polo's time. If I were writing of my travels through this area in the thirteenth century, I would not have mentioned this "Great Wall."

Our lunch was with Provincial Vice-Governor Liu Gan Zhi.

Above: Praying at the entrance to a mosque

We followed the Yellow River (Huang He) for hundreds of miles for our passage to Hohhot, the capital of Inner Mongolia (Nei Mongol in Chinese). Mongolia was one republic until 1921 when Russia and China split this ancient country in half. This created a new country, Mongolia, the northern part of the acquired land, which became the world's second Communist republic after Russia.

It had been a long journey, and we were looking forward to a good meal. Although many restaurants do not look very clean, food poisoning was not one of our problems…up till now. The restaurant we chose was questionable. On the rear wall there was a sign in both English and Chinese that read "Don't Spit, Please." In the kitchen, large hunks of meat were haphazardly thrown in a corner; dishes were casually rinsed not washed; the cook was coughing while he prepared the food and an old man in filthy clothes was the boss. He was the least of our worries. With regard to cleanliness this was a very dubious operation, yet it was not the worst that I had experienced. Somehow, no one got sick.

We found our housing in Hohhot to be in a yurt…the portable housing that Mongolians have used since before Marco Polo. Its design has remained the same. The yurt (ger in Mongolian) is the traditional dwelling of the nomads of Central Asia from Turkey to Mongolia. It is a round, thirty-foot diameter, tent-like structure made from a wooden frame and covered by wool felt. We saw many of these in Afghanistan and Western China. A traditional yurt is very easy to collapse and reassemble in less than an hour, and it can be carried by one or two animals (horses, camels, or yaks). The walls are constructed of several crisscrossed sections of latticework very much like a collapsible baby gate. The sections fold together to facilitate setting up or tearing down. The top ring, a toghona, provides an opening for the smoke of the wood stove to escape and is a source of light during the day. It has holes for the roof poles that fan out like a wheel. This forms the wooden skeleton over which layers of felt cloths are placed. The colder the weather, the more felt and layers of animal hides cover this frame.

The only innovations that have been made since Marco slept in a yurt are that the heating/cooking fires have been replaced by a wood/coal burning stove, and the cloth door is now very often wooden. In the thirteenth century, the rich had their yurts mounted on four wooden wheels and pulled by a team of horses or oxen. This was the Asian nomad's Winnebago.

The sunset that evening displayed for me the quintessential pastoral scene. The fiery sun penetrated a red and purple sky as it drifted towards the horizon and spread into a million glowing embers. Below the sky were the grasslands, a few leafless trees, and shadows of sheep scattered around the landscape. The half dozen now orange/red yurts reflected the sun with beauty never to be captured on a photograph. They call this type of visual experience "breathtaking." I now understand the meaning of this expression. As I walked out of our dinning hall and saw this spectacular vista, I stopped and gulped in a breath of air. Then to complete this idyllic setting, a donkey pulling a cart loaded with a small family moved slowly across our view as if some celestial art director knew exactly what it takes to make a perfect picture.

Sleeping in a yurt when the temperature outside was well below freezing was like participating in a live experiment in thermal physics. The heat diminishes exponentially as a function of distance from the stove at the center of the yurt. Therefore, if you put your sleeping bag in a radial position with your feet towards the fire, they will be too warm and your head will be freezing. If your position is reversed, you have a similar but reversed problem. It was also obvious that if your body was parallel to the outside wall, you were toasted on one side and frozen on the other. There was no ideal location for a sleeping place in a yurt; some part of your body would be uncomfortable. After being in the saddle all day herding horses or sheep, you probably do not give a damn as to what part of your body is cold as long as you can get some sleep.

Of all the peoples and culture I encountered along the Marco Polo trail, I found the Mongolians to be the most hospitable and fun loving. Before we started the afternoon meal, there were many rounds of toasts, Mongolian style. One of our hosts stood up and with a glass of wine (I assumed it was wine) held high, he began to sing a Mongolian song. It was toast to another of the hosts at this giant round table for fifteen. The song lasted a minute or two and was no doubt humorous since all the other local people laughed. After his toast was finished he did not drink the wine but instead handed the glass to the person to whom he had addressed his song. The recipient did his "Gan Bei" (chug-a-lug in Chinese) of the full glass of wine. He in turn would offer another song / toast to a different member at the table until each drinking person at the table had their turn. The melodies, the style of chanting and rhythm used by these rotund Mongolian singers reminded me of the chants sung by the North American Indian. (Didn't the American Indian come from Mongolia across the frozen Bering Sea about 11,000 years ago?) After all this singing, contagious laughing, and drinking, we enjoyed a sumptuous mutton dinner.

I also learned of another interesting tradition in the Mongolian culture. Just as Christians have a baptism and Jews perform circumcision on baby boys, the Mongolian family has a hair-cutting ceremony for their young children. When a boy reaches the age of three and a girl the age of four, a special day is chosen and they have a big party where the child's parents and all their friends and relations show up to watch and have a hand in the ceremony. Everyone wears traditional Mongolian garments, and they crowd into the family's yurt. Men are on one side and women on the other just as in the Jewish tradition of the ritual circumcision except it is the hair that is cut off. The Jews also separate the sexes. The child's father makes a welcoming speech and the cutting begins. The oldest and most revered guest makes the first cut followed by all the others in turn by age. Then the party begins. The guests are treated to the omnipresent mutton, cheese made from mare's milk, and black tea with goat's milk and salt. The father toasts each of his guests and offers them a glass of "airag," a frothy fermented mare's milk called "kumis" in other parts of Central Asia. It doesn't take too many rounds of airag before the singing begins and the merriment explodes. Mongolians seem to be a real party people. It provides a compensatory balance against the harsh conditions of daily life.

The tomb of a beautiful Mongolian princess, who played a very important part in the life of Marco Polo, was in an obscure part of Hohhot. Her name was Cocachin. If it were not for Cocachin, Marco Polo would never have returned to Venice and his book,—and this book as well,—would never have been written. I had to pay her homage and visit her grave.

After spending over seventeen years in China, the Polo brothers, Maffeo and Niccolo, and Niccolo's son, Marco, wanted to go home to Venice. Kublai Khan would not hear of it. He wanted them to remain in his court. About this time Kublai's nephew, Arghun Khan, made a request that he be given a princess of the Baya'ut tribe for marriage. Arghun's deceased wife had requested that after her death he marry someone from her tribe. A beautiful seventeen-year-old princess by the name of Cocachin was chosen. Arghun was the leader of the Persian sector of the Mongolian Empire, five thousand miles from Beijing. It was interesting how these monarchs would communicate. We know that messages were carried by what was the equivalent of America's nineteenth century "pony express." Riders would travel by fast horses or ponies from caravanserai to caravanserai. They could cover up to two hundred or more miles a day. It was also possible that messages could have been exchanged by carrier pigeon, but I found no record of their use by the Mongolians. Pigeons were used as message carriers by Roman warriors.

An overland journey would be too brutal for the delicate princess so it was decided to take her by sea. Reluctantly, Kublai Khan agreed to have the Polo family escort her to Isfahan, Persia. It was a twenty-eight-month journey by sea around the subcontinent of India to Hormuz, Persia. It was another month for the entourage to make the overland voyage to Isfahan and the palace of Arghun only to discover that he had died. So that this journey would not have been for naught, Arghun's son, Ghazan, married Cocachin and the Polos went home to Venice. They arrived in 1294, twenty-three years after their departure.

As official visitors to the capital of Inner Mongolia, we met our pleasant obligation to visit the important tourist sites in Hohhot. This included the Five-Pagoda Temple sometimes called the thousand-Buddha-Pagoda. It in fact has 1563 carvings of Buddha on the outside and none on the inside. The inside ones were all destroyed during the Cultural Revolution.

We found another great lady in Chinese/Mongolian history that lived over 2,000 years ago, Wang Zhaojun. She crossed the Great Wall and married Chanyu of the Han Dynasty and made great contributions to the unity between the Chinese Han and the more primitive Huns from the north. She too was buried just a few miles outside Hohhot in what was called "A Tomb Covered with Green," which it was.

Riding horses with Mongolians on the grasslands of Mongolia, along the Marco Polo trail, was as close as one can get to living in the boots of the thirteenth-century traveler. We spent the morning doing just that. It was a clear, cold day, the world around us was as flat as a giant football field, and the blue sky was untouchable. Our hosts, dressed in their traditional clothes, — gray tunics and big black boots—literally rode circles around us. The horses' hooves puffed up small swirls of brown dust as they pounded the turf. It was a surrealistic scene from a childhood dream, and I was euphorically living it. My father told me stories of running away from home in Massachusetts and working on the King Ranch in Texas. Later he enlisted in the U.S. Cavalry serving in a company under Lt. George Patton. This was the type of adventurous life I too wished to live.

Horses maintain a place of prominence with these descendents of Genghis Khan. Horses are much more important here than in most of the world where they are predominately used as beasts of burden. Horses are pictured on the Mongolian nation's seal. In times gone by, the Mongolian soldiers drank the blood of their mount when they went into battle with little food. Today, they eat the meat, and the mare's milk is a staple in their diet, made into cream, cheese, and butter and most important fermented into "airag," the frothy beer-like beverage consumed the way Westerners have cold drinks or beer on a hot summer's day. It provides these isolated people an escape from the grim grueling life in the grasslands. Horsemanship is one of the "Three Manly Sports" of Mongolians, which also includes wrestling and archery. Competition is held in their own Olympics called Naadam where this summer festival has been held yearly since being initiated by Genghis Khan over 800 years ago.

That morning we had a miniature Naadam festival. Horsemanship was displayed and there were horse races for fun (no betting). Then there were demonstrations of the "Second Manly Sport"…wrestling. Half a dozen local wrestlers came to show us their proficiency in this sport. Mongolian wrestling is an exciting, special event even to the uninitiated. The two wrestlers, wearing leather vests and a short colorful skirt tied around their waists, bend over head to head with hands outstretched grabbing their opponent's arms and shoulders as they sidestepped in circles on the grass. The muscles of their bare arms ripple waiting for the opportunity to make their move. This spinning may sometimes go on for many minutes. Then suddenly one grabs for a grip on his opponent's clothing or tries to overturn the other with the sheer strength of his arms and upper body. The action can be swift; a combatant can go down within seconds. In Mongol wrestling, when one part of the body above the feet touches the ground, the game is over. The winner in his colorful vest, skirt, and black boots tips his cap to the loser and sometimes sings him a song. Life in Mongolia was like living in a Broadway musical. You never knew when they would break out singing. After each match, in the national games, both wrestlers would start flapping their arms like a bird as they bounced on their knees towards the stage for recognition of the winner's triumph. This was their way of mimicking the eagle before and after the match. It was just a few months earlier, on the grassland high in the Karakoram Mountains, that I took a chance at doing the Eagle dance with the Tajik people. We saw traditions such as this again and again throughout Asia.

To my surprise, Michael said he was a wrestler in college, and he would like to have a go at it with one of the contestants. He donned the traditional wrestling vest with a red, yellow, and green-banded skirt over his jacket. They chose the smallest of the Mongolian combatants who was still a bit larger than Michael's welterweight size. They both assumed the proper starting position, standing bent over, head to head holding each other's shoulders. Then the merry-go-round dance began. After about a minute, Michael made the first move trying to grab the other guy's leg. This threw Michael a little off balance and his opponent started to pull down on Michael's shoulder. Michael shifted his weight for more stability but within another minute Michael was on the ground. After another Mongolian match, Mike said he would try again but this also ended with him on the ground. I was impressed as to how well Michael did, considering his weight disadvantage and the fact that he had not practiced wrestling of any type in many years.

The Mongolian wrestling we witnessed was carried out in the same manner as Marco describes in his story of the big beautiful daughter of Kaidu Khan. Even the wrestlers in 1985 wore the same costume that Polo described in his story. All the modern Mongolian wrestlers wore jerkins—a short, close fitting sleeveless jacket usually made of leather—just as they did 700 years before. Polo did not have access to a satellite TV sports channel, so it would not be likely he would have known what wrestlers wore at a match in Mongolia, unless he was there. We did not see any female wrestlers, and Xiao Yun was not interested in challenging any of the men.

That evening we had a Mongolian shindig. Our hosts arranged a full evening of entertainment. There was a troupe of dancers and singers in traditional costumes. The girls wore knee length, pink silk outer dresses with slits up to the waist, edged with bands of gold spangles. Under this, was a floor-length, yellow gown. A silk bandana was around their long pigtailed hair. The men were dressed in matching costumes. They were spectacular in appearance and talent.

The dancers performed to the accompaniment of a band with men and women musicians playing flutes, accordion, a cello, and a few traditional Mongolian string instruments. This was followed by a solo performance by a black-capped Chinese man with a fake "Fu Manchu" mustache, who played an ancient four-stringed instrument, singing what apparently was a medley of very humorous songs. Everyone but Mike and I understood the jokes as the drinking continued, and everyone loosened up. I got up to sing a little-known jazz song I remembered from the 1940's. It was originally sung by Nat King Cole on the radio. The title was "Frim Fram Sauce." The following are a few lines of the lyrics as I remember them:

259 *Wrestlers and Horses*

I don't want French-fried potatoes,
Red ripe tomatoes,
I'm never satisfied.
I want the frim fram sauce with the Ausen fay
With chafafa on the side.
I don't want pork chops and bacon,
That won't awaken
My appetite inside.
I want the frim fram sauce with the Ausen fay
With chafafa on the side.

Of course no one could have possibly understood it, since it was not all English, Mongolian nor Chinese.

Inner Mongolia was like a separate world within China. It was not China in many, many ways—language, music, lifestyle, clothing, topography, sense of humor. It was truly a different world and before 1921 it was part of Mongolia, a different country. Our visit to Inner Mongolia had been warm (not the weather), fun, and a very special experience. I did not want to leave.

Shangdu is 175 miles north of Beijing. It was the summer home of the Kublai Khan. When Marco Polo visited Shangdu he was the guest of the emperor and he and his father and uncle received royal treatment. Let us read how Marco describes this incredible palace:

The Great Khan who now reigns and whose name is Kublai Khan built Shangdu. In this city Kublai Khan had an immense palace made of marble and stone, with halls and rooms all gilt and adorned with figures of beasts and birds, and pictures of trees and flowers of different kinds. It is most wonderfully beautiful and marvelously decorated. This palace is situated within the city, but on one side it is bounded by the city-wall, and from that point another wall runs out enclosing a space of no less than sixteen miles around, with numerous springs and rivers and meadows. Into this park one cannot enter except from the palace. And the Great Khan keeps all kinds of animals in it, namely stags and fallow deer and roebucks, in order to feed his gerfalcons and hawks, which he keeps there in mew. Of gerfalcons alone there are more than two hundred. He goes himself once a week to see them in mew. And often enough the Great Khan rides about this walled park, taking a leopard with him on his horse's croup; when the fancy takes him, he lets it go, and with it takes a stag or a fallow-deer or a roebuck and has it given to the gerfalcons in mew. This is what the Great Khan does for amusement.

And you must know that in the middle of that walled park, where there is very fine wood, the Great Khan has a great palace built, all of cane (bamboo); it is a kind of pavilion, with fine painted and gilt columns, and at the top of each column is a large dragon, with its tail coiled round the shaft; with its head and two legs, the one stretched to the right and the other to the left, it holds up the roof. Inside, the palace is all gilt, and adorned with figures of beasts and birds of exquisite workmanship. The roof is also made of canes, but it is well varnished, with such strong varnish, that no amount of rain can do it any damage. And I will tell you how they make this palace of canes. You must know that these canes are more than three palms in breadth, and are from ten to fifteen paces long. They are slitting two, lengthways, from knot to knot, so that one gets two tiles. And the tiles made from these canes are so thick and large that one can cover and build a whole house with them. This palace I have told you of was all made of canes. The great khan had it built in such a way that it could be moved whenever he wanted. Over two hundred silk cords braced it. The Great Khan lives there three months a year-June, July and August...

MARCO POLO, 1298

The summer palace was razed when Mongolian rule ended; only parts of the ruined structures remain. Around the perimeter one can still see ruins of a few of the beacon towers. Xiao Yun and the other photographers tried to photograph Shangdu but the area was so devoid of photogenic objects they were unable to make visual meaningful records of this ancient paradise. The deserted site had been overgrown with weeds and stood in the marshy bed of a river. The foundations of palace buildings could be traced with the rubble of their marble walls and fragments of lions and dragons and other sculptures that testified to the former existence of an ornamental city as described by Marco Polo. But in reality, it is just a point on a map.

In the fall of 1797, Samuel T. Coleridge composed a poem that came to him, as he said, "in a sort of reverie brought on by two grains of Opium taken to check my dysentery." It was called "Kublai Khan," which described the palaces of Shangdu that he called "Xanadu." The following is the first stanza of the poem that immortalized both Kublai Khan and his summer palace:

In Xanadu did Kublai Khan
A stately pleasure-dome decree:
Where Alph, the sacred river, ran
Through caverns measureless to man
Down to the sunless sea.

The drivers for our three-car caravan had abandoned us in Hohhot. They were driving the cars back to Beijing as the Marco Polo expedition team of six boarded a train, heading south and east following the Great Wall of China to Beijing.

I sat starring out the window overcome with emotion, knowing that the most important phase of my lifelong project was about to end. Monstrous obstacles had been overcome and objectives reached. It was a great feeling of satisfaction. The hills rolled by and I thought about my family. I had not been able to contact my wife and my two youngest daughters since I left Seattle over three months before. Sarah was just a year and a half when I left, and I'd been away for almost a fifth of her life. Jane was still in preschool, and Nancy had to handle everything. The pursuit of my Marco Polo dreams required a big sacrifice for my family and left a big debt for me to repay. I hoped and prayed that they were OK. The train rumbled past a section of the Great Wall and my mind was directed to a new personal goal of getting the recognition for Marco Polo that he had deserved for seven centuries. He and his book were ridiculed by his fellow Venetians during his lifetime and that belittling of his accomplishments has not ended. The train was winding its way through the mountains northwest of Beijing. I would soon be saying good-byes to a group of people who surrounded me on this train and to whom I had become warmly attached. This would not be easy. The sound of the wheels changed as the train made its way across a bridge trestle spanning a river. Marco Polo was escorted along this route by representatives of the Great Khan, and he was treated royally. Michael and I were embraced by people from the voice of the leaders of China, the China News Service, who also treated us royally. They arranged for our access to forbidden places where foreigners were never allowed and arranged for all that we needed. Marco tells about this part of the journey this way:

nd let me tell you in good sooth that when the great Khan heard that Messers Nicolo and Maffeo Polo were on their way back, he sent people a journey of full 40 days to meet them; and on this journey, as on their former one, they were honorably entertained upon the road, and supplied with all that they required.

MARCO POLO, 1298

The Marco Polo itinerary for the entire expedition was established after a few years of research tracking down the many manuscripts of Polo's book and the itineraries established by many authorities on Marco Polo. Most of the routes they identified were different, so I developed a consensus of all this data. This was the path I sought to follow and this was the route that CNS arranged for us to travel. I was moving along on the last few miles of this 13,000 mile journey—a journey that had taken ten years. What will be my next step after I tread in Marco Polo's last footstep in Beijing? The future was hazy, but I knew Marco Polo would be part of it.

I remembered my first visits to Beijing in 1979, trying to contact the authorities for the elusive permission to follow Marco across the Pakistan-Chinese border. I spent a great deal of time pursuing my personal Holy Grail. I came to Beijing almost every two months from 1979 to 1985, and I often stayed at one of the few hotels available to foreigners, the Beijing Hotel, not far from Tienamen Square. Each frustrating day I would return to the hotel coffee shop where I commiserated with my fellow foreigners— business people, journalists, representatives for non-profit organizations, and other Sinophiles. Each of us had a sad story to tell. We called the coffee shop "The Café of Broken Dreams."

This was in the early days, before the Chinese "Dragon" awoke and began inching his way out of the cave in which Mao Tse Tung had forced him to hide. Under Deng Xiao Ping, China gave up the isolation policy of the 1960s and 1970s to pursue its new desire to sit at the table of nations.

I remember the day in 1981 when they installed the first traffic light in Beijing. Before traffic lights, immaculately dressed traffic cops wearing white starched uniforms and white caps directed traffic with their white gloves. On that day, some twenty officers with white bullhorns explained in a cacophony of voices how the traffic lights worked to the thousands of bicyclists who were trying to go through the intersection of the two most active streets in Beijing, Dongchangan and Wangfujing, in front of the Beijing Hotel. They were yelling through the bullhorns: "Red means stop! Green means go!" For thirty years, the Communist government drove into each mind of this population that red was the symbol for their culture and country. Their national flag is red. Mao had the little red book that was read by everyone. Red was good luck. Red meant go! How could they, in one day, change the mindset of the entire Chinese population? Even the people in the western world referred to the Communist Chinese as "Reds." It was a Herculean task but within a few days the taxi drivers and bicyclists learned how to live in the twentieth century and stop when the light was red. Only a few years later this same major intersection in front of the Beijing Hotel no longer had a traffic light. They built an overpass.

Outside the train, the scene was bleak; no houses, no farms, no people. I was excited about ending the project in Beijing but not like those few minutes at the Kunjerab Pass when I placed that first step across the Pakistan-China border. That was the high point of my life. I had always established goals in my life and knew where I was going but it was the drama and the unknown process of how I was to meet my goal that provided me with the real excitement. I had always believed that human beings are divided into two types: those who enjoyed power boats were always focused on where they were going and those who enjoyed sailing were always looking for the challenge of how to get there. Sailing was always my love.

The train rolled across the hills to Beijing.

CHAPTER 27

Sitting on the Marco Polo Bridge
Beijing, October 20 to 24, 1985

And now ye have heard all that we can tell you about the Tartars and the Saracens and their customs, and likewise about other countries of the world as far as researches and information extend. Only we have said nothing about the Greater Sea (Mediterranean) and the provinces that lie around it, although we know it thoroughly. But it seems to me a needless and useless task to speak about places which are visited by people every day. For there are so many who sail all about that sea constantly, Venetians, and Genoese, and Pisans, and many others, that everybody knows all about it, and that is the reason that I pass it over and say nothing of it.

For according what has been said in the beginning of the Book, there never was a man, be he Christian or Saracen or Tartar or Heathen, who ever traveled over so much of the world, as did that noble and illustrious citizen of the City of Venice, Messer Marco the son of Messer Nicolo Polo.

THE LAST WORDS IN MARCO POLO'S BOOK, 1298

I did it. I made it to Beijing on October 20, 1985. After fifteen years of hard work, struggles, frustrations, near disasters, true disasters, exciting accomplishments and most important…miracles, I have finally arrived in Beijing. I left Venice over ten years ago following in the footsteps of the elusive Marco Polo half way around the world and now the journey is complete. In the 700 years since Marco Polo was here, the Middle East, Central and Eastern Asia has changed in many ways, but I sought to see it as Marco Polo saw it.

The director and many of the staff from CNS were at the train station to welcome us at the end of a successful venture. I was elated. For the next few days I had a perpetual smile plastered across my face. They took me to the Beijing hotel for a small banquet to celebrate. There was so much to do. Michael and I sat down to write a news release and a brief synopsis of the project. This was to be distributed at the news conference scheduled for October 22. Copies were to be sent to John O'Connell, our publicity person in Seattle, to announce to the rest of the world what we had done.

I had meetings with CNS to settle our finances.

I called my wife Nancy and told her I was okay and coming home in three days.

We planned a press conference for Tuesday October 22, 1985 at 2:00 p.m. For the next two days we wrote the press kit and notified all the news agencies including the Chinese and international media. It worked, and over 50 people showed up—*AP, UPI, Reuters, NY Times, LA Times, China Daily, Baltimore Sun, ABC, NBC, CBS, and China's CCTV,* U.S. Embassy personnel, and representatives of the Chinese government—an overwhelming success. The conference was held at the Beijing Hotel where we would be available to answer questions and have individual interviews. In addition to Michael Winn and me, we had our fellow travelers from the China News Service: Luo Xiao Yun, Lu Xiang You, Jin Tie Lu and Jin Bo Hong. It was either a slow news day or we really caught the fancy of the world press.

The six-page News Release and synopsis of the journey were handed out. We made our presentation and answered their questions. One of the reporters from *Reuters* told the group about an incident that occurred to him almost ten years earlier: "I was working as a Chinese translator for Berlitz in Washington D.C. when Harry Rutstein came into my office with a letter to be translated into Chinese. The letter was being sent to the agencies in China from whom he needed permission to complete his project. I said to myself, 'This guy must be crazy to expect the Chinese to let him cross into Western China.' Well, here I am today celebrating that achievement."

Not far from downtown Beijing stands an old, grey stone bridge across the Yongding River. Marco wrote about this bridge in *A Description of the World*, and it is now known as the Marco Polo Bridge. It seemed appropriate, so Michael and I took a taxi out to the bridge before we left China. We walked across this magnificent structure. Stone arches along its length provide support for a parade of 484 stone lions carved along the protective rail. Four stone elephants crouch headlong into each end of both railings as if they were keeping them in place. We were impressed, as was Marco.

My excitement, euphoria, and the great sense of accomplishment I felt are really indescribable. Our journey would have been impossible to complete without the help, support, and encouragement of so many people; but I had another thing going…some really damn good luck. The Marco Polo Bridge is an appropriate symbol for the fulfillment of my lifelong dream: it stood the test of time. I am hoping that readers of my story will be encouraged to pursue their own fantasies and aspirations. My odyssey ended happily, safely and with great celebration as I sat triumphantly on the Marco Polo Bridge.

EPILOGUE

My travel, in the footsteps of Marco Polo, started as an adventure. He had told his tale—a fantastic adventure—and changed history. His work inspired me. Having traveled in his footsteps and gained an even better understanding of the breadth of his accomplishments, I want to give this great man the credit he undeniably deserves. The Marco Polo Foundation exists to make that possible. If you would like more information about the Marco Polo Foundation or are interested in hosting a lecture or class on this topic, please contact me through my website: www. MarcoPoloFound.org.

Above: The journey's end at the Marco Polo Bridge, Beijing, China

REFERENCES

AKURGAL, EKREM. *Ancient Civilizations and Ruins of Turkey*. Istanbul. Mobil Oil
     Turk A.S., 1969.

BANIK, ALLEN E. *Hunza Land*. Long Beach, California. Whitehorn Publishing, 1960.

BENEDETTO, L.F. & RICCI, ALDO. *The Travels of Marco Polo*. New York. The Viking Press, 1931.

BIDDULPH, JOHN. "Tribes of the Hindoo Koosh." Karachi. Indus Publications, 1977.

BOULNOIS, LUCE. *The Silk Road*. New York. E. P. Dutton & Co., 1966.

BYRNE, DONN. *Messer Marco Polo*. New York. The Modern Library, 1921.

CLARK, JOHN. *Hunza: Lost Kingdom of the Himalayas*. London. Hutchinson & Co., 1957.

DUPREE, NANCY HATCH. *The Road to Balk*. Kabul, Afghanistan. The Afghan Tourist Organization, 1967.

FODOR'S. *Fodor's People's Republic of China*. New York. David McKay Co., 1979.

HAMBIS, LOUIS. *La Description Du Monde*. Paris. Librairie C. Klincksieck, 1955.

HART, HENRY H. *Venetian Adventurer*. Stanford. Stanford U. P., 1942.

KAPLAN, FREDERIC. *The China Guidebook*. Fairlawn, N.J. Eurasia Press, 1979.

KING, JOHN. *Karakoram Highway*. Victoria, Australia. Lonely Planet Publications, 1989.

KOMROFF, MANUEL. *The Travels of Marco Polo*. New York. The Modern Library, 1931.

KOMROFF, MANUEL. *The Venetian: The Travels of Marco Polo*. Garden City, N.Y. Garden City
     Publishing Co., 1926.

LATHAM, RONALD. *The Travels of Marco Polo*. London. The Folio Society, 1968.

LATHAM, RONALD. *Marco Polo, The Travels*. New York. Penguin Books, 1958.

LATTIMORE, OWEN. *The Desert Road to Turkistan*. Boston. Little, Brown & Co., 1930.

LISTER, R.P. *Marco Polo Travels in Xanadu with Kublai Khan*. London. Gordon and Cremonesi, 1976.

LUO, ZEWEN, ET AL. *The Great Wall*. Maidenhead, England. McGraw-Hill Book Co., Ltd., 1981.

MARSDEN, WILLIAM. *The Travels of Marco Polo the Venetian*. Garden City, N.Y. Doubleday & Co., 1948.

MURRAY, HUGH. *The Travels of Marco Polo*. New York. Harper Brothers, 1864.

MYRDAL, JAN. *The Silk Road: A Journey from the High Pamirs and through Sinkiang and Kansu*. New York.
     Pantheon Books, 1979.

NAGEL'S. *Nagel's Encyclopedia-Guide China*. Geneva. Nagel Publishers, 1979.

NORINS, MARTIN R. *Gateway to Asia: Sinkiang*. New York. The John Day Co. 1944.

OLSCHKI, LEONARDO. *Marco Polo's Asia: An introduction to his 'Description of the World' Called 'Il Milione'*.
     London, England. Cambridge University Press, 1960.

ORION PRESS. *The Travels of Marco Polo*. New York. Orion press, 1958.

ROBERTSON, SIR GEORGE. *Chitral*. Karachi. Oxford University Press, 1977.

RUGOFF, MILTON. *The Travels of Marco Polo*. New York. The New American Library, 1961.

SEARS, J.H. *The Travels of Marco Polo*. New York. J. H. Sears & Co., 1921.

SHAW, ISOBEL. *Pakistan Handbook*. Chico, California. Moon Publications, 1990.

SHOR, JEAN BOWIE. *After You, Marco Polo*. New York. McGraw Hill, 1955.

STEIN, AURIEL. *On Ancient Central-Asian Tracks*. Chicago. The University of Chicago Press, 1944.

TOBE, JOHN H. *Hunza, Adventures in a land of Paradise*. Ontario, Canada. The Provoker Press, 1971.

WALSH, RICHARD J. *Adventures and Discoveries of Marco Polo*. New York. Random House, 1953.

YULE, SIR HENRY. *The Book of Ser Marco Polo: The Venetian concerning the kingdoms and marvels of the east*.
     New York. Charles Scribner's Sons, 1903.

ACKNOWLEDGEMENTS

Joanne Kroll was my coauthor in writing the first book of our travels *In the Footsteps of Marco Polo: A Twentieth Century Odyssey*. Joanne was also the coauthor of the first section of this book, telling the story of the 1975 expedition. Joanne provided the much-needed assistance in the planning and execution of the expedition and was an inexhaustible source of knowledge on all subjects. It was her inspiration and support that provided the impetus to push forward the project from a dream to reality. I will be eternally indebted to her for all her contributions to the Marco Polo Odyssey and for being my friend for so many decades.

Richard Rutstein, I am grateful to my son, Rick, for his keen sense of humor, support he offered the project, and for the tolerance he showed his father.

Michael Winn, my travel partner in Pakistan and China who helped this project in so many ways in addition to his phenomenal photos and the highly acclaimed feature articles in the *Smithsonian* magazine, *Adventure Travel*, and other publications on our adventure in Pakistan. Michael was a major asset to our project.

George Udell, my friend and movie making maven, without whose help the movie *On the Roof of the World with Marco Polo*" would have never happened. George died a few years ago, and he is surely missed.

Charles Vanderpool, Cinematographer, Film Editor, Film Maker Extraordinaire was the one man film crew who created *On the Roof of the World with Marco Polo*.

Nancy Rutstein, my wife and partner on our many trips to China, whose patience and understanding allowed me to follow Marco Polo and who kept the "home fires burning" and our children happy. It was the result of Nancy's efforts that allowed us to get the much needed political help.

Franc Shor, Associate Editor, *National Geographic*, was my mentor for this Marco Polo project. It was Frank Shor who introduced me to ambassadors and other key officials of the countries that I was to visit. Without the help of Frank Shor, the expedition may have failed.

President George H. W. Bush, whose support made the Marco Polo Odyssey possible.

Frances S. Dayee edited the first draft of the manuscript.

Julia Sidorova edited and helped in the revision of the second draft of the manuscript.

Lydia Bird edited one of the final drafts of the full manuscript.

Earl Sedlik offered invaluable help in defining the market for this book.

Deborah Dowd proofread my final draft of the manuscript scrutinizing, modifying, and correcting it with her exceptional knowledge of the English language.

I must also acknowledge the help of the hundreds of people in embassies and the government agencies of Italy, Israel, Cyprus, Turkey, Iran, Afghanistan, Pakistan, China and of the thousands of others along the way who helped with a smile or a hand pointing in the right direction.

Thank you, all.

PHOTO CREDITS

All photographs displayed in *The Marco Polo Odyssey* were taken by the following photographers:
Jin Bo Hong, Independent photographer, Beijing
Lu Xiang You, China News Service, Beijing
Luo Xiao Yun, China News Service, Beijing
Jin Tie Lu, China News Service, Beijing
Michael Winn, Independent photographer, New York
Harry Rutstein, Marco Polo Foundation, Inc., Seattle
Cover photo by Joanne Kroll, Seattle
Cover and book design by Geoff Gray, Seattle